Guide to East Germany

Stephen Baister
Chris Patrick

BRADT PUBLICATIONS, UK
HUNTER PUBLISHING, USA

First published in 1990 by Bradt Publications, 41 Nortoft Rd, Chalfont St Peter, Bucks SL9 0LA, England. Distributed in the USA by Hunter Publishing Inc., 300 Raritan Center Parkway, CN94, Edison, NJ 08810.

British Library Cataloguing in Publication data
Baister, Stephen
    Guide to East Germany.
    1. East Germany Visitors' guides
    I Title II Patrick, Chris
    914.3104879

    ISBN 0-946983-49-6

Front cover: Saalfeld, Thuringia, photo by Anthony Lambert
Back cover: New Year Celebrations at the Brandenburg Gate, Berlin 1989/1990, photo by Ursula Gebhardt
Colour photos by kind permission of Berolina (with the exception of colour pages 1, 12, 15 and 16 where photos are by the authors)
Black and white photos by the authors
Maps by Hans van Well
Typeset from the authors' disc by Patti Taylor, London NW8 ORJ
Printed by the Guernsey Press, Channel Islands

Foreword

The idea of writing a travel guide to East Germany grew out of a holiday in Thuringia in 1989 when we realised that there was virtually no material available in English on the East. At that time the German Democratic Republic still seemed firmly established and there was little or nothing to hint at the events that were to come later that year and lead to the end of the old communist order. This book has therefore been written at a time when its subject has been undergoing unprecedented change. This will have practical consequences for the traveller: street names with communist or socialist references may well be changed; Karl-Marx-Stadt, for example, has already reverted to its old name, Chemnitz, and other similar changes will occur shortly; visa and entry formalities will change or disappear, as will the position in relation to currency and exchange rates.

East Germany is worth visiting for a number of reasons. The first is that at least until recently, and to some extent still, it was interesting in that it was a communist alternative to its western neighbour, and its separate development is itself worthy of attention. The second reason is that many of the greatest historical and cultural centres of the German-speaking world (towns such as Potsdam, Dresden, Leipzig and Weimar) are in the East, as is a great deal of attractive and relatively unspoilt countryside, including for example the Erzgebirge and the woodland areas of Thuringia. Finally, of course, the capital of East Germany, Berlin, is one of Europe's most interesting and beautiful cities.

Whilst this is not intended to be an academic work, every effort has been made to ensure accuracy. Please notify us if you spot any howling errors by writing to us care of the publisher.

S.B. C.P.

Acknowledgments

We should like to express our thanks to the following who have assisted: Friedbert Krebs, Head of the Consular Section of the Embassy of the GDR in London, his wife, Marina Krebs, and all the Krebs family; Michael Juhran, the press officer of the Embassy of the GDR in London; Jürgen Friedrich of Berolina Travel Ltd for photographs and practical information; our friends and the people of East Germany generally for their kindness and hospitality; finally, our publisher for her enthusiasm and support for this project and for her speedy production of the book.

Baltic Sea

(DENMARK)

Sassnitz
RÜGEN
STRALSUND
Warnemünde
Rostock
WISMAR
GREIFSWALD
GÜSTROW
NEUBRANDENBURG
Schwerin
Ludwigslust
Neustrelitz

(FEDERAL REPUBLIC of GERMANY)

(POLAND)

Neuruppin
EBERSWALDE - FINOW
STENDAL
Tangermünde
BRANDENBURG
Potsdam
BERLIN
FRANKFURT an der ODER
Oder
MAGDEBURG
WITTENBERG
Lübben
SPREEWALD
HALBERSTADT
WERNIGRODE
QUEDLINBURG
HARZ
Dessau
LÜBBENAU
Cottbus
EISLEBEN
Halle
TORGAU
Heiligenstadt
MERSEBURG
LEIPZIG
MEISSEN
BAUTZEN
GÖRLITZ
MÜLHAUSEN
Naumburg
Coldite
NEISSE
EISENACH
Erfurt
GOTHA
WEIMAR
Jena
FREIBERG
DRESDEN
ZITTAU
Arnstadt
Gera
Zwickau
CHEMNITZ
THÜRINGER WALD
Ilmenau
ANNABERG - BUCHHOLZ
ERZ GEBIRGE

(CZECHOSLOVAKIA)

GERMAN DEMOCRATIC REPUBLIC

0   20   40   60   80   100
km

Table of Contents

Introduction 1–14

Practical Information 15–27

Berlin 28–71
  – West Berlin 31–41
  – East Berlin 41–71

Potsdam 72–78

Dresden 79–97

Weimar 98–113

Leipzig 114–125

The South West 126–147

The South East 148–164

The West 165–186

The East 187–192

The North 193–212

Biographical Appendix 213–214

Introduction

Basic Facts

East Germany is the popular name by which most people have known the German Democratic Republic (Deutsche Demokratische Republik), frequently abbreviated to GDR (DDR). After 1949 two separate German states grew up, the eastern one belonging to the communist sphere of influence, the western one, properly called the Federal Republic of Germany, being allied to the west and functioning as a capitalist state. After the collapse of East Germany's communist government in late 1989 the two Germanies embarked on a course of reunification.

East Germany covers an area of approximately 108,333km² and has a population of over 16 million. It is bordered by the Baltic Sea to the north, Poland to the east, Czechoslovakia to the southeast, and West Germany to the west.

History

The history of Germany is long and complex, and until the 19th Century is not really the history of one country at all but of a series of small separate states.

The Beginnings of German History

The name Germany comes from an ancient tribe, the Germanii, who did battle with the Romans. Between the 5th and 7th Centuries they became Christian, beginning with the conversion of a Germanic king, Chlodwig, in the year 496, under the influence of SS. Killian and Columbus and subsequently St Boniface.

By the 8th Century the Germanic tribes had been conquered by the Franks, and a fusion of Christian, Frankish and Germanic traditions took place under Charlemagne who made Aachen (in present day West Germany) the centre of his empire, the Holy Roman Empire, a development recognized by the Church on Charlemagne's coronation by Pope Leo at St Peter's on Christmas day of the year 800.

Charlemagne's empire failed to survive his death in 814, following which it divided into three kingdoms. This partitioning, completed by 843, is often said to mark the beginning of modern German history with the establishment of a German-speaking kingdom in the east. This kingdom of East Francia was an unstable association of tribes ruled over by a series of kings from Ludwig in the 9th Century to Otto I, crowned Holy Roman Emperor by the Pope in 962.

The Hohenstaufen dynasty provided a series of emperors who ruled the empire through a period of imperial growth into the 12th and 13th Centuries until the death of Friedrich II, son of Barbarossa, in 1250, after which anarchy and disorder spread until a series of unsuccessful reigns was followed by that of Karl IV (1347-1378) who formulated a system of elections by seven electors (Kurfürsten), three representing the church, and four secular interests.

The Peasants' Revolt
The 15th and 16th Centuries were a period of growing trade and prosperity, but not for the many peasants working the land. Although serfdom had been abolished, they still remained oppressed. In 1524, encouraged by Thomas Müntzer and others imbued with the new ideas of the Reformation, they rose up in an attempt to gain some measure of freedom. The Peasants' Revolt (Bauernkrieg) was put down with great cruelty and violence exemplified by the battle of Frankenhausen in May 1525, after which many of the leaders, including Müntzer, were tortured and executed.

The Reformation
The 16th Century was a time of turmoil for purely religious reasons too. An Augustinian monk, Martin Luther (1483-1546), had become disillusioned with the corruption rife in the Catholic church, epitomised by the practice of selling indulgences, a perversion of the doctrine that salvation could be attained (at least in part) by good works. Luther rejected the supremacy of the Pope and the notion that salvation could be attained only through his church, insisting instead that salvation could be achieved by faith alone.

In 1517 Luther challenged the Pope by nailing to the door of the church in Wittenberg a document setting out 95 theological propositions (theses) that were at odds with accepted Catholic doctrine. In spite of the fact that his ideas gained widespread support, he was excommunicated and had to take refuge in the Wartburg castle in Eisenach. There he worked on the first translation of the Bible from the original Greek into German. The ability to have this translation printed, along with many other theological works, ensured the rapid spread of Luther's ideas. Attempts to put down his Reformation failed, and at the Peace of Augsburg in 1555 both the Catholic and Protestant religions were accepted.

The Thirty Years' War

By the beginning of the 17th Century Germany was little more than a loose federation, and, in spite of the Peace of Augsburg, was divided by religion. The oppression of one religious group by the other was a constant source of tension. In 1618 the Protestant community in Bohemia, feeling unjustly treated, refused to recognise the authority of the emperor. General Tilly was sent to quell the revolt which resulted in the gradual involvement of Denmark, Sweden, England and Holland in a European war that lasted until 1648 and decimated the population. The Treaty of Westphalia, which brought the war to an end, allowed the ruler of each state to determine the religion of his subjects.

The Emergence of Prussia

By the end of the Thirty Years' War, Germany consisted again of a vast number of tiny kingdoms, cities and principalities. One state, however, soon began to lead the way under a powerful ruler, Friedrich Wilhelm, the Great Elector (der Große Kurfürst, 1648-1688). This was the state of Brandenburg-Prussia, a powerful agricultural and industrial entity with a large army and its capital in Berlin. Friedrich Wilhelm's son, Friedrich III, established in place of this a new kingdom of Prussia (Preußen), and declared himself to be King Friedrich I, the first king of Prussia.

After his death in 1713 and the reign of his son Friedrich Wilhelm, the throne fell to Friedrich II, better known as Frederick the Great, who continued to develop Prussia as an economic and military power. In 1740 he felt strong enough to send troops into Silesia and take it from Austria, a position that remained unchanged even after the Seven Years' War. By 1722 he had also acquired parts of Poland, such that by the time of his death in 1786 Prussia was a substantial European power in its own right. It was also a major centre of European culture.

The Napoleonic Wars

The French Revolution in 1789 had an effect that went well beyond the frontiers of France. Ideas of freedom and democracy spread, and monarchy was no longer seen as the only method of rule. In 1804 Napoleon crowned himself emperor of France and embarked on a series of military campaigns with a view to acquiring an empire to go with the title. Austria and Prussia fought to maintain their independence but failed. By the Treaty of Tilsit of 1807, signed after Prussia's defeat at the battle of Jena, Prussia lost substantial territories and was obliged to pay vast reparations.

The Growth of Nationalism

There followed a period of reform in Prussia, begun by the October Edict of October 9, 1807, and carried through by Scharnhorst, Hardenberg, von Stein and Gneissenau. At the same time a new sense of national pride began to develop, exemplified by works such as Herder's *Germanien*, Schiller's *William Tell*, and a series of lectures given by the philosopher, Johann Gottlieb Fichte, from 1807-1808. Fichte's *Addresses to the German Nation* were written to awaken "in the minds and hearts of Germans throughout the country a spirit of determined activity", and they did so by fanning the flames of national pride. The defeat of Napoleon at the battle of Waterloo at the hands of the English (under Wellington) and the Prussians (under Blücher) contributed to the new sense of nationalism.

In 1815 the Congress of Vienna was convened to establish the frontiers of Europe after the defeat of Napoleon. Attempts to forge a united Germany failed, but again Prussia emerged as a dominant force, acquiring areas of Poland and Cottbus, Wittenberg, Torgau, Merseburg, Naumburg and Weissenfels. A German Confederation (Deutscher Bund) was formed under the leadership of Austria, thanks in part to the influence of the Austrian, Metternich. Under the Austrians, there followed a period of political suppression and apathy known as the Biedermeier period.

Revolution

In 1830 there was again revolution in France, and this had its counterparts in Leipzig, Dresden and elsewhere. These uprisings achieved little, but news of a further revolution in France in 1848, following as it did strikes and demonstrations in Berlin in 1847, produced renewed demands for greater freedom and democracy which resulted in the fall of Metternich and the loss by Austria of its leading position in the German Confederation. Friedrich Wilhelm IV of Prussia called upon an elected assembly to formulate a constitution and attempt to form a new German nation from which Austria would be excluded.

The Unification of Germany

However, unification was still some way off. In 1858 Wilhelm I came to the throne of Prussia and set about the task of breaking from Austria once and for all and establishing a new German nation. In doing this he relied on the help of Otto von Bismarck (1815-1898) whom he made Minister-President in 1862. He waged war against Austria in 1866 and expelled it from the old Confederation which was rapidly replaced by a new Norddeutscher Bund (North German Confederation) which came into being in 1867 under Prussia. The king of Prussia was made President, and the Chancellor was Bismarck.

In the meantime socialism was becoming a growing political force. The communist party had its first congress in 1847; the communist manifesto was adopted in 1848; the Social-Democratic Workers' Party was founded in Eisenach in 1867, led by August Bebel and Wilhelm Liebknecht.

A unified Germany posed a considerable threat to France, and tension between the two countries grew, culminating in the Franco-Prussian war of 1870. Victorious Prussia extended its sphere of influence by acquiring the territories of Alsace and Lorraine. The German Empire (Deutsches Reich) was proclaimed in 1871 with Wilhelm I as Kaiser (emperor). It was again a loose affair, made up of some 20 different states, governed by a Bundesrat (dominated by Prussia) and an elected Reichstag. A common currency was introduced along with common weights and measures to facilitate trade.

In 1890 Bismarck resigned after differences of opinion with Wilhelm II who succeeded Wilhelm I in 1888. A period of instability followed, and Germany weakened such that by the turn of the century the country faced isolation, encircled as it was by hostile powers in the form of France, Russia and England.

World War I

On June 28 1914 Archduke Franz Ferdinand was assassinated in Sarajevo by Serbian extremists. Austria invaded Serbia; Russia and France went to Serbia's aid. Germany invaded France by marching through Belgium, causing Britain to intervene on behalf of its ally. Soon the whole of Europe was plunged into a fruitless war that ended in a total defeat for Germany and the loss of millions of lives.

By the Treaty of Versailles that ended the war in 1918 Germany lost Alsace and Lorraine back to France and substantial territories to Poland; the Austro-Hungarian empire was dissolved, and a new map of Europe was drawn with whole new nations such as Czechoslovakia and Yugoslavia appearing. Apart from territorial losses, Germany suffered the humiliation of being compelled to pay vast reparations.

The Weimar Republic
A defeated Germany began to rebuild itself under the leadership of Friedrich Ebert, and a National Assembly was elected to draft a new constitution. Because of unrest in Berlin the government was forced to flee to Weimar where the Weimar constitution was formulated in 1919, giving its name to what was to be known as the Weimar Republic. This was unstable, in particular economically, partly as a result of the reparations which the German people could ill afford. Inflation and unrest prevailed.

In 1923 the National Socialists (Nazis) under Hitler attempted to gain power in Munich. They failed, and Hitler spent 13 months in prison, time he used to compose his work of political invective rather than theory, *Mein Kampf* (My Fight). But bad economic conditions fostered German nationalism, and by 1930 the Nazis were the largest political party. Hitler was appointed Chancellor in 1933. Only a matter of weeks later a fire gutted the Reichstag building. Hitler denounced the attack as a communist conspiracy and suspended the constitution. In 1934 he proclaimed the German Reich with himself as its leader (Führer) and was able to proceed unchecked with the elimination from Germany of all opposition (especially communist or socialist) and with the elimination of the Jews whom he blamed for Germany's decline.

World War II
In 1936 German troops moved into the demilitarised Rhineland. In 1938 they marched into Austria, then Czechoslovakia. Chamberlain's appeasement of Hitler at a meeting in Munich was short-lived. On September 1 1939 German troops invaded Poland, compelling France and Britain to declare war.

In 1941 Hitler invaded the Soviet Union in the face of a non-aggression pact he had signed with Stalin. However, his troops were no more able to sustain a prolonged war with Russia than Napoleon's had. The war with Russia consumed more and more resources, until a combination of the Russian winter and ferocious resistance by the Soviet people, coupled with the USA and Britain liberating France, ultimately brought about Hitler's defeat in May 1945. Germany fell under the occupation of Soviet, American, British and French troops.

The Birth of the GDR

Tensions soon mounted after the end of the war between the western powers and the Soviet Union under Stalin. Germany became the focus of those tensions, culminating in Stalin's blockade of the western sectors of Berlin from 1948-1949 in an attempt to force the allies to abandon their occupation zones of the former capital. The division between east and west became final when West Germany declared itself to be the Federal Republic of Germany and East Germany proclaimed itself the German Democratic Republic in 1949.

The two states developed separately, the west as a capitalist state and the east as a communist state under the Socialist Unity Party of Germany (SED). The GDR joined Comecon in 1950 and the Warsaw Pact in 1955.

Disparities between the standards of living in the two neighbouring states soon led to problems. The western mark and western economy soon became more powerful than their East German counterparts, and key workers began to leave the east for the west, often actively encouraged by the west to do so. On August 13 1961 the GDR government took steps to secure its frontier and erected the Berlin Wall. Gradually the border between East and West Germany was almost totally sealed, and contact between the two countries ceased during the years known as the cold war.

Relations between the two states only began to improve as a result of Willy Brandt's Ostpolitik (Eastern policy) of the early 1970s which allowed limited contact between families and friends who had not seen one another for years.

The road to reunification

In 1989 Hungary (which citizens of the GDR could visit freely) decided to open its borders with western Europe, and a large number of East Germans took the opportunity to leave and seek a new life in West Germany. This precipitated a government crisis which culminated in the resignation of the leader, Erich Honecker. His replacement, Egon Krenz, was unpopular as he had been a hard line communist and had been for many years in charge of the Stasi, the East German secret police. His attempts to assuage popular demand by opening the frontiers and allowing unrestricted freedom of travel came too late to save the situation. The Berlin Wall was opened on November 9 1989, and although many who left for the west returned, many key people (in particular doctors) did not, leaving the GDR weaker than it had been for two decades. Revelations of widespread corruption among party leaders made matters even worse. Krenz resigned after only a few months in office. He was replaced by Hans Modrow and a young progressive lawyer, Gregor Gysi, but being members of the SED, they too failed to gain the confidence of the people who saw no future for their country other than in reunification with their richer counterpart in the west. Elections were held on March 18 1990, resulting in victory for the conservatives (Alliance for Germany) and making the reunification of the two Germanies inevitable.

Geography

Geographically, East Germany can be divided into three areas: the Baltic coastline, the northern lowlands and the southern region of hills and woodland.

The Baltic coast is the northernmost frontier of East Germany covering some 340km from the bay of Lübeck in the west to Rieth and the Polish border in the east. Economically it is important as the location of the ports of Rostock, Wismar and Stralsund and as a popular place for holidays. It is largely made up of areas of dunes and chalky cliffs.

The northern lowlands account for some two thirds of the area of East Germany. A fertile area runs behind the coastline and is important for agriculture. Behind that lie the flat, undulating Mecklenburg lake plateau and the low-lying plains and marshes of Brandenburg and the Spreewald. The Spreewald is so beset by marsh and water that boats remain an important form of transport, and some houses still stand on stilts. It is an important area for market gardening, as well as for tourism.

The lowlands extend to a line just north of the Harz mountains in the west and Halle and Cottbus in the central and eastern parts. The Harz dominates the east. The southwest corner is covered by the Thuringian basin, an area of woods and hills. Further east lies the Vogtland (undulating wooded hills), and towards Czechoslovakia, the Erzgebirge, ore-rich hills and mountains, and one of the East's most attractive and unspoilt regions. Other popular tourist areas in the south are Saxon Switzerland, an area of flat-topped mountains, the Lausitzer Bergland, a highland area of granite ridges and valley basins, and the sandstone Zittau mountains.

About 30% of the total land area of East Germany is woodland, much of it still unspoilt and under-visited.

The main waterways (still important for transport) are the Saale (427km), and the longest river, the Elbe, 566km of which flow through the East. The river Oder is important, as, with the Neiße, it forms the border with Poland in the east. The longest canal in the country is the Oder-Spree-Kanal (83km).

Another attraction of the East is its many lakes. A large number can be seen around Berlin, but the largest are Lake Müritz in Mecklenburg, and Lake Schwerin, near the town of Schwerin in the northwest.

The climate is temperate. The average temperature is 8.5°C, ranging from 0.7°C in January to 18°C in July, and the mean annual rainfall 585mm. Temperatures can rise to as high as 33°C in summer and reach as low as -25°C in winter.

Economy

In spite of a lack of raw materials and a deficient infrastructure, the East German economy is not at all the complete failure it has often been described as in the west. It is the second largest after the USSR among all the CMEA countries. It has until recently had the highest living standards of all the east bloc countries, higher too than some west European countries.

Until recently the economy and industry were subject to rigorous central planning, a state planning commission being responsible for the five year and annual economic plans implemented by state monopolies.

Since the war the principal industries have been metals, chemicals, machinery, electronics and shipbuilding. Agriculture is also important, and although it too has been under state control and subject to central planning, there are privately owned farms.

In the wake of the events of late 1989 and the collapse of the conservative-style communism of Erich Honecker and his contemporaries, considerable economic liberalisation and a move towards a capitalist economy has taken place.

Life and People

The people of East Germany are racially and culturally the same as those in West Germany, and that has always been the major problem for the East. In spite of the fact that East Germany provided its citizens with a relatively high standard of living, job security, a reasonably good standard of housing, and a good health and education service, people inevitably compared their way of life to that of the richer West Germany. This, coupled with the inability to travel freely, ultimately precipitated the downfall of the SED government in the March 1990 elections.

Many ordinary East Germans have had a somewhat idealised picture of life in the west and have yet to come to terms with the fact that not everyone in the west can have everything that is seen in the shops, and that the price of a consumer oriented society is frequently paid by unemployment and a lack of state provision.

The pattern of everyday life is much as in West Germany. Work begins early, often as early as 6.30am or 7.00am, and the streets are often quiet after 9.00am, by which time most people are at work. Just under half of the workforce is made up of women, a reflection of socialist equal opportunity policy, but also of economic necessity. Wages are low by western standards, something like an average of 1,200 marks a month. Even with both partners working, this is estimated to produce an average income per annum per household of only £8,000. However, prices are very low and the social wage high. For example, nobody pays individually for health care or education, and rents, transport and food costs are low.

As East Germany has been a communist society since 1945, a visitor there is struck (as in the Soviet Union) by the lack of choice of consumer goods. Until recently it took 15 years to get a car, and there have always been shortages of luxury products, although there are none of the vast queues one sees in Poland or the USSR. A benefit of a society that is not governed by the free market is the almost complete absence of advertising, and historical or cultural sites are rarely blemished in the way they are in the west by hoardings or souvenir shops.

There has always been freedom of religion in East Germany, but active religious practice has been frowned upon in the SED, membership of which has been a prerequisite for a successful political or professional career. 42% of the population are protestant, only 7% catholic.

Politics and Constitution

Until recently, East Germany was a communist state, the leading role in its political life being played by its communist party, the Socialist Unity Party of Germany (SED). The general secretary of the SED has always been the effective leader of the country.

Political authority was vested in the Volkskammer (People's Chamber) which was elected every 5 years and approved all laws and decrees. It in turn elected the Staatsrat (Council of State), the highest organ of state, which decided fundamental policies and acted as a sort of cabinet. The Volkskammer also elected the Ministerrat (Council of Ministers) which had executive responsibility for carrying out policy.

The national flag is a black, red and gold horizontal tricolour with the national emblem (hammer and compasses surrounded by a sheaf of corn) in the centre. Few flags now still bear the old national emblem; the same flag now flies in both East and West.

Clearly, in the light of the proposed political and monetary union of East and West Germany, the whole political structure of East Germany is at present subject to complete review.

The Sorb Minority
About 0.7% of the East German population are Sorbs, a Slav people encountered mainly in the Cottbus and Dresden areas and in the area around the Spreewald and Lausitz. They have their own language (variously referred to as Sorbian, Wendish or Lusatian) which is a distant relative of Polish.

Their separate cultural rights are preserved under Article 11 of the East German constitution. They have their own nationalist organisation (Domowina) and hold a major cultural festival in Bautzen every 5 years and a festival in the Spreewald every September.

Culture and the Arts
The cultural history of East Germany is inseparable from that of the West. However, the East has its particular attractions that reflect its different development as well as outstanding examples of work of a type to be found throughout the German-speaking world.

In architecture, there are abundant examples of the Romanesque style (1025-1230) notably in the Harz (eg St Servatius in Quedlinburg). The altarpiece at Erfurt cathedral is an example of sculpture from the same period, and the Goldene Pforte (doorway) of Freiberg cathedral is also noteworthy. Examples of the Gothic period (1200-1500) are Naumburg cathedral with its Naumburger Meister sculptures (1250-1260), the Barfüßerkirche in Erfurt, and the late Gothic churches of St Nicholas in Stralsund and Wismar.

Hall churches (Hallenkirchen), found throughout Germany, were the standard method of church building from around 1350. These churches are distinguished by the fact that the nave and aisles are of equal height and are covered by a huge roof over the whole construction. Notable examples are the Marktkirche St Marien in Halle, the cathedral at Freiberg and St Severus in Erfurt.

The Renaissance (16th Century) saw the rise of secular building, notably for example in Dresden, and of a flourishing of German art in the works of Dürer, Holbein and Cranach. Saxony in particular flourished, and a great deal of building and expansion occurred, including for example in Görlitz, Erfurt and Gera.

The Baroque period (17th Century to 1750) was a period which again put the emphasis on ecclesiastical art of an especially lavish kind after the Thirty Years' War. The St Hedwig cathedral in Berlin and the Hofkirche in Dresden are the product of this age, as are a number of palaces (the Zwinger in Dresden, for example). The Rococo (1730-1780) represented a decorative refinement of the Baroque that found its expression in the elaborate interiors of Sanssouci in Potsdam and the Berlin opera house.

The classical style of the late 18th and early 19th Centuries is represented in the simple grandeur of the Brandenburg Gate and the Schauspielhaus and a whole range of buildings in Berlin. The 18th Century was also the period when German Romanticism flourished, exemplified in the paintings of Caspar David Friedrich, many of places in the Greifswald area. The later Realist painters (Adolph von Menzel and Max Liebermann) portrayed a more brutal, everyday life.

The turn of the century saw the coming of Jugendstil (the German equivalent of art nouveau), a brief period of fanciful design and elegance (exemplified in the theatre at Cottbus) followed by the Expressionist art of Otto Dix, George Grosz and the Blauer Reiter group founded by Kandinsky, and die Brücke, a group centred around Dresden.

Walter Gropius's Bauhaus, a simple, even stark building erected in Dessau (1925-1926), gave its name to a whole new school of art and design that aimed to give expression to the new modern age.

East Germany also has important musical associations. Michael Praetorius was born in Kreuzberg, Thuringia, in 1571 and worked as an organist and composer in Halberstadt, Frankfurt an der Oder, Dresden, Magdeburg and Leipzig. Heinrich Schütz, the so-called father of German music, was born in Köstritz in

Saxony in 1585 and died in Dresden in 1672. Johann Sebastian Bach (1685-1750) was the most famous of a Thuringian family which for two centuries produced a series of composers, conductors and organists. J.S. Bach lived and worked in Eisenach, Arnstadt, Leipzig and Köthen. Handel was actually born as Georg Friedrich Händel in Halle where he studied law and was cathedral organist.

Weber, composer of *Der Freischütz*, is inextricably associated with Berlin (where the opera was first peformed) and Dresden (where it has been most frequently performed).

Richard Wagner was born in Leipzig and studied there, and from 1843-1849 was conductor of the Dresden opera. Liszt was court conductor at Weimar. Richard Strauss followed some time later after a period as court musician at Meiningen. He also conducted in Berlin. A number of his operas had their first performances in Dresden.

German literature has a history going back to the Middle Ages. However, the history of modern German literature, and indeed the modern German language, goes back to Luther's translation of the Bible, undertaken in the Wartburg. The 18th Century Enlightenment period saw a flourishing of German literature, and especially drama, epitomised in the work of Lessing. Weimar in particular became a literary centre: the poet Wieland taught there, and the author of German fairy tales, Musäus also worked there. Its best known literary residents, Goethe and Schiller, established Weimar as the leading cultural centre in Germany in the late 18th Century.

Jena became the centre of early Romanticism, a movement commenced by the Schlegel brothers and joined by Novalis (who lived in Weissenfels) and Tieck (a Berliner). Later, de la Motte Fouqué, E.T.A. Hoffmann and Chamisso continued a Romantic tradition in Berlin.

In the 19th Century, the poet Heinrich Heine visited the Harz and recorded his experiences in his lyrical *Die Harzreise*. His political poem, *Die Schlesischen Weber*, records the uprising among the Silesian weavers in 1844. The same topic is at the centre of Gerhart Hauptmann's Naturalist play *The Weavers*, a play which is still often performed in East Berlin.

The 20th Century is perhaps best known for the work of Thomas Mann (who ultimately left Germany) and his brother Heinrich who remained in the East and whose *Professor Unrat* provided the plot for the film *The Blue Angel*. Bertolt Brecht, a committed communist, settled in East Berlin and remained there until his death in 1956.

In its forty odd years of existence East Germany has made a distinctive contribution to culture and the arts. Building and architectural skills have necessarily been devoted to the task of post-war reconstruction (at its best in Berlin and the Semper opera in Dresden); most modern architecture is unimaginative and reminds the traveller of that of a post-war new town in the UK. Painting and sculpture tend towards didacticism and realism (eg in the work of Heinrich Drake, the sculptor, and Ernst Hassebrauk, the painter). Post-war literature aimed primarily at the consolidation of socialism, as can be seen from the works of Anna Seghers and Johannes R. Becher. Literature critical of the state (such as *The King David Report* by Stefan Heym) was discouraged or banned, and a number of writers left. However, with the publication in the 1970s of Ulrich Plenzdorf's *The New Sufferings of the Young W* (the title was a pun on Goethe's most famous novel), a work expressing the discontent of a young man growing up in East Germany, a gradual development towards a more critical approach began, culminating in the publishing in 1989 of *The Troika* by Markus Wolf, an autobiographical novel by a former diplomat and politician in which he considers growing up under socialism through the eyes of three young men.

Cloister at Magdeburg cathedral, Germany's earliest Gothic church

Practical Information

Visas
Normal Visit Visa
In order to obtain a visa it is necessary to plan a day-by-day schedule and pay for accommodation before leaving for East Germany. When hotels/camping sites have been paid for, visitors receive a voucher, on presentation of which it is possible to get a visa either at one of the East German border crossings or, before departure, at any GDR embassy abroad.

UK visitors should apply, with confirmation voucher and passport, to the Consular Section of the Embassy of the German Democratic Republic, 34 Belgrave Square, London SW1X 8QB (office hours Mondays — Fridays 10.00am to 12.30pm, closed Wednesdays). In the USA, visas can be obtained from the Visa Section, Embassy of the German Democratic Republic, 1717 Massachusetts Avenue NW, Washington DC 20036 (office hours Mondays and Fridays 9.30am — noon; Wednesdays 1.00pm to 3.00pm.).

The visa costs DM15.00 per person, but there is no charge for children under 16 travelling on their parents' passport.

Day Visas from West Berlin
It is possible to obtain a visa on the spot for anyone visiting East Berlin or East Germany from West Berlin for one day only. Day visas are issued at the road crossing point at Friedrichstraße/Zimmerstraße (Checkpoint Charlie) or at the Friedrichstraße station for visitors travelling from West Berlin by U-Bahn (underground) or S-Bahn (suburban railway).

This visa costs DM5 and visitors are required to change a minimum of DM25 into East German marks. Visitors must leave by midnight.

Transit Visas
Visitors travelling through East Germany en route to West
Berlin or any other country can be issued with a transit visa by
border guards. The cost is DM5.

Booking Accommodation
Perhaps the simplest way to book accommodation in East
Germany is to do so well in advance via a travel agency. In the
UK the East German travel service, Berolina, has full details of
package holidays to East Germany and can also arrange personal
tours. Berolina Travel Ltd. is at 22a Conduit Street, London
W1R 9TB (tel: (071) 629 1664). Most local travel agencies can
also arrange holidays.

In the USA, any travel agency can contact the Reisebüro der
DDR and make arrangements for travel and accommodation.

Other possibilities for arranging accommodation include
writing to the Reisebüro der DDR in East Berlin, writing
directly to the hotel(s) you would like to stay in or visiting the
Reisebüro der DDR in East Berlin. If you write to the
Reisebüro you must send full details of name, date of birth,
passport number, citizenship and the dates and places you hope
to visit. If you visit the office in East Berlin in person, on a day
visa from West Berlin, you will be expected to give full details
of your trip at window 13 on the second floor. If there are no
problems, you will receive hotel vouchers, on payment of the
full cost, within half an hour to an hour. The office is open
Mondays to Fridays from 8.00am to 8.00pm and on Saturdays
and Sundays from 9.00am to 4.00pm. The address is: Reisebüro
der DDR, Generaldirektion, Alexanderplatz 5, PSF 77 Berlin
1026. Writing directly to hotels may take some time, and unless
the letter is in German there is a possibility that you will not
receive a reply. Although travel restrictions and booking
requirements are being relaxed, the available accommodation is
restricted. Booking is still therefore advisable.

Visiting relatives or friends
It is possible to stay with friends or relatives in East Germany,
but arrangements need to be made well in advance. If you plan
to stay partly in hotels and partly privately, you need to submit
your schedule, including the name and address of the people
you plan to stay with, to the Reisebüro der DDR (address
above). Again payment for hotel accommodation must be made
in advance, and a handling fee of DM30 per adult from the UK

(DM50 from the USA) must be made. From completion of these formalities to receiving an entry permit takes six to eight weeks, but on payment of an extra DM20 (DM25 in the USA) an express service is available, permitting you to receive the relevant documents in around 10 days.

Anyone not staying in state-run hotels must exchange a minimum of DM25 per day per adult, DM7.50 for children under 15, and DM15 for pensioners. Again, this procedure is likely to be simplified in the near future.

Registration

It is still obligatory to register with the police within 24 hours of arrival in any district in East Germany. All the large hotels will arrange this automatically, but anyone staying privately should go in person to the nearest main police station and get their passport stamped. This procedure needs to be repeated every time a new Bezirk (administrative region) is entered.

Money

Until July 1990 the East German Mark is still a different currency to that of West Germany. It is usually referred to as the Ostmark or Mark der DDR. The Mark is divided into 100 Pfennig. Notes come in denominations of 100, 50, 20, 10 and 5, and coins come in units of 20, 10, 5, 2 and 1 Mark and 50, 20, 10, 5 and 1 Pfennig.

Until recently the Ostmark could only be exchanged at the same rate as West German Marks. Now they are freely convertible. As prices in East Germany are low, it is advisable to change only small amounts at a time; for the same reason, try to use small denominations of notes and keep plenty of small change.

Avoid the temptation to buy East Marks in the West. It is illegal to import or export currency. You will be required to declare all currency brought into or out of the country, so keep receipts for any money changed or spent.

Money can be changed at most Interhotels as well as at certain commercial banks. The rates are fixed.

Once in East Germany there are generally three methods of payment:
1. In East German money — generally accepted in normal shops and restaurants;

2. In Western currency — this is compulsory in shops selling luxury goods, so-called Valuta-Restaurants and the large hotels; 3. Credit card — only for use where payment is made in Western currency. Although in theory any western currency can be used, the West German Mark is by far the easiest to use. As East and West Germany are now committed to monetary union the East German mark will be withdrawn from circulation after July 1990.

Insurance

Under reciprocal medical services agreements British citizens receive emergency medical and dental treatment free of charge. Medical insurance is not therefore essential. Other nationals may need to insure privately.

Getting there

The most convenient method of travel is by air to West Berlin (Tegel airport) from where you can travel by bus and underground (U-Bahn) to one of the border crossings. At the time of writing there are no direct flights from any UK airport to East Berlin, although KLM fly from Heathrow via Amsterdam to East Berlin's Schönefeld airport.

It is possible to travel by train. It takes about 18 hours from London (including the Channel crossing).

It is also possible to enter via the ports of Rostock or Saßnitz or by car at one of the specified border crossings.

Border crossings

The easiest way to cross into the East is via the Friedrichstraße crossing point at Friedrichstraße station (on the U-Bahn and S-Bahn). Apart from a visa you will also need to fill out a statistical card (Zählkarte) and a customs and currency declaration form (Zoll- und Devisenerklärung).

Another convenient crossing point is that at the corner of Friedrichstraße and Zimmerstraße generally known as Checkpoint Charlie. It is commonly used by coaches and cars, but is also open to pedestrians.

There are at present 27 other border crossings (Grenzübergänge) connecting West Berlin with East Berlin or other parts of East Germany, but they remain restricted to use by East and West Germans.

Other authorised border crossings are as follows:-

Through West Germany
Selmsdorf (Lübeck to Wismar or Schwerin)
Salzwedel (Ülzen to Magdeburg)
Herrnburg (Lübeck to Schwerin)
Zarrentin (Hamburg to Berlin)
Schwanheide (Büchen to Boizenburg)
Horst (Lauenburg to Boizenburg)
Oebisfelde (Wolfsburg to Gardelegen)
Marienborn (Helmstedt to Magdeburg)
Worbis (Göttingen to Erfurt)
Wartha (Kassel to Eisenach)
Gerstungen (Bebra to Eisenach)
Meiningen (Schweinfurt to Erfurt)
Eisfeld (Coburg to Erfurt)
Probstzella (Kronach to Saalfeld)
Hirschberg (Hof to Schleiz)
Gutenfürst (Hof to Plauen)

Through Czechoslovakia
Bad Brambach (Cheb to Plauen)
Schönberg (Cheb to Oelsnitz)
Zinnwald (Teplice to Dresden)
Bad Schandau (Decin to Dresden)
Schmilka (Decin to Dresden)

Through Poland
Görlitz (Luban to Görlitz)
Frankfurt/Oder (Poznan to Frankfurt/Oder)
Forst (Zary to Cottbus)
Pomellen (Szczecin to Angermünde)
Grambow (Szczecin to Pasewalk)
Guben (Zielona to Cottbus)
Tantow (Szczecin to Berlin)

Transport – between cities
The cheapest method of travel inside East Germany is by train.
The East German rail system (Deutsche Reichsbahn) is,
however, very old-fashioned, and the trains slow and unreliable.
If possible, for long journeys use the D-Züge (quicker than the
Schnellzüge or Personenzüge, and generally appearing in red
print on railway timetables). You will have to pay a supplement
(Zuschlag). Journeys on the main lines are relatively efficient;

it takes, for example, under three hours from Berlin to Rostock, and 2½ hours from Berlin to Leipzig or Dresden. Travel on branch lines is, however, much slower; it takes, for example, one hour to go from Dresden to Meißen and three hours from Leipzig to Eisenach.

For short journeys buses are often preferable to trains. Freiberg, Augustusburg and Annaberg-Buchholz, for example, can all be reached conveniently by bus from Chemnitz.

Cars can be hired, but at a relatively high price. You should book in advance as only a limited number of hire cars are available. Whether driving a hire car or your own you should ensure that you drink no alcohol whatsoever. Speed limits are 50kph in built-up areas, 80kph outside built-up areas and 100kph on motorways. Other speed limits are indicated by round red signs containing the speed limit in a central white disc.

A yellow diamond-shaped sign gives you the right of way. Generally, approach crossings and junctions with care, as road markings are often bad, obscured or non-existent. Traffic lights frequently have a green arrow attached as a permanent fixture and pointing right. Where there is such an arrow you can filter right even if the lights are against you, provided it is safe to do so.

If travelling in an area where there are trams, you will find that they stop to set down passengers in the middle of the road. You should stop behind the tram until all passengers have got on or off the tram.

The police have the power to impose summary fines of between 10-1,000 marks for traffic offences. Foreigners must pay in western currency. Drink-drive offences can mean not just a fine but imprisonment.

If you take your own car you will need a green card. Be prepared for your car to take a fair amount of punishment: even on the motorways, the road surfaces are bad, and roads are badly marked, badly lit and badly repaired. In towns cobbled streets, even on relatively main thoroughfares, are common.

Keep a full tank of petrol. Filling stations are often some way apart and are irregular in their opening hours.

Transport - within towns

Getting around in towns is generally easy by bus and/or tram. Tickets must be bought before getting on.

Taxis are generally hard to find, and it is best to ask a hotel or restaurant to order one for you. Rates are low.

As a pedestrian, do not forget that it is an offence to cross the road against a 'red man', and that it is also an offence not to use a pedestrian crossing where one is available nearby.

Accommodation
There is still a chronic shortage of accommodation in East Germany, and indeed it is said that there are only some 90,000 hotel beds in the whole country. You should therefore book any trip well in advance and be prepared to accept whatever accommodation you are offered, from luxury hotel to simple room without bath. The large luxury hotels are generally part of the Interhotel chain which has hotels in Berlin, Potsdam, Magdeburg, Halle, Leipzig, Dresden, Erfurt, Weimar, Chemnitz, Gera, Jena, Suhl, Thuringia, Oberhof and Rostock. Other towns have cheaper hotels, but these often do not have a bathroom — not even a shared one. However, all hotels tend to be clean and the beds quite comfortable.

There is a system of youth hostels (Jugendherbergen), but they are generally for use by organized groups and reserved well in advance.

Camp sites are generally open from the beginning of May to the end of September. Some are strictly reserved for citizens of East Germany, but there are sites taking foreigners in Berlin, Cottbus, Dresden, Erfurt, Frankfurt/Oder, Halle, Chemnitz, Leipzig, Neubrandenburg, Potsdam, Rostock, Schwerin and Suhl, as well as in holiday areas on the Baltic coast, in the Mecklenburg Lake District and in the Harz mountains. Full details are published in a leaflet (International Camp Sites in the German Democratic Republic) obtainable from Reisebüro der DDR or Berolina. Camping equipment must be brought by the camper; equipment cannot be hired locally.

Post & telephone
There are plenty of post offices and slot machines selling stamps. Stamps can also generally be bought at the larger hotels. Interhotels also have telex and, increasingly, fax facilities.

Telephones are more complicated. The system is old fashioned and inefficient. The code for any particular place will vary depending on where you are calling from, and it is only in the large towns and cities that you can dial direct rather than going through the operator.

Shopping

Anyone visiting East Germany from the West is struck by the lack of consumer goods for sale. Shopping opportunities are limited. Quality imported food and alcohol as well as luxury goods generally come from the West anyhow and can only be bought for western currency in the Intershops. Books and records are good value, as are glassware and lace. Souvenir shops are virtually non-existent. Queues are common. The general rule is, if you see something you want to buy, buy it while it is there: you can never assume in East Germany that because something is available in one town or one shop it will necessarily be available in the next.

Language

German is spoken, and you should not rely on people speaking English in the same way as you might in West Germany. Similarly, menus, information in museums and galleries, signs and so on, will be in German and only rarely accompanied by an English translation. If you know no German, take a dictionary and a phrase book, and perhaps a menu reader to help you order in cafés and restaurants. Note that ß is pronounced as ss.

Food and drink

The food in East Germany is typically mid-European, with an emphasis on meat and potatoes, and in the south dumplings, and on quantity rather than quality. There is a notable lack of fresh vegetables in restaurants, particularly in the larger towns and cities. Vegetables, and for that matter salad, are often pickled. Pork tends to feature on menus more frequently than any other meat, but chicken is also popular. Sausage (Wurst) comes in many shapes and sizes, and is frequently served with dumplings. Fish is not common, except at special fish restaurants (usually called Gastmahl des Meeres). A common starter is a fish and vegetable soup, Soljanka. In many restaurants, the price of a main course includes unlimited pickled cabbage and green beans; customers help themselves from large dishes laid out on a central table.

A speciality of the Berlin area is Eisbein, pig's trotter, traditionally eaten with sauerkraut. It is fatty and not for the faint-hearted. The Harz is known for its dairy products, the Spree for dishes incorporating horse-radish and Thuringia for its dumplings (Klöße). Throughout East Germany cakes and ice cream are good and widely available.

Breakfast is often served early and may finish as early as 8.30am. It will generally consist of dark bread and rolls, cheese and cold meats, boiled eggs and yoghurt. Coffee is more common than tea. Fresh fruit and fruit juice are rare, except in the most expensive hotels.

The main meal of the day is lunch, which again starts earlier than in most parts of Europe. Most restaurants begin serving at 11.00am and continue until around 2.00pm. By contrast, the evening meal tends to be more of a substantial snack than a cooked meal, with the emphasis on bread, cheese and meat or sausage.

In the larger towns it may be possible to eat Czech, Russian, Bulgarian or Cuban food, but, except in Berlin, there are no Chinese, Indian or other exotic restaurants.

Beer is by far the most common drink. It is of the Pils lager type, generally good, and drunk in quantities of half a litre or a litre. Wine is widely available, and originates almost entirely from the East bloc. East Germany itself produces white wine which tends to be over-sweet or insipid. Red wine from Bulgaria or white wine from Hungary are better bets. If you want a dry wine, ask for something 'herb'; most of those available are 'lieblich' (sweet). East German champagne (Rotkäppchen) is, however, both excellent and cheap. A fairly wide range of schnaps and fruit brandies is also available, many of which are of high quality.

Eating and drinking places fall into several categories:

- Gaststätte: restaurants serving full meals, beer and wine; most, however, do not object to serving drinks only.
- Restaurant: hot and cold food and drinks served; not usually possible only to drink.
- Weinstube/Weinkeller: wine bars/wine cellars, serving drinks, principally wine and spirits, and light food.
- Bierstube/Bierkeller: beer bars, serving mainly beer, with light snacks also.
- Eiscafé/Eisdiele: ice cream cafés, which normally serve a wide range of ice creams, including many with alcoholic sauces, coffee, tea, and sometimes also cakes.
- Konditorei/Café: most cafés serve coffee, tea, cakes and spirits; many of the larger cake shops (Konditorei) do the same. Normal practice is to choose the cake(s) you want from the counter, and then give the numbered slip you receive to your waiter or waitress.

A problem about eating in East Germany is the overall shortage of restaurants. It is often necessary to queue in order to get a place, and once seated you may be expected to share a table. If possible, it is best to book in advance. Cellar restaurants (Ratskeller), which traditionally run under town halls throughout Germany, tend to be easier to get into than many other restaurants because of their sheer size.

Be careful about the opening times of restaurants too: even if a restaurant is open until 11.00pm, it may stop serving hot food at 9.00pm and food of any sort at 10.00pm.

In many restaurants it is expected that you leave your coat at the cloakroom or on a peg near the door. If you sit down in a coat or put it on the back of your chair, you will probably be asked to remove it.

There is no hard and fast rule for tipping, but locals tend to round up the bill by about 10%, but no more, when they pay. The usual way to do this is to say how much change you expect, rather than to leave money on the table.

Opening times

Shops are generally open Monday to Friday between 9.00am and 6.00pm, except in Berlin where hours tend to be 10.00am to 7.00pm. On Saturdays large stores are open in the morning, usually until 1.00pm, but all shops are closed on Saturday afternoons and Sundays.

Museums and galleries have no fixed closing day, but many tend to close on Mondays. Similarly, many restaurants and drinking places are closed on Mondays and/or Tuesdays.

Special interest holidays

There are various special interest holidays which can be taken in East Germany, either as packages or organised privately. The following are worth bearing in mind:-

Music Holidays

Berolina organises spring and autumn music tours taking in performances at the Schauspielhaus (Berlin), the Semperoper (Dresden), and the Gewandhaus or opera (Leipzig). Visits can also be arranged to Handel's house at Halle and the museum devoted to the work of the organ builder, Silbermann, at Freiberg.

People interested in the life and work of Bach may organise visits to Leipzig, Eisenach, Arnstadt and Weimar. Halle is an obvious place to visit for anyone interested in Handel, and Heinrich Schütz was born in Bad Köstritz near Gera.

For those interested in organs and organ music Berolina will arrange tours with recitals incorporating Arnstadt, Weimar, Mühlhausen and Erfurt.

Among East Germany's numerous music festivals are the Musik-Biennale held biannually in Berlin (February), the DDR-Musiktage, the Handel Festival, the Telemann festival, Bach festivals at Köthen, Greifswald and in Thuringia, the Gewandhaus-Festtage in Leipzig (September-October), the Hallesche Musiktage in Halle (October-November) and the Gottfried Silbermann Week (September).

Spas
Spa treatment has long been a feature of German life, and East Germany has a number of famous spa and health resorts. Cures can be booked through Berolina or Reisebüro der DDR. Stays are normally 21 days, and the price usually includes accommodation with full board, dietary advice and a weekly medical examination.

Among East Germany's many spa towns are Bad Salzungen in the south, a salt-springs spa resort, Bad Elster in the Weiße Elster valley, with its mineral springs, Bad Brambach, with its radon mineral springs, Bad Liebenstein, the largest resort for cardiac patients in the country, the Heinrich Heine diet sanatorium clinic at Potsdam-Neufahrland near the Krampitzsee and Lehnitzsee, and Graal Müritz on the Baltic coast not far from Rostock.

The Reformation
East Germany is the site of a number of towns with deep associations with the Reformation. Wittenberg and Eisleben are especially important for anyone interested in Luther, as is Eisenach, the site of the Wartburg where Luther worked on his translation of the Bible; Thomas Müntzer was born in Stolberg in the Harz and also had associations with Allstedt, Frankenhausen, Erfurt, Halberstadt, Halle and Zwickau.

Again, tours based on the life and work of Luther are arranged by Berolina.

Sport
The Thuringian woodlands, Harz mountains, Saxon Switzerland and Erzgebirge are all good walking areas and also suitable in parts for skiing in winter. Several areas along the Baltic, including Warnemünde and the island of Rügen, are popular for sailing, although facilities are not so far well developed for tourists.

Trains
It is still possible to encounter working steam trains, but chance sightings cannot be relied upon now as they could even five years ago. Holidays for rail enthusiasts can be arranged through Berolina. One example of a normal gauge steam railway can be visited at Erfurt. On certain weekends in summer a steam train runs on a stretch of local line starting from the main station.

Most of the narrow-gauge railways are located in holiday areas and are often used to link the main railway network to tourist destinations. Popular narrow-gauge railways include the Molli line (Bad Doberan to Kühlungsborn), the Harzquerbahn (Wernigerode to Nordhausen), the Erzgebirgsbahn (Cranzahl to Oberwiesenthal) and Osterzgebirgsbahn (Freital-Hainsberg to Kipsdorf), the Lößnitztalbahn (Radebeul to Moritzburg and Radeburg) and the Zittauer Bimmelbahn (Zittau to Oybin and Jonsdorf).

Narrow-gauge railways have also traditionally been run by the Young Pioneers (a communist youth organisation now gradually disappearing) (for example in Dresden, Halle, Plauen, Cottbus and Chemnitz). Dresden is also the site of a well known transport museum.

Galleries and Museums
It is impossible to list all the galleries and museums that can be visited, but almost every town has some sort of gallery or museum, and the range of interests covered is wide. The Museum Island in Berlin contains art galleries and museums of antiquities, and Dresden has some of Germany's most famous paintings. Museums of science and technology (e.g. the hygiene museum at Dresden and the museum at Magdeburg) are also well presented and widespread.

Zoos
East Germany has numerous zoos, the principal ones being in Berlin, Cottbus, Dresden, Erfurt, Frankfurt/Oder, Gera, Halle, Chemnitz, Leipzig, Magdeburg, Neubrandenburg, Potsdam, Rostock, Schwerin and Suhl.

Sources of information
The main UK source of information on holidays in East Germany is Berolina (22a Conduit Street, London W1R 9TB). They stock maps of the major cities and pamphlets and brochures on individual towns and areas.

View from the Nikolaiviertel in Berlin; in the background the Red Town Hall and the TV tower

Traditional organ-grinder, Alexanderplatz, Berlin

The Teahouse at Sanssouci, Potsdam

Cecilienhof, Potsdam

The ruins of the Frauenkirche, Dresden

The Buchenwald Memorial

More specialist information can be obtained from the Embassy of the German Democratic Republic, 34 Belgrave Square, London SW1X 8QB or on business matters from the Department of Trade and Industry. Another useful source of information is the Britain-GDR Friendship Society, 129 Seven Sisters Road, London N7 7QG. There is limited literature in English on East Germany (other than academic or specialist works), but recommended general reading includes David Childs's *The GDR: Moscow's German Ally* (London, 1988), Mike Dennis's *German Democratic Republic: Politics, Economics and Society* in the Marxist Regimes series (London & New York 1988), Martin McCauley's *The German Democratic Republic since 1945* (London 1983), and *The German Democratic Republic*, an East German work produced by Panorama DDR. Other recommended reading is *Honecker's Germany*, edited by David Childs (London 1985), *The German Democratic Republic: the search for identity* by Henry Krisch (London and Colorado 1985), *The German Democratic Republic: a developed socialist society*, edited by Lyman H. Legters (Colorado 1978) and *25 Years On: The Two Germanies* by Stanley Radcliffe (London 1972), a comparative study of East and West. Generally Panorama — Presseagentur of 1054 Berlin, Wilhelm-Pieck-Straße 49 — is a good GDR source of material in English as well as German.

There are several German language guides to East Germany, the main ones being *Reisebuch DDR* (VEB Tourist Verlag Berlin), an East German publication, again obtainable from Berolina, and *Baedeckers Reiseführer*, a West German publication which, however, is largely a reconstruction, and in parts a total repetition, of the East German publication.

Transport Map of East Berlin

Figures indicate
travelling time in minutes

S **U**

Berlin

Background

Berlin celebrated its 750th anniversary in 1987, a date based on the first documented record in 1237, not of Berlin, but of a town on the site of what is now part of Berlin, Cölln. The first documentary record of Berlin itself came seven years later in 1244. The symbol of Berlin, the bear, can be traced back to its use on the seal of the city in 1280.

Most people think of Berlin as the former capital of a united Germany, but in fact its status as a capital city was brief. In the 15th Century it was the major city of the Brandenburg-Prussia province, but in the 18th Century Frederick the Great set up his court in Potsdam, making that city the centre of cultural and political life.

Berlin's importance really began after Bismarck's unification of Germany when it became the capital of the German Empire after 1871. It remained the capital even after World War I and the collapse of the empire and became a major centre of art and culture as well as science and industry during the years of the Weimar Republic (1919-1933).

In 1920 the city boundaries were extended to take in the outlying area and form Groß-Berlin (Greater Berlin). With its 4 million inhabitants Berlin became the second largest city in Europe, rivalling in importance London and Paris.

The position of Berlin was further consolidated after Hitler came to power in 1933 and made it the administrative centre of his Third Reich. It was the focus of world attention at the 1936 Olympic Games (the stadium still survives in West Berlin) which Hitler sought to make a showcase for the world in spite of the imprisonment and murder of those who continued to resist National Socialism and the persecution of the Jews that culminated in the 'Kristallnacht' (so called after the sound of breaking glass) of November 9-10 1938 when the Nazis embarked on the systematic destruction of the synagogues.

After months of bombing, the Third Reich in Berlin capitulated in 1945, General Werdling surrendering to Marshal Zhukov in Berlin Karlshorst on May 8.

Under the terms of the London Protocol of 1944 made between the USA, Britain and the USSR, Berlin was given special status, a position that was ratified (with the assent of France) by the Potsdam Agreement signed in August 1945. Berlin, which became an island in the Soviet Occupied Zone of Germany, was divided into four sectors under the joint control of an Allied Control Council, each sector remaining under occupation by one of the Allies, the Soviet Union occupying the eastern zone.

When the Federal Republic of Germany (West Germany) was proclaimed in 1949, West Berlin (the British, French and American sectors) became one of the member states. In 1947 the West German Bundestag declared that Berlin was the capital of the Federal Republic, although Bonn, for practical reasons, became the seat of government. In the same year the Soviet Occupation Zone became the German Democratic Republic with East Berlin as its capital.

Tension between East and West inevitably focused on Berlin. Stalin had tried to bring about the downfall of West Berlin by blockading its road and rail links in 1948-49, a measure that failed as a result of the elaborate air-lift that kept the western sectors alive. In 1953 discontent among the citizens of East Berlin culminated in demonstrations on June 17, with citizens demanding better conditions and free elections. The demonstrations were quelled by Soviet troops, a fact that caused relations between the two halves of the divided city to deteriorate further. In spite of this, however, people moved freely between East and West. The West attempted to attract key workers from the East and many people emigrated from the East to the West through Berlin. Currency too flowed out as people came to the West to buy food and consumer products not available in the poorer East. To arrest this trend the border between East and West Berlin was sealed on August 13 1961 and the Berlin Wall was constructed, at first a primitive frontier that was gradually strengthened until it became virtually impregnable. It remained a barrier between the people of East and West Berlin until Erich Honecker was deposed in 1989 and his successor, Egon Krenz, ordered the borders to be re-opened on November 9 1989. By 1990, with Germany set on a course of reunification, Berlin was again spoken of as the capital of a united Germany.

WEST BERLIN

West Berlin, with a population of some 1,850,000, is made up of the American, British and French sectors created after the end of World War II. Although it is a state of the Federal Republic of Germany it remains technically under the control of the Allies and has a separate parliament (the Abgeordnetenhaus) which meets in the town hall, Schöneberg.
Although there is now freedom of movement between East and West Berlin, most of the Berlin Wall (46km long) is still in place and should be seen. Construction started on August 13 1961, and a more and more elaborate structure grew up over the years until it became virtually impenetrable. The Wall was effectively opened to allow free movement on November 9 1989. It is best viewed from the Brandenburger Tor, although large sections are now being removed.

Haus am Checkpoint Charlie

The House at Checkpoint Charlie (Friedrichstraße 44) deals with the history of the Berlin Wall and the fate of those who tried to cross it, some with success, others less fortunate. Its approach is very much coloured by cold war era thinking. Open every day from 9.00am — 8.00pm.

West of the Brandenburg Gate

The Straße der 17. Juni (named after the East Berlin rebellion against the government in 1953) leads away from the Brandenburg Gate to the Siegessäule.

Siegessäule

The Siegessäule (Victory Column) was built between 1869-1873 after a design by Heinrich Strack to commemorate Germany's successful military campaigns of 1864, 1866 and 1870 against France. The gilded goddess on the top is by Friedrich Drake. The hall underneath the column contains a mosaic frieze, the work of Anton von Werner (open April to November Mondays 1.00pm —7.00pm, Tuesdays — Sundays 9.00am — 7.00pm).

Reichstagsgebäude

Close to the Wall and the Brandenburg Gate is the Reichstag Building. The Reichstag was the German parliament, and it was the fire here on the night of February 27 1933 that led to the arrest, trial and execution of a young Dutchman, van der Lubbe, and the arrest of the Bulgarian communist, Georgi Dimitroff. Although Dimitroff successfully defended himself against charges of conspiracy, the fire was used by Hitler as an excuse to pass laws giving totalitarian powers to himself and his Nazi party.

The building itself was built between 1884 — 1894 by Paul Wallot whose design was chosen from 183 entries in a competition. The original building had a dome which has never been restored. Today the Reichstag contains a chamber to seat 650 and offices and meeting rooms for the use of the Bundestag (one of West Germany's two houses of parliament).

There is a permanent exhibition 'Questions for German History'. The Reichstag is open Tuesdays to Sundays 10.00am — 5.00pm.

Kongreßhalle

The nearby Kongreßhalle (Congress Hall) was a gift to Berlin from the United States. The design is by an American architect, Hugh A. Stubbins. Built in 1956 and 1957, it was regarded as adventurous at the time because of the curious V-shaped roof structure. Unfortunately a large part of the roof collapsed in 1980, although the building is now functioning again. (Not open to the public.)

Schloß Bellevue

The Bellevue Palace, between the Siegessäule and the Spree, was built in 1785-1786 for Prince Ferdinand of Prussia, Frederick the Great's youngest brother. Since June 18 1959 it has been an official residence of the President of the Federal Republic. The gardens are open until dusk, but the palace itself cannot be visited except by special arrangement.

Hansaviertel

The Hansaviertel, again not far from the Siegessäule, is a residential area developed between 1955-1957 as a model of good modern architecture. 53 architects from all over the world (including Alvar Aalto, Oscar Niemeyer and Walter Gropius) produced designs for blocks of flats and houses. Also in the Hansaviertel is the Akademie der Künste (Academy of Arts). The best way of seeing this area is to take the U-Bahn to Hansaplatz or the S-Bahn to Bellevue and walk along Klopstockstraße and Bartningallee.

Philharmonie

The Philharmonie, near the Wall (Matthäikirchstraße 1, nearest U-Bahn station Potsdamer Platz), is the home of the Berliner Philharmonie, one of the world's finest orchestras.

The building is an exciting modern concert hall, with the audience almost surrounding the orchestra, and was built under Hans Scharoun between 1960 and 1963.

Neue Nationalgalerie

The New National Gallery is another modern building, close to the Philharmonie (Potsdamer Straße 50). It is a harsh modern building of black metal and glass, cuboid in shape, and the work of Mies van der Rohe. It is devoted entirely to modern painting and sculpture. (Open Tuesdays to Fridays 9.00am — 5.00pm, Saturdays and Sundays 10.00am — 5.00pm)

Martin-Gropius-Bau

In the Niederkirchnerstraße, just outside Tiergarten in Kreuzberg (one of Berlin's poorer areas), is the Martin Gropius Building, built between 1877-1881 by Martin Gropius in collaboration with Heino Schmieden. It is used for exhibitions.

Kurfürstendamm

The Kurfürstendamm is West Berlin's most famous and most prestigious boulevard. It first became a road in the 16th Century and was used as a route to the Jagdschloß in Grunewald. In the 19th Century it was expanded into a larger, wider thoroughfare at the instigation of Bismarck. Commemorative plaques recall that the writers Max Hermann-Neiße and Robert Musil lived at Nos. 215 and 217 respectively. At the bottom end at the corner of Joachimstaler Straße is Café Kranzler, Berlin's best known café.

Although it is common to find people simply strolling along the Ku'damm (as the locals call it) it really is little more than a modern shopping street and has little to offer that 20 minutes or so will not suffice to satisfy. The shops are ludicrously expensive.

Kaiser-Wilhelm-Gedächtniskirche

The Kaiser-Wilhelm Memorial Church dominates Breitscheid-platz at the bottom of the Kurfürstendamm and is the symbol of West Berlin. It is an odd mixture of ancient and modern, consisting in part of the ruin of a church built here in the 1890s which was destroyed in the war, and a modern building, dating from 1961, the work of Emil Eiermann. The modern church is an octagonal building, most impressive in the dark when the inside lights produce a kaleidoscopic pattern of light. A free-standing campanile in the same style stands on the other side of the preserved ruin.

The interior is also impressive. A simple altar is watched over by Karl Hemmeter's Resurrection. Concerts are often given on the organ (Karl Schuke, 1962) on Saturdays evenings at 6.00pm.

Weltkugelbrunnen

The Globe Fountain nearby (constructed 1983) is an eccentric fountain of bronze and granite on different levels. It defies description.

Europa Centre

The Europa Centre is often cited as a tourist attraction of West Berlin but in fact is nothing more than a multi-storey block of shops and offices. Its only features of any real interest are the I-Punkt restaurant with its excellent views and the Uhr der fließenden Zeit (flowing time clock), a water clock, created by Bernard Gitton in 1982. Also here are Die Stachelschweine (the Porcupines), the West's best known satyrical cabaret.

Zoo and Aquarium

The Berlin zoo on Hardenbergplatz, opposite the main railway station of the West (Bahnhof Zoo), was started in 1841. Among its 11,000 inhabitants (over 1,500 species) are Bobby, the gorilla, and a panda, Bao Bao. The aviary is said to be the largest in the world. The entrance on Budapester Straße is particularly striking, a sort of pagoda roof in far eastern style supported by two elephants. The aquarium (its entrance is also on Budapester Straße) contains over 60,000 fish and reptiles.

The zoo is open every day from 9.00am — 5.00pm, and the aquarium from 9.00am — 6.00pm, but on the last Saturday in each month until 9.00pm.

Deutsche Oper

The Deutsche Oper (Bismarckstraße 35, U-Bahn, Deutsche Oper), is the opera house and company of West Berlin. From the outside it is a rather dreary concrete and glass building in the shape of a cube, but lit up at night it can be attractive. The original opera on this site was built in 1912 by Heinrich Seeling, and some original materials have been incorporated into the reconstructed building by Fritz Bornemann. Outside stands a moving sculpture, the work of Hans Uhlmann.

Schloß Charlottenburg

This palace and its associated buildings lie in a well kept park. The main palace faces onto Luisenplatz (at the end of Otto-Suhr-Allee). The palace itself was begun in 1695 as a summer residence for the elector's wife (the later queen, Sophie Charlotte, after whom it is named) to plans by Arnold Nering. It was expanded between 1701-1707 by Eosander von Göthe to become a symmetrical building facing onto a large courtyard. The two side wings contain offices, but the main building is open for visitors who can walk round the appartments of Friedrich I, Sophie Charlotte, and Friedrich Wilhelm I and II. Especially noteworthy is the Chinese room by Knobelsdorff, decorated in the Chinese fashion in 1788 for Friedrich Wilhelm II.

The so-called Knobelsdorff wing of the palace houses a gallery of Romantic art which contains works by Caspar David Friedrich and others. The Langhans extension on the end of the west wing (the former theatre) houses a museum of pre- and early history.

An equestrian statue to the Grand Elector (der Große Kurfürst) dominates the cobbled square facing Luisenplatz. Like many German statues of this type it follows the classical model. It is the work of Andreas Schlüter, who modelled it, and Johann Jacobi, who cast it. It sank in the Havel while being removed for protection during the last war but was salvaged and erected here in 1952.

The palace gardens, worth a visit in themselves, contain a number of smaller buildings including the Schinkel-Pavillon, built as a summer house and now containing pictures and sculptures of the Schinkel period; the Belvedere, a tea pavilion by Langhans, now the home of a substantial collection of porcelain; and a Mausoleum in the form of a temple, originally designed as the resting place for the body of Queen Luise.

The palace complex is open Tuesdays to Sundays from 9.00am — 5.00pm. Note that the mausoleum is only open April-October.

Ägyptisches Museum

The Egyptian Museum (Schloßstraße 70) opposite Charlottenburg is devoted to Egyptian history from about 5000 BC — 3000 AD and is open Mondays — Thursdays 9.00am — 5.00pm and Saturdays and Sundays 10.00am — 5.00pm.

Antikenmuseum
The Museum of Antiquities directly opposite (Schloßstraße 1) is
open Mondays — Thursdays from 9.00am — 5.00pm and at
weekends from 10.00am — 5.00pm.

Around the Radio Tower
International Congress Centre
Near Theodor-Heuss-Platz, south of Masurenallee, is Berlin's
International Congress Centre (ICC), a vast area used for
international exhibitions and trade fairs. The two main halls can
seat 5,000 and 2,000 people. The ICC itself is linked to the
exhibition areas by a bridge.

Radio Tower
The radio tower (Funkturm) dominates the skyline. It is a steel
structure built 1924-1926 by Heinrich Straumer and has a
restaurant and viewing platform.

Olympic Stadium
The Olympiastadion was built between 1934-1936 for the XIth
Olympic Games held in Berlin in 1936. An oval structure with
a capacity of 100,000, it was supposed to be a showpiece for the
world of Hitler's Third Reich. It was here that the black athlete
Jesse Owen beat his 'Aryan' opponents.

Le Corbusier House
South of the Olympic Stadium (in the Heilsberger triangle
between the stadium and Heerstraße) is the Le-Corbusier-
Haus, a 17-storey block of 530 flats. It was designed as a town
'under one roof' with shops, post office etc. as well as living
accommodation.

Beyond the centre
Grunewald
The Grunewald is Berlin's largest woodland and forest area
covering some 30km². Divided between the districts of
Wilmersdorf and Zehlendorf and stretching for over 5km
towards the Havel and almost 10km south of Heerstraße to the
Wannsee, it is a favourite place for excursions, especially in
summer. In the northern part the Teufelsberg is an artificial hill
made out of the rubble of World War II. The area also takes in
some of Berlin's most attractive lakes, the Grunewaldsee,
Krumme Lanke and Schlachtensee.

Kleinglienicke

Kleinglienicke is the name of a parkland area in the extreme southwest of West Berlin in the Wannsee area. The palace and gardens (Schloß und Park Kleinglienicke) are the work of Schinkel and his pupils, Ludwig Persius and Ferdinand von Arnim, and the landscape gardener, Peter Lenné.

Pfaueninsel

The Pfaueninsel (Peacock Island), 1.5km long and 500m across, is a small island just off the mainland at Wannsee. At various times it has been used for the breeding of rabbits and as a laboratory. However, it attracted the attention of Friedrich Wilhelm II who erected a summer residence there. Friedrich Wilhelm III then adopted it, and in 1822 Peter Lenné designed a park on it. The castle (Schloß) was built in 1796 in Romantic style, a folly designed to look like a ruin, the two towers connected by a bridge. As it was the work of a carpenter, a man called Brendel from Potsdam, wood is the principal building material. Even the bridge was wood until it was replaced by a more stable metal structure in 1807.

It takes about an hour to walk round the island which apart from the castle is the site of a number of eccentric buildings. The island itself is reached by ferry.

Wannsee

The Wannsee, a large lake on the Havel, is again in the southeast corner of West Berlin and is another popular place for excursions. The lake is famous for its sailing boats and yachts and for water sport generally. The beach is one of the largest on any lake anywhere in Europe. Nearby (close to No. 3 Bismarckstraße) is the grave of the German writer Heinrich von Kleist who committed suicide here on November 21 1811. The words engraved on his headstone ('Now, immortality, thou art wholly mine') are taken from one of his plays, *Prinz Friedrich von Homburg*.

Spandau

Spandau, in the northwest, is known to many English people because it where the British army in Berlin is largely stationed. It was also the site of the prison where Rudolf Hess was imprisoned until his death in 1987 (after which the prison was demolished).

Zitadelle

The Citadel (Zitadelle) on the banks of the Havel is Spandau's greatest attraction. The tower (Juliusturm) dominates the skyline and may go back to the 12th Century. The Citadel itself mostly dates from 1560-1594 and shows in its design the Italian influence of the Venetian architect Chiaramello de Gandono. It is open Tuesdays to Fridays 9.00am — 4.30pm and on Saturdays and Sundays from 10.00am — 4.30pm. (Note: often closed in winter.)

Die Nikolaikirche

The Church of St Nicholas is Spandau's other main attraction. The present brick church with its high roof and imposing tower dates back to the second half of the 14th Century. The high altar was a gift from the architect Graf Rochus zu Lynar in 1582. Its intricacy contrasts with the simplicity of the interior.

Museums and galleries

Like East Berlin, West Berlin is full of galleries and museums. Information about the main ones is given below.

Dahlem

Die Staatlichen Museen in Dahlem, Lansstraße 8/Arnimallee 23-27 (U-Bahn Dahlem Dorf), are several museums under one roof. The picture gallery (Gemäldegalerie) contains a high quality and representative collection of paintings from all over Europe (works include paintings by Bosch, Breughel, Raphael, Botticelli, Lippi, Cranach and Rembrandt). Notable are the Breughel painting depicting Dutch proverbs, the altar paintings of Rogier van der Weyden and Cranach's *Fountain of Youth*.

The engravings collection (Kupferstichkabinett) containing works by Dürer, Breughel and Rembrandt (to name three of many) and 27 of Botticelli's illustrations to Dante's Divine Comedy is also worth a visit, as is the sculpture gallery with over 3,000 items including work by Donatello, Luca and Andrea della Robbia. Note the fine Spanish collection.

Also at Dahlem are the Museums of Indian Art and Islamic Art, the Museum for East Asian Art, and a Museum of Anthropology.

All are open Tuesdays to Sundays 9.00am — 5.00pm.

Berlin Museum

The Berlin Museum (Lindenstraße 15) is one of Berlin's most accessible and attractive museums. It is housed in an old court building (das Alte Kammergericht) constructed in 1735 under Friedrich Wilhelm I. It is devoted to the history of Berlin, but also has a splendid bar and restaurant that open for Sunday lunch. Museum opening times are Tuesdays to Sundays 11.00am — 6.00pm.

Bröhan Museum
The Bröhan Museum (Schloßstraße 1a), close to Schloß Charlottenburg, is a collection of artefacts covering the period 1899-1939. It is essential visiting for any lover of art nouveau. It is open Tuesdays to Sundays from 10.00am — 6.00pm.

Gedenkstätte Plötzensee
The Plötzensee Memorial (Hüttigpfad) is the West's homage to the victims of Hitler. The location was chosen because Plötzensee was the prison where so many of Hitler's victims were executed.

Musical Instruments Museum
The Musical Instruments Museum at Tiergartenstraße 1 contains some 2,000 instruments from the 16th Century onwards. Open Tuesdays to Saturdays from 9.00am — 5.00pm and Sundays from 10.00am — 5.00pm.

Sugar Museum
An unusual museum devoted to sugar and recognisable by its turret in the form of a sugar beet. It is in Amrumer Straße 32 and is open Tuesdays to Sundays 10.00am — 5.00pm.

Other places of interest
Botanical Gardens
Situated in Königin Luisenstraße the Botanical Gardens contain over 18,000 different species of plants (outdoors as well as in greenhouses). Opening times for the gardens and greenhouses vary according to times of year, so check local information for exact details.

Markets
There are something like 70 markets a week held in West Berlin. Among them are the Berliner Trödelmarkt (Straße des 17. Juni, Saturdays and Sundays 8.00am — 3.00pm), the flea market at the disused Nollendorfplatz U-Bahn station (11.00am — 7.30pm daily), the Winterfeldtmarkt (near Gleditschstraße) held on Wednesdays and Saturdays, and the Markt am Maybachufer

(Kottbusser Brücke, Tuesdays and Fridays from noon —
6.30pm). Avoid the squalor of the Krempelmarkt held on
wasteland between the National Library and Checkpoint Charlie
underneath the new monorail track which is used largely by
Poles desperately trying to make a living by selling cheap Polish
cigarettes and electrical goods for western money.

Where to stay
By contrast with East Berlin, there are numerous hotels in all
parts of West Berlin and at every standard. At the top end of the
market is the Bristol Hotel Kempinski, Kurfürstendamm 27.
Other hotels are the Grand Hotel Esplanade, Lutzowufer 15, the
Inter-Continental, Budapester Straße, the Steigenberger in Los-
Angeles-Platz, the Palace in the Europa Centre and the
Schweizer Hof, again in Budapester Straße. A cheap hotel with
shared rooms is the Budget-Hotel, Alt-Moabit 89. There are
hotel accommodation agencies at Bahnhof Zoo, the airport and
in the Europa Centre.

Where to eat
Again, there are many restaurants, especially in the area around
and just off Kurfürstendamm. For cheap meals there are plenty
of places that serve pizza and pasta, and Turkish and Yugoslav
restaurants are also good value.

Getting about in West Berlin
If you are staying in the West for a weekend you can buy a
family ticket covering the U-Bahn and buses for DM10. You
can also buy day tickets for DM9 per person. Otherwise, avoid
buying individual tickets (at DM 2.70 each) but get the cheaper
Sammelkarten (one ticket gives you five trips). Any ticket is
valid for one journey at a time in any one direction by the
shortest route. Information and maps can be obtained from the
BVG kiosk outside Bahnhof Zoo station.

Entertainment
Music
Classical concerts are most often held in the Berliner
Philharmonie, Matthäikirchstraße 1 and in the Haus des
Rundfunks, Masurenallee. The opera (Deutsche Oper) is at
Bismarckstraße 35.

# West Berlin

Pop concerts tend to take place in the Deutschlandhalle, Messedamm 26. The Metropol, Nollendorfplatz 5, is good for rock and pop. There is sometimes Irish music in the Irish pub in the Europa Centre.

Theatres
Principal theatres include: Schiller-Theater, Bismarckstraße 110 (and workshop theatre for smaller productions); Schloßpark-Theater, Schloßstraße 48; Freie Volksbühne, Schaperstraße 24; Hebbel-Theater, Stresemannstraße 29; Komödie, Kurfürstendamm 206; Renaissance-Theater, Hardenbergplatz 6; Schaubühne am Lehniner Platz, Kurfürstendamm 153; Theater am Kurfürstendamm, Kurfürstendamm 209; Theatermanufaktur am Halleschen Ufer, Hallesches Ufer 32; Vagantenbühne, Kantstraße 12a.

Night Life
There is an enormous number of clubs, discos and bars, again many of which are in the Kurfürstendamm area. They vary a great deal in price. Among them are Big Eden, Kurfürstendamm 202, Dschungel, Nürnberger Straße 53, Metropol, Nollendorf-platz 5, and the Quartier Latin, Potsdamer Straße 30. Many bars only close for about an hour a day.

Information
Up to date information on what is going on is given in the magazine, Berlin-Programm.

General and tourist information can be obtained from Berlin Tourist Information, Europa Center (open daily 7.30am – 10.30pm).

EAST BERLIN
East Berlin, at present still properly called 'Berlin, Capital of the German Democratic Republic' to distinguish it from West Berlin, is the home of 1.2 million East German citizens. Apart from its importance as the seat of government and administration in East Germany, it is a major international centre for culture and the arts and is important industrially with major factories and enterprises manufacturing electrical and electronic goods, machinery, textiles and chemicals. The river Spree runs through the city the surroundings of which are famous for their woods and lakes.

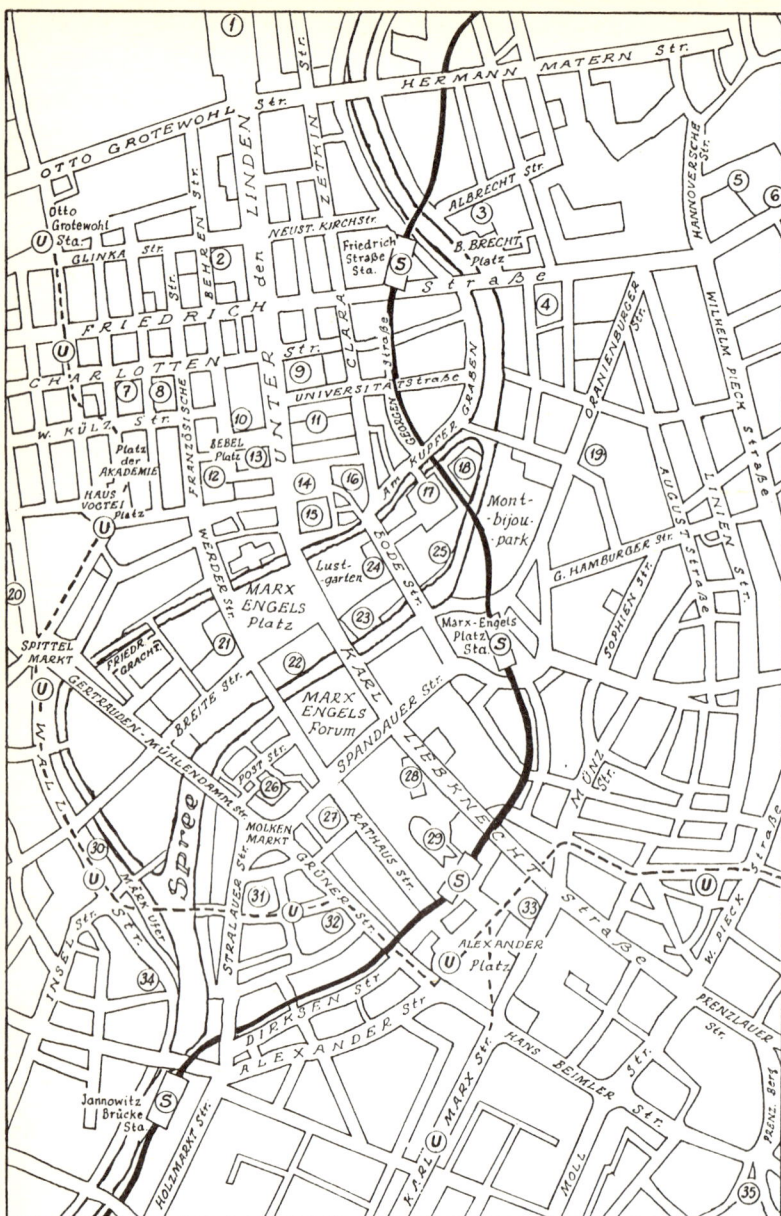

BERLIN - East

0   300

m

N

EAST BERLIN - KEY

① Brandenburg Gate
② Comic Opera
③ Berliner Ensemble
④ Friedrichstadtpalast
⑤ Dorotheenstädtischer Cemetery
⑥ Brecht-Haus
⑦ Schauspielhaus
⑧ Französicher Dom
⑨ German State Library
⑩ Old Library
⑪ Humboldt University
⑫ St. Hedwig's Cathedral
⑬ German State Opera
⑭ Neue Wache
⑮ Museum of German History
⑯ Maxim Gorky Theatre
⑰ Pergamon Museum
⑱ Bode Museum

⑲ Synagogue
⑳ Spittelkolonnade
㉑ Council of State
㉒ Palace of the Republic
㉓ Berlin Cathedral
㉔ Altes Museum
㉕ National Gallery
㉖ Nikolaikirche and Nikolaiviertel
㉗ Red Town Hall
㉘ Marienkirche
㉙ Television Tower
㉚ Otto-Nagel-Haus
㉛ Ministerrat
㉜ Klosterkirche
㉝ Hotel Stadt Berlin
㉞ Märkisches Museum
㉟ Volkspark Friedrichshain

Ⓢ Station
Ⓤ U-bahn Station

Visiting Berlin
One-day walk through East Berlin

Most of the principal sights and monuments of Berlin can be seen in a day's walk by a visitor on a one-day visa. Starting from Friedrichstraße station turn right under the railway bridge and you will see the Hotel Metropol ahead on your right and the International Trade Centre (tinted glass and concrete) on your left.

Unter den Linden

Just a few minutes walk away from Friedrichstraße Station, the history of old Berlin starts at the junction of Friedrichstraße and Berlin's best known street, Unter den Linden. The name of the street, literally translated, means 'Beneath the Lime Trees' and the lime trees are still there as they have been since the 17th Century. The original street was designed and laid out between 1618-1648 by the Elector, Friedrich Wilhelm of Brandenburg. Initially it consisted of a promenade planted with 1,000 lime trees and 1,000 nut trees. The buildings now lining it go back largely to the 18th Century by which time plane trees and chestnut trees had also been added and the pedestrians had been protected from the traffic by iron barriers.

Brandenburger Tor

To the right, looking west, Unter den Linden comes to an abrupt halt with the Brandenburger Tor (Brandenburg Gate), the only one of the old city's gates that is still standing. It remained a symbolic gate dividing East from West until it was opened as a border crossing point in December 1989. The gate is decorated with reliefs depicting a procession of the goddess of peace. A statue of Minerva, goddess of wisdom, occupies a niche on the north side, and Mars, the god of war, a niche on the south. The Brandenburger Tor (1788-1791) was modelled by Carl Gotthard Langhans on the Acropolis and is a clear statement of 18th Century classicism. The quadriga, a chariot drawn by four horses, which sits on top of the monument facing east, was added in 1793 by one of Berlin's best-known sculptors, Johann Gottfried Schadow. The chariot is driven by the goddess of victory. She has survived not only World War II, after restoration work, but also a period of imprisonment in France. Napoleon plundered the quadriga in 1806 and it was only returned to Berlin in 1814 after being recaptured by the victorious Marshal Blücher.

Quite close to the gate at Under den Linden 67, next to the Soviet embassy, is a bronze plaque commemorating the life and

work of architect Karl Friedrich Schinkel, who lived here
between 1823 and 1839 and has a museum dedicated to his work
in one of Berlin's recently restored churches (the Friedrichswerdersche Kirche — see p.54). On the other side of Unter den
Linden, at Schadowstraße 10/11, is the house of another famous
Berlin architect, Johann Gottfried Schadow (1764-1850).

The State Library

The first substantial building of note on the northern side of
Unter den Linden is the Staatsbibliothek (German State
Library), a neo-baroque edifice (1903-1914), housing between
five and six million books and manuscripts. It is East Germany's
equivalent of the British Library and is said to grow by 80,000
new acquisitions a year.

Access to the interior is restricted to tours on the first Sunday
of every month, but visitors may enter the courtyard at the
front, in which, on the left, is a large stone with Bertolt Brecht's
poem summing up the communist view of history: 'Der junge
Alexander eroberte Indien./Er allein?/ Cäsar schlug die Gallier./
Hatte er nicht wenigstens einen Koch bei sich?/ Philipp von
Spanien weinte, als seine Flotte/ Untergegangen war. Weinte
sonst niemand?/ Friedrich der Zweite siegte im Siebenjährigen
Krieg. Wer/ Siegte außer ihm?' (Young Alexander conquered
India. Did he do it alone? Caesar defeated the Gauls. Didn't he
even have a cook with him? Philip of Spain cried when his fleet
sank. Didn't anyone else cry? Frederick the Second won the
Seven Years' War. Who won apart from him?)

Statue of Frederick the Great

The central promenade of Unter den Linden is the setting at
this point for an equestrian statue of Frederick the Great
mounted on a high plinth. The work of Christian Daniel Rauch
from the year 1851, it was brought to Berlin from Sanssouci in
Potsdam in 1980. It depicts the king mounted on Condé, his
favourite horse.

Humboldt University

The academic tone of this stretch of Unter den Linden is
confirmed by the Humboldt University next door. Again the
building is a product of the 18th Century. Originally built as a
palace for Prince Heinrich, the brother of Frederick the Great,
it became a university in 1810. Many of Germany's greatest and
best-known scholars taught or studied here: philosophers such
as Hegel and Fichte, philologists such as the brothers Grimm
(Jakob wrote an influential grammar of the German language

and propounded Grimm's Law on German sound shifts, as well as co-authoring the now world-famous fairy tales), the physicists Einstein and Planck, and Karl Marx. Engels is said to have attended lectures as an occasional guest and Lenin to have been a reader in the library. The two statues just outside the wrought-iron railings of the university commemorate the philologist Wilhelm von Humboldt and his brother Alexander von Humboldt, the naturalist and explorer whose statue bears the words 'Al segundo descubridor de Cuba. La Universidad de la Habana 1939' (To the second discoverer of Cuba. The University of Havana 1939).

Alte Bibliothek
The Alte Bibliothek (Old Library) opposite the University and facing Bebelplatz is the old Royal Library. Built by Unger between 1774-1780 with an impressive baroque façade, it was traditionally referred to by Berliners as 'die Kommode' (the chest of drawers). Lenin was one of its best known readers. It is now part of the Humboldt University.

Bebelplatz
Between the Alte Bibliothek and the Opera Café on the south side of Unter den Linden is the Bebelplatz, named after August Bebel, one of Germany's early socialist leaders. Previously known as the Opernplatz, the square was the scene of book-burning by the Nazis on May 10 1933.

German State Opera House
On the same side of Unter den Linden stands the Deutsche Staatsoper (German State Opera), Berlin's main opera house, again in the classical mode, based on the principles of a Corinthian temple. The original building by Knobelsdorff (1741-1743) burnt down in the early 19th century and was subsequently reconstructed by Langhans in 1843. Further disaster struck during World War II, and the present restored building owes its splendour to extensive work carried out in the mid-1980s. Statues of the Greek dramatists, Aristophanes, Euripides, Menander and Sophocles, emphasise classical values but the interior is rococo.

At the side of the opera is the famous Operncafé, a two-storey baroque building dating from 1833. It brings to an end the south side of Unter den Linden and is a good place to stop for a rest. In good weather you can sit outside and look across to the Gorky Theatre and the Neue Wache.

Maxim-Gorki-Theater
Set back behind the University and the Neue Wache is the Maxim Gorky Theatre, a simple building that used to house the Berlin Academy of Singing. It was built in neo-classical style (1825-1827) on designs by Schinkel. Mendelssohn gave a performance of Bach's *St Matthew Passion* here as part of his revival of Bach's work, and Liszt gave his first Berlin concerts here.

Neue Wache
The Neue Wache (New Watch — 1816-1818) is now a Monument to the Victims of Fascism and Militarism. From here you can observe the changing of the guard at 2.30pm every day. Soldiers of the People's Army have kept watch here continuously since May 1 1962. The exterior of the Neue Wache is Roman but the interior has been decorated according to the designs of an East German architect, Lothar Kwasnitza, and the setting for the tomb of the unknown soldier is in Byzantine style. Earth from Buchenwald and Mauthausen and from the battlefields of Moscow, Stalingrad, Normandy and elsewhere contained in urns lies beneath the tombstones dedicated to the unknown soldier and the unknown resistance fighter. An eternal flame burns in their memory.

Zeughaus/Museum of German History
One last military site in Unter den Linden is the Zeughaus (Arsenal), which now houses the Museum of German History (Museum für Deutsche Geschichte). Built between 1695 and 1706 and based on a design of the French architect François Blondel, it is one of Berlin's finest examples of baroque architecture. The presentation of history is moulded by the principles of Marx and Lenin: the development of Germany is depicted as it has affected, and been affected by, the workers and peasants, and not just as an account of the actions of monarchs and statesmen. It is open Mondays to Thursdays from 9.00am — 6.00pm and on Saturdays and Sundays from 10.00am — 5.00pm.

Concerts are given in summer in the courtyard in the centre of the building, the Schlüterhof, named after the architect who designed many of the statues incorporated in the Zeughaus.

Marx-Engels-Brücke/Schloßbrücke
The Schloßbrücke (currently known as the Marx-Engels-Brücke) crosses the Spree at this point and connects Unter den Linden with Marx-Engels-Platz. It is the work of Karl

Friedrich Schinkel, and the decorative statues (by Emil Wolff, Hermann Schievelbein, Heinrich Möller, Ludwig Wichmann, Friedrich Drake, Gustav Bläser, August Wredow and Albert Wolff) commemorate the liberation from Napoleon. Glance down on the north side of the bridge and you are sure to see seagulls perched on one of the wooden posts.

Marx-Engels-Platz
Marx-Engels-Platz (Marx-Engels Square), across the Spree canal, extends on both sides of the road, and is bordered in the north by the Altes Museum, to the east by the cathedral and on the south side by the Palast der Republik and the Council of State.

Berlin Cathedral
Just before crossing the Spree you come to Berlin's largest church, the Berliner Dom (Berlin Cathedral). The original building was built between 1746 and 1750 according to designs by Knobelsdorff, Johann Boumann and Frederick the Great, and was replaced in 1894 by the present cathedral, the work of Julius Carl Raschdorff. It lay in ruins for many years after the war (and for a long time after Berlin's principal Catholic church had been restored), until reconstruction work began in the early 1980s. It was re-consecrated in 1983 and now functions partially as a church and partially as a museum. The museum is worth a visit to see the Kaiserliches Treppenhaus (Imperial Stairway), although many of the exhibits on show here are not originals but reproductions, often of works of art housed elsewhere. On the side facing the square a freestanding door has recently been erected. The reliefs represent the story of the Prodigal Son and the whole door is known as the Versöhnungstür (Door of Reconciliation). It is the work of Siegfried Krepp, and was undertaken between 1979 — 1989. The opening times of the cathedral are Monday to Saturday 10.00am — noon and 1.00pm — 5.00pm, and Sundays noon — 5.00pm. Concerts of church music are often given on Friday evenings.

Palace of the Republic
Marx-Engels-Platz south of the main road is the site of one Berlin monument that was never restored and has now disappeared for ever. Before being renamed, the square used to be called Schloßplatz (Palace Square) after the palace known as the Berliner Schloß. Built around a massive courtyard, the palace was for several centuries a royal and imperial residence. The whole edifice was reduced to rubble in World War II and

the site was smoothed out to create a new empty square that was the scene of public meetings and Christmas fairs before construction began on the Palast der Republik (Palace of the Republic) which was opened in 1976. 180m long, this modern building with its reflecting glass contains a theatre, cinemas, cafés and a hall for 5,000 people. It also houses the Volkskammer (People's Chamber) with its 541 seats for members and space for diplomats, journalists and visitors. The Volkskammer came into being in 1948 and approved the first constitution of East Germany. It is a parliamentary body but until recently had little power compared to the Staatsrat (Council of State). Over one of the entrances there is a massive GDR emblem: sheaves of wheat to represent workers of the land and a hammer and compasses to represent industrial workers.

Marx-Engels-Forum
The Spree itself divides the Palace from the Marx-Engels-Forum, a large square dedicated to the memory of Marx and Engels at a formal ceremony conducted by Erich Honecker on April 4 1986. The area is dominated by two enormous statues of Marx and Engels, the work of Ludwig Engelhardt. The forum is also the setting of a five-section marble wall, the work of the sculptor Werner Stötzer. The sections depict the exploitation of man by his fellows, contrasting with Margret Midell's bronze reliefs depicting Glück und Geborgenheit (Joy and Salvation). The salvation is not that of Christianity, but salvation from class war, and the tableau as a whole is designed to represent a society free from oppression.

Karl-Liebknecht-Straße
The street that leads through Marx-Engels-Forum and that continues the route begun by Unter den Linden is Karl-Liebknecht-Straße. Liebknecht, a student at the Humboldt University (then called the Friedrich-Wilhelm University), was a leading figure in opposing Germany's role in World War I. His pamphlet, *The Main Enemy Stands at Home* condemning the warmongery of the time, won much support but also made him many enemies. Like Rosa Luxemburg he was murdered in 1919 for his revolutionary politics and left-wing beliefs. The wide road now named after him used, in imperial times, to bear the name of Kaiser Wilhelm.

Marienkirche
Continuing along Karl-Liebknecht-Straße you come to one of Berlin's oldest churches, standing uneasily in the shadow of the

TV tower that dominates Alexanderplatz. First records of the Marienkirche (St Mary's Church) date back to 1294, although the towers were added in the 15th Century, and there are many other later additions. The church has a rather stark interior but a wonderful sense of simplicity and unity. The organ by Joachim Wagner goes back to the 1720s, and the font, in front of the altar, dates from as far back as 1437. The dance of death fresco, a doom painting on the walls below the towers at the back of the church, is believed to have been painted after the plague of 1484. The church was struck by two bombs in World War II but was one of the first Berlin monuments to be restored, work having begun as early as 1945. The extravagant pulpit with its winding stairs and baroque decorations was worked on by Andreas Schlüter between 1702-1703.

The church is open Mondays to Thursdays 10.00am — noon and 1.00pm — 5.00pm, and Saturdays from noon — 4.30pm. Organ recitals are occasionally given on Saturdays.

On the side of the church facing Karl-Liebknecht-Straße a statue of Martin Luther, dating from the end of the 19th Century and the work of Otto and Toberentz, has been erected. It is only a shadow of the pre-war monument, which included a large platform with figures of other leaders of the Reformation, including Melanchthon, surrounding Luther.

Alexanderplatz

Alexanderplatz was immortalised in one of Berlin's most famous novels, *Berlin Alexanderplatz* by Alfred Döblin, published in 1929 when Berlin was at the centre of European culture. It tells the story of Franz Biberkopf, just released from a four-year sentence at Tegel prison, trying to integrate himself back into Berlin life. He fails, and ends his days in a lunatic asylum working as a porter. The novel, and the later film based on it, are not just about the fate of Biberkopf but are a damning depiction of Berlin life at the time.

Today's Alexanderplatz bears little resemblance to that of Franz Biberkopf and Alfred Döblin. Popularly called just Alex, its present design goes back to 1966-1967 and now looks dated. It is a vast empty area dominated by the television tower at one end and the 39-storey Interhotel Stadt Berlin, the second tallest building in East Berlin, at the other.

The name Alexanderplatz comes from Tsar Alexander I of Russia who visited Berlin in 1805. Given that royal names tend to have been replaced, it is surprising that this one has survived

— perhaps a testimony to the extent to which Alex has beome a part of Berlin life.

From the top of the Interhotel or television tower you can see that the square is laid out in a sort of coloured swirling pattern that cannot be seen from the ground. Apart from this, the principal attraction of the square is its famous Weltzeituhr (world time clock), a peculiar and rather unimaginative structure of metal and concrete that tells the time in places throughout the world. It was inaugurated in 1969 on the GDR's 20th anniversary.

Alexanderplatz was also Berlin's first real shopping centre after the war, and the Centrum was East Germany's first department store.

Hotel Stadt Berlin

One of Berlin's most popular restaurants, the Zille Stube, can be found on the first floor of the Hotel Stadt Berlin building. Heinrich Zille was one of the city's best loved satirical artists and cartoonists around the turn of this century and he remains popular in East and West Berlin. A statue of Zille sketching stands in the Köllnischer Park (see p.63). Most of his drawings are of overweight Berliners, and the captions are in Berlin dialect.

Television Tower

The Fernsehturm (television tower) that has become the symbol of East Berlin is 365m in height. The viewing platform, 207m above Alex, is situated in the massive round ball below the mast. The entrance to the viewing platform can be found by the S-Bahn station at Alexanderplatz and it is there you buy your ticket to go up to the café and platform. Be prepared for queues of up to an hour, especially in summer. On a clear day, when you can see as far as 50km, the wait may well seem worthwhile, and further compensation can be found in the rotating café (one revolution per hour). The round globe-like structure can be seen all over Berlin, East and West, and was designed to show West Berlin that the Eastern capital was established and there to stay. On a sunny day, a peculiarity of the structure is that the sun often shines on the ball in such a way as to form a bright cross that adds to the drama of the building. The tower is open daily 9.00am — 11.00pm.

The outbuildings contain a tourist information centre and there is a permanent Berlin exhibition in one of the rooms, open daily 10.00am — 7.00pm. Here too you can find a café, a cheap

self-service restaurant and also the Stadtrestaurant, one of East
Berlin's better restaurants.

Red Town Hall

The name of the Rotes Rathaus (Red Town Hall) comes not
from the fact that it was communist but from the colour of the
bricks used in its construction. This imposing symmetrical
building with its central tower 74m high was built between 1861
and 1869 under the direction of Friedrich Waesemann. At first
floor level there is a frieze in red terracotta depicting scenes
from the history of Berlin, the work of Alexander Calandrelli,
Ludwig Brodwolf, Otto Geyer and Rudolf Schweinitz.

Like most traditional German town halls, the Rotes Rathaus
has a restaurant in the cellar (Rathauskeller). It runs under the
whole length of the building and is a Bierrestaurant at the north
end and a Weinrestaurant at the south end.

Neptune Fountain

As you pass in front of the town hall heading away from
Alexanderplatz, you will see to your right the Neptunbrunnen
(Neptune Fountain), designed and built in 1891 by Reinhold
Begas and depicting Neptune surrounded by cherubs and sea-
creatures. Two other famous Berlin statues near the town hall
depict less conventional subjects: both *die Trümmerfrau* (the
rubble lady) and *der Aufbauhelfer* (the reconstruction worker)
celebrate the work done by ordinary people after the war to
rebuild Berlin from its ruins.

Nikolaiviertel

Not far from the town hall and distinguished by its two
matching spires, is the oldest church in Berlin, the Nikolaikirche
(Church of St Nicholas), which has given its name to a whole
new part of Berlin, the Nikolaiviertel (St Nicholas quarter).
According to the earliest remaining records the church goes
back to 1264; this original building was burnt down in a great
fire in 1380, although restoration work began almost straight
away. In 1559 the church aligned itself with the Reformation
and on its 300th anniversary Schinkel assisted in improvements
and further renovation.

Everything except the outer walls was destroyed in the
wartime bombing, and the church and its surroundings lay
virtually in ruins until work began in 1981 to reconstruct not
just the historic church but the whole area in which it stood.
The church is now a museum, focusing on the history of
medieval Berlin-Cölln, and including many early examples of

the use of the Berlin bear on bowls, weather vanes and other articles. It is open Tuesdays to Sundays 10.00am — 6.00pm.

Not just the church but the whole Nikolaiviertel is a sort of living museum. Many houses and shops have been rebuilt on historical principles and even the modern building has been designed to blend in, giving the whole area a pleasing sense of harmony. One interesting example is the Theodor-Fontane-Apotheke just opposite the church, named after the novelist who worked as a chemist's apprentice in Spandauer Straße in Berlin between 1836-1840. The area was conceived partly to reinstate just such a sense of history in what was the heart of old Berlin, but there was a practical purpose too: providing housing for 1,500 Berliners who now live in the modern flats that overlook the pedestrian streets, the Spree and Marx-Engels Forum.

Most of the restored historical buildings are either shops or restaurants. As a result this is now one of Berlin's prime eating areas. Zum Nußbaum (The Nut Tree) is a small restaurant that was immortalised in drawings by Zille. The original used to stand on the other side of the Spree in the town of Cölln but has been reconstructed here. Drawings of it by Zille and by Otto Nagel were used in attempting to reconstruct its original appearance.

Das Knoblauchhaus is one of few historic buildings to have survived the war, although it has undergone substantial renovation. Knoblauch is the German word for garlic, but the house is named after Johann Christian Knoblauch, an affluent needle manufacturer, who had the house built for his family in 1759. It now houses a small museum (dealing with the history of the Knoblauch family) and a pleasant restaurant and Weinstube.

The Ephraim Palais was built at about the same time, 1761, for another rich family, that of the banker Veitel Heine Ephraim, court jeweller to Frederick the Great. It is now used for special exhibitions and concerts, and again has a pleasant café and restaurant.

Among the Nikolaiviertel's many other restaurants, cafés and Weinstuben are Zum Paddenwirt (The Frog Innkeeper), Zur Rippe (The Rib) and, back facing the Marx-Engels-Platz, Mutter Hoppe (Mother Hoppe), a basement restaurant serving traditional German food and good beer at reasonable prices. Again facing the Marx-Engels-Platz, but rather more conventional and up-market, is the Zum Marstall (The Stables) restaurant. Being on the first floor it offers good views. Quite close by, in the Poststraße but on the second floor, apparently buried among flats, is East Berlin's first pizzeria.

Council of State

On the south side of Marx-Engels-Platz stands the building that housed the Staatsrat, the Council of State of East Germany. The main entrance (Eosander Portal) was taken from the ruins of the Schlüterhof, the main courtyard of the old Schloß. It is oddly a symbol of socialism rather than monarchy and emperor, because it was from the balcony above this gateway that Karl Liebknecht addressed a revolutionary gathering of workers, soldiers and sailors on November 9 1918. The Council of State itself consisted of 26 members, elected by the members of the Volkskammer every five years. Broadly speaking it fulfilled the functions more generally assumed by a President. The office of Chairman of the Council of State was East Germany's highest office.

Friedrichswerdersche Kirche

Across the Jungfernbrücke, Berlin's oldest drawbridge (1798), and just off on the right, you come to the Friedrichswerdersche Kirche, a beautifully proportioned church by Schinkel and opened as a museum in his honour on Berlin's 750th anniversary in 1987.

St. Hedwig's Cathedral

A little further on but set back behind what is now Französische Straße, the continuation of Werderstraße, is Berlin's main Catholic church, the St-Hedwigs-Kathedrale. St Hedwig, a German saint not widely known in the English-speaking world, was born in Bavaria in 1174, the daughter of Berthold III of Andechs, and married the duke of Silesia, Henry I (the Bearded). After the defeat of Silesia in the Seven Years' War, for the first time large numbers of catholics became integrated into the German empire. Well-known for her charitable works, Hedwig devoted a great deal of time to setting up religious foundations, the best known of which was the Cistercian house at Trebnitz, just north of Breslau (now Wroclaw in Poland). The nobility of this design is detracted from by the suspicion that the enterprise only came to fruition as the result of the use of convict labour. Hedwig died in 1243 and was canonised in 1267.

The original cathedral was built between 1747 — 1773 modelled on the Pantheon in Rome and is believed to have been based on designs by Georg Knobelsdorff and sketches by Frederick the Great. However, it was only completed in 1773 under the direction of Johannes Boumann. Again it suffered heavily during World War II but was restored between 1952 and 1963 with money provided by the church but with substantial financial assistance from the East German government. The interior is a bold design, combining the classical features of the old church with some exciting innovations. The church is an early example of liturgy in the round with the congregation facing the altar on three sides. A wide winding staircase leads down into a crypt, with several side chapels and many modern works of art, that now functions as a place for private prayer and services attended by smaller congregations. The cathedral is generally very well attended on Sunday mornings, and the 10.00am mass attracts many who come to hear the music, often with an orchestra. Organ recitals are also given every Wednesday for half an hour from 3.00pm. The cathedral is open to visitors Mondays to Saturdays 10.00am — 5.00pm and Sundays 12.30pm — 5.00pm.

Platz der Akademie

West of St Hedwig's lies the Platz der Akademie, (Academy Square), formerly known as the Gendarmenmarkt (Gendarmerie Market) and the site of the Französischer Dom (French Cathedral) and the Deutscher Dom (German Cathedral), both built in the first decade of the 18th Century and facing one another symmetrically across the enormous square. The square is still sometimes known by its former name which is derived from the fact that the Gens d'Armes regiment had a watch here in the 18th Century. The name was changed in 1950 to celebrate the 250th anniversary of the Akademie der Wissenschaften (Academy of Sciences) which stands on the east side of the square.

Although both cathedrals were badly damaged during the war, the French cathedral was fully restored by 1983 and now houses the Huguenot Museum. The Huguenots settled in and around Berlin following the Edict of Potsdam of 1685 and contributed to both the commercial and cultural life of the city. The museum has permanent exhibitions on the Huguenots and the Reformation and Counter-Reformation in France, and a library and archive on the Huguenots in Prussia and Mark Brandenburg, including details of Theodor Fontane, whose ancestors were Huguenots from Nîmes.

The French cathedral also houses a 60-bell glockenspiel which plays automatically for a few minutes every day at noon, 3.00pm and 7.00pm. Concerts are also given on Tuesdays at 2.00pm and Saturdays at 3.00pm. A good view of the glockenspiel and also of the centre of Berlin can be obtained by climbing the 250 steps to the top of the tower.

On the west side of the building (entry via a separate door) is the Französische Friedrichstadtkirche (French church), a simply decorated non-conformist church, architecturally unusually broad and low. It is open to visitors Tuesdays to Saturdays noon — 5.00pm and Sundays 1.00pm — 5.00pm.

The German Cathedral, still in the process of restoration, was built for the Reformed Lutherans and will also be a museum. During the course of the original building on July 28 1781 the whole dome spectacularly collapsed. The disaster was recorded in an etching by Johann Rosenberg, and the 17 year old Schadow also drew the scene (the drawing is in the Berlin Museum in West Berlin). A massive new hotel is being built just behind the German Cathedral and is to be called the Dom Hotel (Cathedral Hotel).

In addition to these two huge cathedrals, the Platz der Akademie is dominated by the enormous Schauspielhaus (Theatre), yet another work of Schinkel's built between 1818 and 1821, but again only restored as recently as 1984 and now functioning as a concert hall, home of the Berlin Symphony Orchestra. The main concert hall can take an audience of 1,900 as against Schinkel's modest seating for 600, while a smaller hall is used for chamber music.

A statue of Schiller by Begas (1868) was re-erected on the square in 1988. The marble figure of the poet and playwright is surrounded by four female figures, representing poetry, drama, history and philosophy.

Glinkastraße

Two streets to the west of the Platz der Akademie runs Glinkastraße, named after the 19th Century Russian composer who came to Berlin several times and died here in 1857 after a performance of his opera, *Ivan Sussanina*. His time here is marked by a stone memorial at number 9-11, on the corner with Mohrenstraße, bearing some of his own words: 'Es ist das Volk, das die Musik schafft. Wir Komponisten arrangieren sie nur' (It is the people who create music. We composers only arrange it).

Otto-Grotewohl-Straße

Otto-Grotewohl-Straße, further to the west and close to the Berlin Wall, was formerly Wilhelmstraße where the Chancellery, the foreign ministry and the ministry of the interior of the Third Reich stood. Here too was the huge underground bunker where Hitler and Eva Braun committed suicide. Nothing of this history remains to be seen, however; the site was flattened at the time the Wall was built, many of the stones of the former

buildings were used to build the War Memorial in Treptower Park, and a housing estate is now being constructed on the waste ground.

Komische Oper
Also in this area is Berlin's second opera house, the Komische Oper (Comic Opera). The company has a lighter repertoire than the German State Opera, and performs in a modern building next to the Grand Hotel on Behrenstraße.

Berlin's museums
Museuminsel
Berlin's oldest and most important museums are to be found in or around the Bodestraße on the so-called Museuminsel (Museum Island) surrounded by the Spree. The island, formerly part of the town of Cölln, was dedicated to 'art and classical antiquity' by a royal decree in 1841. Building began two years later, but the island did not reach full fruition until the completion of the Pergamon Museum in 1909. All the museums are open Wednesdays, Thursdays, Saturdays and Sundays from 10.00am — 6.00pm and Fridays from 10.00am — 6.00pm. The Pergamon Altar and the Middle East collection can also be visited on Mondays and Tuesdays.

Pergamonmuseum (Entrance: Kupfergraben)
The Pergamonmuseum is the most famous of Berlin's museums and, rather like London's British Museum, is devoted to ancient art and culture. The classical collection contains Greek and Roman sculptures, paintings and mosaics covering twelve centuries. The museum is best known for the fact that it contains the complete façades of a number of classical monuments, notably the Milet Market Gate dating back to 165 AD, a massive structure in marble complete in virtually every detail and occupying the whole side of one room. The Pergamon altar, after which the museum is named, dominates another room. Dating from 180-159 BC it was built in the reign of Eumenes II and has been reconstructed at the top of an imposing flight of steps. The upper part is a perfectly symmetrical classical colonnade, and the lower part a relief depicting a battle between the gods and the giants. Another relief depicts the legend of Telephos, the founder of Pergamon. The Pergamon altar is the largest Greek monument remaining intact to have been excavated and removed from its site (now in

Turkey). Sculpted in marble, it was excavated in 1878-1886 by the archeologist Carl Humann and brought to Berlin in 1902.

Apart from a substantial classical collection, the Pergamon contains large Middle Eastern, Far Eastern and Islamic collections. The Middle Eastern collection rivals those in the Louvre and the British Museum and concentrates on items from the 8th Century BC to the time of Christ. Particularly famous are the Ischtar Gate and the Processional Parade of Babylon, 2,500 years old, and the giant sculptures from Sumeria, Assyria and Mesopotamia. The collection also houses some 30,000 cuneiform tablets. The Far Eastern collection concentrates mainly on China and Japan and contains exhibits of lacquerware, ceramics and porcelain covering a span of some 4,000 years. The Islamic collection, filling 18 rooms, displays books, rugs and carpets, ivory and ceramics and contains the façade of the desert palace of Mshatta in Jordan dating back to the 8th Century, a present from the Turkish Sultan to the German Emperor, and the prayer niche of the mosque of Bey Hakim in Konya from the 13th Century.

Bodemuseum (Entrance: Monbijoubrücke)
The Bodemuseum, formerly the Kaiser-Friedrich-Museum, but re-named in 1956 after its founder, Wilhelm von Bode, also concentrates on the ancient world. It contains a substantial Egyptian collection, one of the finest in the world, with over 30,000 papyrus items and a large number of parchments, wooden tablets and other documents. The early Christian and Byzantine collection contains works of art from Greece, Italy, Asia Minor and Eastern Europe from the classical age to medieval times. Especially noteworthy is the tombstone depicting a nursing mother (4th Century) and the icon of Archdeacon Euplius (about 1500).

The sculpture collection contains works from both medieval and modern times and generally of German origin, although there are also examples of the work of Donatello, Luca and other Italian masters. Note the crucifix from the Moritzkirche in Naumburg, the works of Anton Pilgram and the *Adoration* by Tilman Riemenschneider.

The coin collection contains over 100,000 Greek and over 50,000 Roman coins as well as a substantial collection covering Germany, the East, India and the Islamic world, and a collection of bank notes and over 20,000 medals from the Renaissance to the 19th Century.

The Bodemuseum also houses a picture collection concentrating on German, Dutch and Flemish art (Cranach,

Ruysdael and Ostade are, for example, represented), but there are also works by Poussin (a self-portrait), Gainsborough and Raeburn, as well as Canaletto and Guardi.

Finally the Bodemuseum houses a museum of early and prehistory, best known for Heinrich Schliemann's collection of artefacts excavated in Troy between 1871 and 1890.

Nationalgalerie (Entrance: Bodestraße)
The Nationalgalerie (National Gallery) was built in the late 19th Century in the form of a Corinthian temple and was the first museum to re-open after the war in 1949. On the whole the paintings and sculptures housed here are more modern than those in the Bode collection, the majority being 19th and 20th Century. German artists such as Schadow, Feuerbach and Liebermann are represented as well as French painters, including Courbet, Cézanne and Dégas, and the sculptor Rodin. The 20th Century collection houses notable paintings by the Dresden group of artists known as Die Brücke (The Bridge), and the *Altes Liebespaar* by Otto Dix.

Altes Museum (Entrance: Lustgarten)
The Altes Museum (Old Museum) is a classical building with an Ionic portico of 18 columns approached by a broad flight of steps, designed by Schinkel. Damaged during the war, it only re-opened in 1966. It concentrates on 20th century art and has a substantial collection of work by GDR artists such as Otto Nagel, Hans Grundig and Werner Tübke.

The collection of engravings, begun in 1831 at the instigation of Wilhelm von Humboldt, contains 57 illustrations by Botticelli to Dante's Divine Comedy. There are also prints and drawings by Cranach, Rembrandt, Schadow and Käthe Kollwitz.

Neues Museum
The Neues Museum (New Museum) was built by August Stüler, a pupil of Schinkel, between 1843 and 1855; it was damaged in the war and is still undergoing repairs.

Other museums
A visitor who only has a day to spend in Berlin will do well to complete the walk suggested above and visit the museums on the island. There are, however, many other museums of general and specialist interest.

Otto-Nagel-Haus
The Otto-Nagel-Haus (Märkisches Ufer 16-18), named after the Berlin artist who died in 1967, is devoted to proletarian, revolutionary and anti-fascist art and to the work of Nagel himself. Other artists who supported the cause of socialism or resisted Hitler are also represented, notably Käthe Kollwitz, Otto Dix and Kurt Schumacher. The house is open Sundays to Thursdays from 10.00 am — 6.00 pm.

Märkisches Museum
The Märkisches Museum (Am Köllnischen Park 5) is the largest museum of local and regional history in East Germany, with 38 rooms devoted to the history of Berlin, the former town of Cölln and of the surrounding area of Mark Brandenburg. The majority of exhibits relate to the history of the city, but there are also rooms dealing with theatre, arts and crafts and paintings of Berlin scenes and themes. One room is dedicated to the realist novelist Theodor Fontane, and contains items of the writer's furniture, and the museum also houses the papers left by Gerhart Hauptmann, the dramatist.
    Opening times are Wednesdays to Fridays 10.00am — 6.00pm; Saturdays and Sundays 10.00am — 5.00pm.

Museum Berliner Arbeiterleben um 1900
The Museum of Working Life in Berlin at the Turn of the Century (Husemannstraße 12) is a reconstructed 19th Century house and, strictly speaking, part of the Märkisches Museum. It depicts the working and living conditions of ordinary people in Berlin at the turn of the century. It is open Tuesdays, and Thursdays to Saturdays 1.00am — 6.00pm and Wednesdays 11.00am — 8.00pm.

Museum für Naturkunde
The Museum of Natural History (Invalidenstraße 43) has geological, fossil and dinosaur exhibits (including the largest known skeleton of a brachiosaurus) as well as rooms dealing with evolution and zoology. Included in the primate exhibition is a model of the gorilla known as Bobby. It is open Tuesdays to Sundays from 9.30am — 5.00pm.

Postmuseum
The Postal Museum, at the corner of Leipziger Straße and Mauerstraße, deals with the history of the German postal and telephone service. (Opening times Tuesdays to Saturdays 10.00am — 6.00pm)

Berlin also offers a rich choice of small museums commemorating the life and works of individuals who have helped to shape German history and culture, and in particular that of East Germany. These include:

The **Brecht-Haus** (Chauseestraße 125) is dedicated to the dramatist and poet Bertolt Brecht and is the house where he and Helene Weigel last lived and worked together. There are tours for up to 8 people about every half hour and the museum is open Mondays to Fridays 10.00am — 1.00pm and 3.00pm — 6.00pm.

The **Johannes-R-Becher-Haus** (Majakowskiring 34) is another literary museum situated in the house of the writer Johannes R. Becher, a founding member of the German communist party and Minister of Culture in the GDR from 1954-1958. Opening times: Tuesdays and Fridays 2.00pm — 7.00pm and Thurdays 8.00am — 1.00pm.

The **Arnold-Zweig-Gedenkstätte** (Homeyerstraße 13) is dedicated to the writer, Arnold Zweig (brother of the better known Stefan Zweig), first President of the Academy of Arts of the GDR. Zweig lived and worked in the house until his death. It was opened as a museum in 1987, the centenary of his birth.

The **Ernst-Busch-Gedenkstätte** (Leonhard-Frank-Straße 11, Berlin Pankow) commemorates the work of the Berlin actor and singer who died in 1980. Opening times: Tuesdays 9.00am — 1.00pm and Wednesdays 2.00pm — 7.00pm.

The **Wilhelm-Pieck-Gedenkstätte** (Wilhelm-Pieck-Straße) contains items connected with the life of Pieck, chairman of the German communist party in 1945 and president of the GDR from 1949 — 1960. Visitors must inquire at the Institut für Marxismus-Leninismus at Wilhelm-Pieck-Straße 1.

The **Ernst-Thälmann-Gedenkstätte** in the Karl-Liebknecht-Haus in Rosa-Luxemburg-Platz commemorates the life of the famous communist leader who was imprisoned by the Nazis in 1933 and died at Buchenwald (see p.112). Visiting: as for the Wilhelm-Pieck-Gedenkstätte.

The **Robert-Koch-Museum** (Clara-Zetkinstraße 96) commemorates the 19th Century physician who won the Nobel prize for medecine in 1905 for his work on tuberculosis.

The **Gedenkstätte Berlin-Karlshorst** in the Fritz-Schmenkel-Straße is the building in which Hitler's army surrendered to Soviet troops on May 8 1945. It contains over 15,000 documents relating to the Soviet Union's fight against Germany. Opening times: Tuesdays to Fridays 9.00am — 1.00pm and 3.00pm — 6.00pm; Saturdays 9.00am — 2.00pm but closed the last Saturday in the month; Sundays 9.00am — 4.00pm.

The **Mori-Ogai-Gedenkzimmer** has recently been opened at Hermann-Matern-Straße 39 to commemorate the time the Japanese novelist (author of *The Wild Geese*, *The Dancer* — both now also films) spent studying medecine in Germany (1884-1888). Visitors must make arrangements with their hotel or with the oriental faculty of Humboldt University.

Other places to visit – south of Alexanderplatz
Court Building
In the centre of Berlin, just beyond the Nikolaiviertel in Littenstraße is Berlin's main court building (Stadtgericht). It was completed in 1904 to a design by Otto Schmalz and contains over 600 rooms. Its principal feature is the huge double staircase in the main hall, one of Berlin's best examples of Jugendstil. Although technically open to the public, security at the court is strict and foreigners are not generally admitted. However, the staircase can be seen from inside the main door without entering the main hall itself.

Klosterkirche
The Monastery Church (Klosterkirche) is situated close to the court in the Klosterstraße. Once one of the finest and best-preserved medieval (1250) buildings in Berlin, it derives its name from the so-called Grey Monastery belonging to the Franciscans. Its bombed remains have been preserved as a war memorial.

Zur letzten Instanz
The pub and restaurant Zur letzten Instanz (The Last Appeal), Waisenstraße 14-16, is an historic reconstruction of an inn first mentioned in 1525. It is known for its Eisbein, a traditional German dish of pig's trotter.

Ministerrat
Coming out of the Littenstraße and turning right into Stralauerstraße you come to the Ministerrat (Council of Ministers) building at the corner of Stralauerstraße and Klosterstraße. The building itself is undistinguished, but is of note as the meeting place of the Council of Ministers, the principal organ of government in East Germany.

Leipziger Straße/Spittelkolonnaden
The Spittelkolonnaden were constructed in 1776 by Carl von Gontard. The simple classical form of this semi-circular

colonnade is a welcome relief to the otherwise stark modernity of the high rise flats that dominate the Leipziger Straße. It was completely destroyed in the last war and is a total reconstruction. The Leipziger Straße is a product of the 1970s. The gigantic blocks of flats vary from 14 to 25 storeys in height; the ground floor of each block is generally taken up with shops and offices.

Märkisches Ufer

The Märkisches Ufer is the area running along the banks (Ufer) of the Spree Canal where it rejoins the Spree proper. The Ermelerhaus is one of the main attractions here. Ermeler was a tobacco dealer who acquired the house in 1824 and had it decorated in a grand style, including maps showing the extent of his world-wide interests in the tobacco trade. In 1914 the house became the property of the city, and in 1928 became an extension of the Märkisches Museum. The ground floor is now a café, and the upper floor a wine bar. The whole house used to stand in the Breite Straße but was transplanted here after World War II.

Next door is the Otto-Nagel-Haus (see p.60), and overlooking the Spree itself the Märkisches Museum (p.60). At the side of the museum is the Köllnischer Park, an open air museum whose most famous attraction is the Heinrich-Zille-Denkmal, a statue showing the famous Berlin illustrator and cartoonist drawing in his pad with a young Berliner peering over his shoulder. It is the work of Heinrich Drake. The brown bears kept in an enclosure in the park are another popular attraction.

Other places to visit – east of Alexanderplatz
Karl-Marx-Allee

Karl-Marx-Allee (formerly Frankfurter Allee) was re-named Stalin-Allee immediately after World War II and the style of building is distinctly Stalinesque. The street is wider than Unter den Linden and is dominated by tall and stark blocks reminiscent of buildings in Moscow constructed in the Stalin era. The buildings here date from just after the war and represent some of the earliest building undertaken by the GDR. This intimidating but splendid boulevard leads after some 2km to the Frankfurter Tor (Frankfurt Gate), the site of Berlin's old eastern gate, beyond which it resumes its historic name, Frankfurter Allee.

Lenindenkmal

North of the Karl-Marx-Allee is the Leninplatz dominated by the Lenindenkmal (Lenin Memorial), a 19m high statue of Lenin made of red Ukranian granite. Work on the Lenin Memorial started in 1969 and the completed statue was dedicated on April 19 1970 shortly before the centenary of Lenin's birth. It was designed by Nikolai Tomsky of the Soviet Academy of Arts.

Volkspark Friedrichshain

The Volkspark Friedrichshain is one of Berlin's oldest parks and is situated just beyond Leninplatz. It was laid out to designs by Peter Lenné and Gustav Meyer and contains a number of socialist monuments including the Gedenkstätte für die Interbrigadisten which commemorates those who fought against fascism and Franco in the Spanish Civil War, the Denkmal für den gemeinsamen Kampf polnischer Soldaten und deutscher Antifaschisten, commemorating the people of Poland who fought against Hitler as well as the Germans who opposed Hitler. The third memorial, the Denkmal für die Roten Matrosen (Memorial to the Red Sailors), commemorates communist seamen who fought and died for the revolution in 1918. Also to be found here is the Märchenbrunnen (Fairy Tale Fountain) decorated with scenes from Grimm's Fairy Tales, including Rotkäppchen (Little Red Riding Hood, and incidentally the trade mark of East Germany's best champagne).

Other places to visit – north of Alexanderplatz
Ernst-Thälmann-Park

This park, named after the socialist leader murdered by the Nazis, lies in the Prenzlauer Berg area of Berlin close to where the Berlin Wall used to divide East from West. It is reached by taking the S-Bahn to Ernst-Thälmann-Park station. The focus of attention in the park is the Ernst-Thälmann memorial, a bronze bust by the Soviet sculptor, Lev Kerbel (14m high). The bust itself is flanked by two tablets, one bearing words of Thälmann himself, the other a tribute from Erich Honecker. The park is also the location of a planetarium, a gift to the city of Berlin from Carl Zeiss of Jena.

Weißensee

Weißensee is an area of Berlin that takes its name from the White Lake (Weißer See) that is reached by following the Greifswalder Straße and Klement-Gottwald-Allee away from

Ernst-Thälmann-Park. It is a popular place on hot weekends for swimming and sunbathing.

Other places to visit – near Friedrichstraße

Walking north along Friedrichstraße away from the station there are a number of more unusual Berlin sights to be seen. The Haus der Presse (press club) on the eastern side of Friedrichstraße was built in 1910 by the architects Heinrich Schweitzer and Alexander Dipenbrock and is distinguished by its five Doric columns made of Jannowitz marble. Behind it is the Metropol Theatre, one of Berlin's leading comic theatres.

A little further up Friedrichstraße on the west side is Bertolt-Brecht-Platz, a square taking its name from the German poet and dramatist (1898-1956) who chose to live and work in East Germany rather than the West after the war. His works are highly political and unequivocally left wing. The Berliner Ensemble theatre where Brecht worked is still devoted largely to performances of his plays.

The Friedrichstadtpalast on the east is again a place of entertainment, housing a variety and review theatre.

Dominating the skyline behind Friedrichstraße is the Charité, Berlin's largest and most famous hospital. It was built for victims of the plague in 1710 but the present building is the result of post-war reconstruction.

Also not far from here in the Schumannstraße is the Deutsches Theater, Berlin's leading theatre, which grew to fame under Max Reinhardt in the 1920s. It opened with a production of Schiller's *Kabale und Liebe* in 1883 and became a State Theatre in 1945.

Just beyond the point when Friedrichstraße becomes Chausseestraße lies one of Berlin's best known cemetries, the Dorotheenstädtischer Friedhof. It was designated as a cemetry in 1762 and lay outside the city boundaries beyond the Oranienburg gate, as burials inside the town were not permitted. Many of Berlin's most famous citizens are buried here including Brecht, the composer Hanns Eisler (1898-1956), the philosopher Hegel (1770-1831), the novelist Heinrich Mann (brother of Thomas Mann), the architects Rauch, Schadow and Schinkel, and the novelist Anna Seghers. There is also a grim tablet commemorating those who died resisting fascism, among them the theologian Dietrich Bonhoeffer. The neighbouring French cemetry (Französischer Friedhof) is the place where the artists Daniel Chodowiecki (1784-1834) and Heinrich Greif (1907-1946) are buried.

The Brecht-Haus at Chausseestraße 125 was opened in February 1978 to mark the 80th anniversary of Brecht's birth (see p.61).

Synagogue

Not far from here at Oranienburger Straße 30 is the Synagogue, a burnt out ruin that has been left as a memorial. The plaque in German bears the words: '5th September 1966. This synagogue is 100 years old and was set on fire by the Nazis during Kristallnacht on 9th November 1938. During the Second World War 1939-1945 it was destroyed by bombing attacks in 1943. Never forget. Board of Berlin's Jewish Community, September 1966'.

Further towards the centre of the town two other reminders of the strong Jewish community in Berlin can be seen: a memorial to the Jews killed by the fascists, on the site of the first Jewish old people's home in Berlin at the southern end of Große Hamburger Straße, and on the nearby college building a commemorative tablet to Moses Mendelssohn, founder of the first Jewish school in Berlin.

Berlin's only working synagogue is the Friedenstempel at Rykerstraße 53. Because it is set back from the street it escaped the fate of the 191 German synagogues that were attacked on Kristallnacht (76 were completely destroyed), and was saved from attack during the war because of its use as a stable.

Treptower Park area
Treptower Park

Another major park is the Treptower Park reached by taking the S-Bahn to the station of the same name. It was laid out by Gustav Meyer between 1876 and 1882 and was originally situated outside the city boundary. A large area of the park is taken up by the war memorial to the fallen Soviet heroes (Ehrenmal für die gefallenen sowjetischen Helden), built between 1947 and 1949. The centrepiece of the memorial is an 11.5m sculpture of a Soviet soldier with a German child in his left arm and a sword in his right hand, resting over a broken swastika. It is approached through two granite portals in the shape of dipped flags. Between the two are the graves of 5,000 Soviet soldiers killed in 1945 in the battle to capture Berlin. Under the Russian soldier there is a round mausoleum containing the names of the dead soldiers. A mosaic depicts the people of the USSR mourning their dead. Facing the soldier is a sculpture of the Motherland (Russia) in the form of a woman mourning the loss of her sons.

Beyond the monument is the Archenhold observatory built in 1896 and still functioning, and nearby a monument to Yuri Gagarin and Sigmund Jähn, the first Soviet and East German cosmonauts.

Kulturpark

The nearby Kulturpark is an amusement park with the usual big dipper, roller coaster and other fairground attractions and a selection of restaurants serving different regional food. Overlooking the Spree is the Altes Eierhäuschen (Old Egg House), an historical Lokal (pub).

Other places to visit - near the zoo

Tierpark

The Tierpark (zoo) is best reached by U-Bahn from Alexanderplatz to Tierpark Station. The zoo was founded in 1954 and constructed with the help of ordinary Berliners who worked on it in their spare time. One day it is said that 1,000 people turned out to work with hoes and spades. Of special interest is the Alfred-Brehm-Haus, one of the largest animal houses in the world, maintaining a lush tropical environment. Over 100 species of birds can be seen in the 16m high domed tropical hall. Another enclosure with an open rock face houses Sumatran tigers.

Schloß Friedrichsfelde

The baroque Friedrichsfelde Palace, with its famous wood carved staircase, is close to the zoo and was built between 1690 and 1719 by Johann Arnold Nering and Martin Heinrich Bühme and restored in 1981. There are tours three times a day at 10.00am, 1.00pm and 3.00pm.

Gedenkstätte der Sozialisten

The Gedenkstätte der Sozialisten, near the U-Bahn Friedrichsfelde Ost, was designed by Mies van der Rohe (1924-1926). It is dedicated to the memory of prominent socialists and is the place of burial of Karl Liebknecht, Rosa Luxemburg, Wilhelm Pieck, Ernst Thälmann, Otto Grotewohl, Walter Ulbricht and others. Pieck himself dedicated it in 1926.

Entertainment in East Berlin

East Berlin is famous for its musical and theatrical life. Generally ticket prices are cheap if you book directly yourself but the costs are similar to those in the West if you book through the hotels or tourist offices and pay in hard currency.

Music

Berlin's two opera houses are the Deutsche Staatsoper, Unter den Linden 7, a substantial mainstream opera house with a company that enjoys an international reputation, and the Komische Oper, Behrenstraße 55-57, which concentrates on light and comic opera, operetta and musicals.

Berlin's principal orchestra is the Berliner Sinfonie-Orchester whose principal conductor is currently Kurt Sanderling. Again it enjoys an international reputation. Concerts are generally given in the concert hall of the Schauspielhaus in the Platz der Akademie. The Berliner Staatskapelle, which concentrates on earlier music, performs in the Apollo-Saal of the opera house.

Theatre

The Deutsches Theater, Schumannstraße 139, is the largest theatre and has a mainstream classical repertoire.

The Maxim-Gorki-Theater, Unter den Linden, Am Festungsgraben 2, concentrates on Russian, Soviet and GDR drama.

The Berliner Ensemble, Bertolt-Brecht-Platz 1, just off Friedrichstraße, focuses mainly on the work of Brecht but also performs a great deal of other modern theatre.

The Volksbühne in Rosa-Luxemburg-Platz has a relatively light repertoire of comedy and entertainment, and a small alternative theatre on the third floor.

The Puppentheater (puppet theatre), Greifswalder Straße 81-84 in the Kulturhaus in Ernst-Thälmann Park draws on a rich repertoire based on the folklore of Germany, Russia, Bulgaria and other East European countries.

Die Distel (The Thistle) is Berlin's best-known satirical cabaret. It performs either at the Admiralspalast (Friedrichstraße 101) or in the Venus, Degnerstraße 9 in Berlin Hohenschönhausen. Its programme was, until recently, regarded as risqué, but it is now having difficulty keeping up in the new liberal atmosphere. The humour is highly political and not easily accessible to a foreigner without both good German and a knowledge of contemporary life in East Germany.

The Metropol Theater, Friedrichstraße 101-102, is another source of light entertainment, including musicals and operetta.

The Friedrichstadtpalast, Das Ei, Friedrichstraße 107, again concentrates on dance, music and revue theatre.

Where to stay

Berlin's most modern and luxurious hotel is the Grand Hotel, Friedrichstraße 158. Other international hotels include the Metropol, Friedrichstraße 150, conveniently close to Friedrichstraße station; Palasthotel, Karl-Liebknecht-Straße 5; Stadt Berlin, Alexanderplatz; and Unter den Linden, Unter den Linden 14. Cheaper hotels include the Hotel Adria, Friedrichstraße 134, the Hotel Newa, Invalidenstraße 115; and the Hospiz Am Bahnhof Friedrichstraße, a Christian-run hotel at Albrechtstraße 8.

Where to eat

The better 'international' restaurants are to be found in the large hotels. They generally accept payment only in foreign currency but now also tend to take credit cards. The ordinary restaurants in and around the centre accept East German currency and are much cheaper but the better known ones may need a reservation.

Typical Berlin-style restaurants include Zur letzten Instanz, Waisenstraße 14; Zillestube in the Stadt Berlin Hotel; Nanteeck in the Palast Hotel; and many restaurants in and around the Nikolaiviertel, including Zum Nußbaum, Gerichtslaube, Am Paddenwirt, Zur Rippe, Weißbierstube, Mutter Hoppe, and the Ratskeller under the town hall.

The centre also has many bars and cafés. In summer try the cafés with outdoor terraces in Alexanderplatz and along Karl-Liebknecht-Straße, and sample a typical Berlin drink, Berliner Weiße, a refreshing type of beer, usually served with a dash of blackcurrant juice.

A little way outside the centre, Prenzlauer Berg is also a good place to look for restaurants, especially for the budget-conscious. Eating places in this area include: Offenbach Stuben, Stubbenkammerstraße 8; Café Flair, Stargarder Straße 72; and Café Papillon, Greifenhagener Straße 16. Husemannstraße also has several good restaurants, including Restauration 1900, at no. 1.

Berlin has a number of restaurants serving non-German dishes, including: Prag, Leipzigerstraße 48; Sophia, Leipzigerstraße 46; Warschau, Karl-Marx-Allee 95; Haus Budapest, Karl-Marx-Allee 91; Haus Bukarest, Frankfurter

Allee 13; Havanna in the Hotel Metropol; and Wolga, Friedrichstraße 176.

Getting about in East Berlin

East Berlin has a safe and convenient transport network, including buses, trams, an underground (U-Bahn) and an overground railway (S-Bahn). The S-Bahn links Friedrichstraße station with Marx-Engels-Platz and Alexanderplatz, from where a network spreads out north, south and east. The U-Bahn can be joined close to Checkpoint Charlie, and continues to Alexanderplatz and beyond.

Both the U-Bahn and the S-Bahn operate long hours, the former from 5.00am — 11.30pm, and the S-Bahn from 4.00am — 1.00am. A one-day pass can be bought at all S-Bahn and U-Bahn stations, giving the holder the right to use any of the city's public transport. Alternatively individual tickets can be bought from machines at each station.

Events

Many special events and festivals are held in Berlin throughout the year. Major annual events include: Berlin Theatre and Music Festival (September/October); GDR Music Days (every two years in February); Berlin Rock-Summer and Theatre-Summer (July/August); Zoo festival (August). In addition each of the districts in the city has its own local festival sometime between May and September.

Information

For exact details of events and information on any other points, it is best to check with Berolina or Reisebüro der DDR for the latest information. Once in Berlin, details can be obtained from the tourist office at the foot of the television tower on Alexanderplatz. A monthly guide entitled *Wohin in Berlin* (Where to go in Berlin) is also available, and gives full details of all theatrical, musical, artistic, sporting and other events in the city.

Excursions from Berlin
Köpenick

Köpenick can be reached on the S-Bahn. Apart from being a residential and industrial area, it is the site of the Schloß

Köpenick can be reached on the S-Bahn. Apart from being a residential and industrial area, it is the site of the Schloß Köpenick, a palace that now houses the Kunstgewerbemuseum with its permanent exhibition of art and craft objects from medieval to modern times and furniture from Germany, Holland, France and Italy. Especially noteworthy are the rooms displaying works from the 1920s and 1930s and from the Jugendstil period. It is open Wednesdays to Saturdays from 9.00am — 5.00pm and Sundays from 10.00am — 6.00pm.

Müggelsee

The Müggelsee is Berlin's largest lake and a popular place for a day trip, especially in summer when it is warm enough to swim in. It can be reached easily from Friedrichshagen or Rahnsdorf S-Bahn stations. The lake is overlooked by a tower, the Müggelseeturm, which stands on the Müggelberg hill. There is a good but popular restaurant there with space for 700, but it tends to be overcrowded.

This is also a popular area for walking; boat trips on the lake offer a less energetic alternative.

Bernau

Bernau too can be reached by S-Bahn. This old town, now at the outer edges of Berlin, is famous for its old town wall, some of which remains intact.

Erkner

Erkner again is reached on the S-Bahn. Apart from being the site of the Gerhart-Hauptmann Museum, it also has two attractive lakes, the Dömeritz-See and the Flaken-See.

Excursions with the Weiße Flotte

The Weiße Flotte (White Fleet) runs cheap excursions by boat to a number of attractive destinations around Berlin. Trips start from Treptow (near the park and Treptow S-Bahn Station), Grünau, Köpenick and Neue Mühle.

Potsdam (see pp.73-78), **Chorin** (see pp.191-192) and the **Spreewald** (see pp.187-189) can also be reached on day-trips from Berlin.

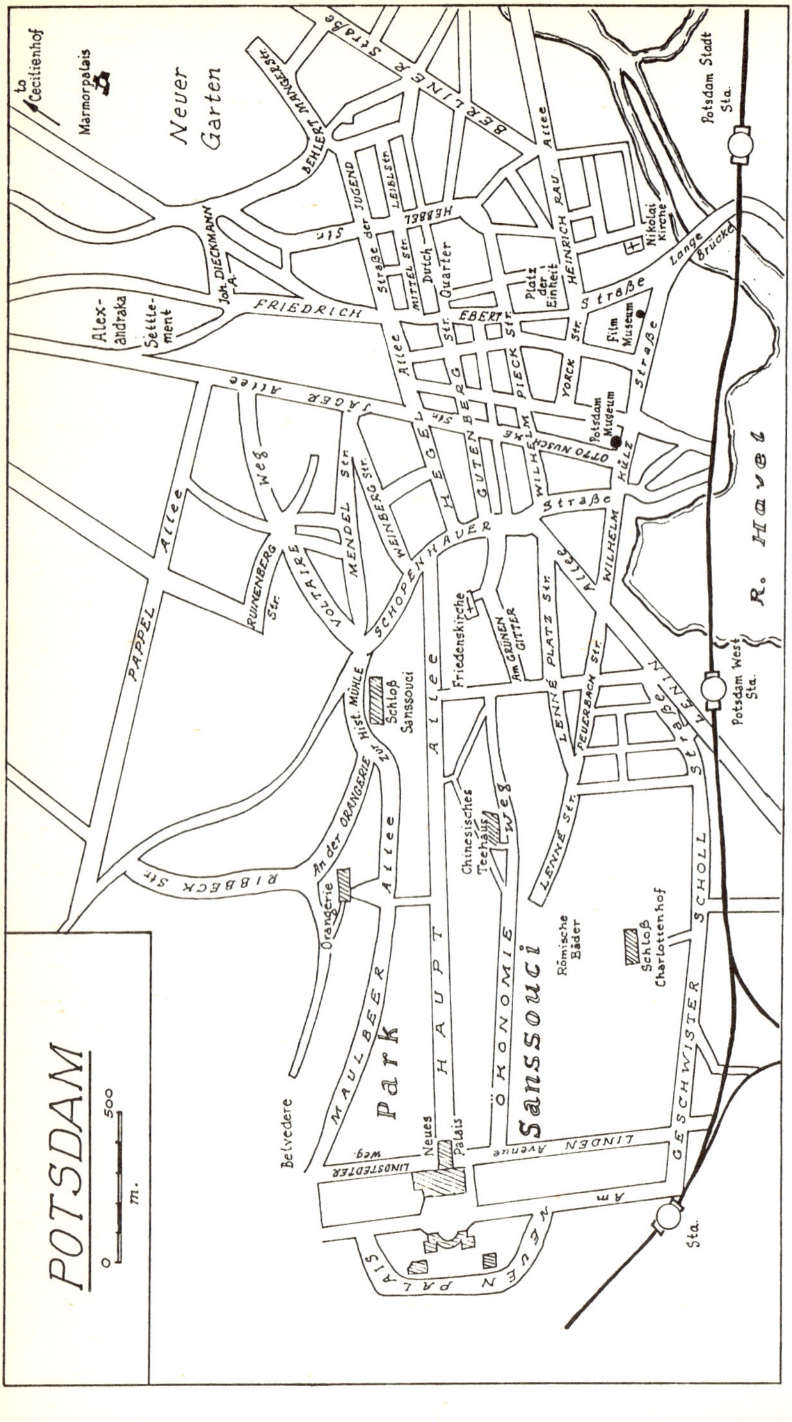
POTSDAM
0
500
m.
to Cecilienhof
Marmorpalais
Neuer Garten
BERLINER Straße
MANGERSTR.
BEHLERT
Joh. DIECKMANN A.
Alexandraka Settlement
FRIEDRICH
Straße der JUGEND Str.
LEIBL Str.
HEBBEL
MITTEL Str.
Dutch Quarter
EBERT Str.
Platz der Einheit
HEINRICH RAU Allee
Nikolai Kirche
Lange Brücke
Potsdam Stadt Sta.
Straße
Film Museum
YORCK Str.
PIECK Str.
Potsdam Museum
OTTO NUSCHKE
WILHELM KÜLZ Straße
R. Havel
JÄGER Allee
HEGEL
GUTENBERG Str.
Weg
MENDEL Str.
WEINBERG Str.
SCHOPENHAUER
VOLTAIRE
RUINENBERG Str.
PAPPEL Allee
Friedenskirche
Am GRÜNEN GITTER
PLATZ Str.
WILHELM Allee
LENNÉ
FEUERBACH Str.
Potsdam West Sta.
Hist. MÜHLE
Zur
Schloß Sanssouci
HAUPT Allee
Chinesisches Teehaus
ÖKONOMIE Weg
LENNÉ Str.
An der ORANGERIE
RIBBECK Str.
Orangerie
MAULBEER Allee
Park Sanssouci
Römische Bäder
Schloß Charlottenhof
GESCHWISTER SCHOLL
Belvedere
Neues Palais
LINDSTEDTER Weg
LINDEN Avenue
Am NEUEN PALAIS
Sta.

Potsdam

All visitors to Berlin should try to set aside time to visit
Potsdam. Not only does it have in Sanssouci one of the most
beautiful palaces in Europe, it is also internationally known for
the Cecilienhof, the site of the 1945 Potsdam Conference, where
Churchill, Truman and Stalin drew up the borders which have
so profoundly shaped Europe ever since. In addition, the old
town retains several buildings of note and manages to combine,
more happily than in many towns in East Germany, its
traditional atmosphere as an historic garrison town with modern
shops and restaurants.

Background

Although the first settlements in the area date back to Slavonic
colonisation in the 8th Century, the town was of no great
importance until the Elector Friedrich Wilhelm (1620-1688)
began to develop Potsdam as the royal seat of the Brandenburg-
Prussian state from 1660 onwards. The Edict of Potsdam, giving
permission to settle to Huguenots fleeing from persecution in
France, led rapidly to economic expansion, a trend that was
furthered by Friedrich Wilhelm I (1713-1740), who initiated the
building of several new areas within the town boundaries and
the setting up of textile and munitions factories.

It was under Friedrich II (1740-1786), however, that Potsdam
came into its own as a royal residence and major military town.
Anxious to establish a haven of civilisation and enlightenment
outside Berlin, Friedrich tore down many of the old town
buildings and had them re-erected in a baroque style to match
the Palace of Sanssouci, which he had begun to build in 1745.

On October 24 1806 Napoleon led his army into Potsdam, and
the town remained under French occupation until a group of
cossacks from the Russian army drove out the French in 1813.

In 1838, however, with the opening of the Potsdam-Berlin railway (the first railway line in Prussia), an invasion which has proved considerably longer lasting began: for day-trippers from Berlin and the surrounding area Potsdam became, and has remained, a favourite destination.

During the 19th Century Potsdam's importance as an industrial centre and a focus of the working class movement grew steadily. It was here that in 1912 Karl Liebknecht was elected to the Reichstag in the 'Emperor's constituency' of Potsdam-Spandau-Osthavelland, and from here that the Emperor fled to Holland in 1918. The land and buildings of Sanssouci finally became public property in 1927.

Following the liberation of Potsdam by the Russian army in April 1945 and the surrender of the German army the following month, the Potsdam Agreement between the three victorious powers of the Anti-Hitler coalition, the USA, the USSR and Great Britain, was signed on August 2 at the Cecilienhof, and before the end of the year Potsdam had become the capital of the province of Brandenburg in the Soviet Occupied Zone.

Subsequently Potsdam has expanded as a centre of learning, and today has several colleges and academies, including the College of Film and Television. Its attractions as a tourist centre have been enhanced by a great deal of reconstruction work over the last 10 years, but at the same time it remains both a modern working town, providing jobs and cultural and recreational facilities for its 137,700 inhabitants, and a garrison town with one of the largest Soviet bases in the country.

Sanssouci

The Park of Sanssouci, which is entered from the town side but extends over an area of around 3km² to the west, is worth exploring at a leisurely pace. Not only are the grounds themselves a pleasure to walk in, they also provide a setting for more buildings of note than can be taken in during a brief visit. If time is limited, stick to the Sanssouci Palace (Schloß Sanssouci) itself and perhaps the Chinese teahouse (Chinesisches Teehaus); but if time allows, a walk taking in also the orangery, the New Palace (Neues Palais), the Villa of Charlottenhof, the Roman Baths (Römische Bäder) and the Peace Church (Friedenskirche) is highly recommended.

The park, which is a mixture of formal flower beds, fountains and lawns, surrounded by less formal wooded areas, was begun in 1744 but enlarged by Peter Lenné during the reigns of Friedrich Wilhelm III and Friedrich Wilhelm IV. The Great

The Central Library of German Classical Literature in the Green Palace, Weimar

Statue of Goethe in the Naschmarkt, Leipzig

Colditz village

Colditz Castle

Traditional wooden Christmas figures from the Erzgebirge

Fountain (Große Fontäne), which springs to a height of 40m when it is working (summer only), is a spectacular foreground to the Sanssouci palace.

The building of the palace is accredited to the architect Knobelsdorff, although he followed very closely the sketches devised by Friedrich II himself. The one-storey rococo building was erected at the top of a series of terraces on which vines were originally planted and is best appreciated from the front; the entrance is, however, in the colonnaded courtyard to the rear of the palace.

Although the interior can only be seen on a guided tour, this should not deter anyone interested in 18th Century art, design or history. Particularly noteworthy are the marble hall with its Corinthian pillars, the music room and the Voltaire room, with its monkey and parrot decorations, so-called because Voltaire is said to have stayed here when visiting Friedrich II.

It is at Sanssouci that one of history's most famous cryptic exchanges allegedly took place (in French):

Note from Friedrich II to Voltaire:
$$\frac{P}{\text{voulez-vous}} \quad \text{à} \quad \frac{ci}{100}$$

Reply from Voltaire to Friedrich II: G a
('Voulez-vouz souper [sous P] à Sanssouci [cent sous ci]?' 'J'ai grand [G grand] appétit [a petit].')

A little beyond the palace and to the left of the main path is the Chinese Teahouse (built 1754-1757), an unusual circular pavilion surrounded by gilded sandstone figures representing Chinese men and women drinking tea and making music. Further to the south lies the Charlottenhof, built some 70 years later (1826-1829) to plans by Schinkel. While the staircase is widely acknowledged as noteworthy, less orthodox but equally interesting is Alexander von Humboldt's work/bedroom, built in the form of a tent. The Roman Baths (1829-35), close to the Charlottenhof, are built in the Italian villa style.

The New Palace (built 1763-1769 by Büring and Gontard) stands at the end of the main path and is a fine example, recently restored, of late baroque. The palace remained the summer residence of Wilhelm II until his flight in 1918, and much of the interior preserves its original rich decoration. Again guided tours are obligatory and include the marble hall, the marble gallery and the palace theatre. One of East Germany's most pleasant cafés, where coffee, cakes and ice-cream can be enjoyed in palatial surroundings, is to be found in the New Palace (separate entrance on the south side — ring the bell and wait for an answer).

Heading back towards the entrance, this time to the north of the main path, you will encounter the Orangery (1851-1862) built on the instructions of Friedrich Wilhelm IV who wanted Sanssouci to 'look like Rome'. Its design is reminiscent of Italian Renaissance palaces, and the Raphael room contains 47 copies of paintings by that artist.

Although a pleasant building in itself and a further sign of Friedrich Wilhelm's liking for things Italian, being built in imitation of the San Clemente basilica in Rome, the Friedenskirche (1845-1854) is most often visited because of the Apsis mosaic (1108). This originated in San Cipriano on Murano island near Venice, but was brought to Potsdam in 1834 and subsequently installed as a feature of the church.

The Sanssouci Palace and the New Palace are open daily 9.00am — 5.00pm; Charlottenhof, the Orangery (Raphael room), the Chinese tea house and the Roman Baths are open between April and September daily 9.00am — 5.00pm.

Cecilienhof Palace

The Cecilienhof Palace, built between 1913 and 1917 in English mock-Tudor style, is now a hotel and a memorial to the 1945 Potsdam Agreement. The room where the historic conference between the leaders of the anti-Hitler forces took place has been preserved as it was in 1945, and can be visited daily between 8.00am and 5.15pm. It is also possible to stay in the hotel, although it is a popular venue and booking can be difficult. The palace is set in an area of parkland, known as the New Garden (Neuer Garten), which is also open to the public. It contains a number of monuments, including a mock pyramid, and also houses the Marble Palace (Marmorpalais), built 1787-1792, and now functioning as an Army Museum. It can be visited daily except Mondays 9.00am — 5.00pm.

Other sights

Potsdam offers a wealth of other attractions, the most popular of which are mentioned below. Much of the appeal of the town lies, however, in its pleasant location on the river Havel, which expands here into a number of lakes. Walks in many of the town's parks and gardens are enhanced by the proximity of water, and for those wishing to explore the area less conventionally, the Weiße Flotte operates boat tours in summer on the Havel (departure from the side of the Hotel Potsdam).

Potsdam's distinctive character can also be appreciated on a walk down Klement-Gottwald-Straße in the centre of town. The original 18th Century houses have now been tastefully restored and the street turned into a lively pedestrianised shopping area.

The Nikolai Church (Nikolaikirche) in the centre of Potsdam, built by Schinkel and Persius between 1830 and 1837, is one of Germany's most important classical buildings. Although badly damaged during the war, it is now completely restored and is frequently used for concerts and recitals. Next to the Nikolai Church stands the former town hall (1753- 1755), now the Hans Marchwitza arts centre.

Although eclipsed at Potsdam by Sanssouci, the picturesque Babelsberg palace and park would, in many other towns, feature as major attractions. The palace, built by Schinkel in English neo-Gothic style (1834-1835) and extended by Strack (1843-1849), is now a museum of early history.

Potsdam's international links are visible both in the Dutch Quarter (Holländisches Viertel) and the Alexandrovka Settlement (Alexandrowka Siedlung). The former consists of 134 brick houses which were built under the direction of the Dutch architect Boumann between 1737 and 1742 in order to house Dutch immigrants. The houses are currently being re-furbished and many have been re-painted, although not in ox blood as they were originally. Further to the north, the Alexandrovka Settlement was built in 1826 for 12 Russian singers out of the original 62 who had formed a choir in Potsdam at the time of the Russian army's liberation of the town from Napoleon's French soldiers. The wooden houses are in Russian style and situated close to the Alexander Nevsky Church (Alexander-Newski-Kirche — 1829).

Cinema enthusiasts will not want to miss the National Film Museum, housed in the former Royal Stables (Marstall). German cinema was born in the Babelsberg district of Potsdam, and stars such as Greta Garbo were launched into stardom by the UFA (formerly Babelsberg) film company. Anyone interested in the history of science should visit Telegraph Hill (Telegrafenberg), with its meteorological observatory, geodesic institute and the imposing Expressionist Einstein Tower (Einsteinturm) where, in the presence of Einstein, experiments were started to verify the theory of relativity.

How to get there

Potsdam can most conveniently be reached either on a bus tour
from West Berlin (tours leave daily from the Kurfürstendamm)
or by train from East Berlin's Lichtenberg station. Double-
decker trains, known to Berliners as 'sputniks', leave hourly and
take around one hour to do the journey.

Where to stay

In addition to the Cecilienhof Hotel described above, Potsdam
has an Interhotel, the Hotel Potsdam, situated at the Lange
Brücke (Long Bridge) near the river Havel. The Potsdam Youth
Hostel is at Eisenhartstraße 5.

Where to eat

The Hans Marchwitza arts centre has a restaurant, wine bar and
dance bar, and the Weinbergterrassen at Gregor-Mandel-Straße
29 also offers meals, a wine bar and dancing. The Klement-
Gottwald-Straße and the surrounding streets is, however, the
most popular area for restaurants, cafés and bars, and a stroll
around here should uncover something to meet most tastes;
restaurants in the area include Gastmahl des Meeres (fish),
Klement-Gottwald-Straße 72; Am Stadttor, Klement-Gottwald-
Straße 1/2; Bolgar, Klement-Gottwald-Straße 36.

Potsdam's equivalent of the 'Berliner Weiße' is known as
'Potsdamer Stange' and is widely available in bars and cafés. The
area is also famous for its fruit wines thanks to the
neighbouring fruit-growing area at Werder.

Events

Potsdam hosts a number of annual events, the most popular of
which is the Park Festival; every year for 10 days in June
numerous musical events are held in the palaces and garden at
Sanssouci. Other events include the crockery market on the last
weekend in September, and a festival of light in the middle of
August.

Information

Further details of these and of other cultural and sporting
events, as well as general tourist information, can be obtained
from the information office at Friedrich-Ebert-Straße 5.

DRESDEN

Jerome K. Jerome in *Three Men on the Bummel* described Dresden as 'the most attractive town in Germany'. That was at the turn of the century, and although the character of the town is now different, changed by the ravages of World War II and the architecture of modern utilitarianism, Dresden remains one of the great attractions of East Germany, especially for the lover of art and music.

Background

The name of the town goes back to a Sorb word, Drezdany or Dresdany, meaning the place of the people of the wooded swamp. The first recorded mention of the name is in 1206 in a document describing how the Margrave of Meissen was called in to settle a dispute between a local nobleman and the bishop of Meissen. The first documented mention of it as a town is in 1216.

By 1275 the town had grown to some importance. It was ruled by the Wettiner nobles who gave it protection and was the site of an important bridge across the Elbe. It came to be ruled by the Albertine line of the Wettiners in 1455, and by 1485 it had become established as their town of residence.

In 1685 a great fire destroyed much of the town on the north bank of the Elbe. The old town there was replaced by the Neue Stadt bey Dresden which became a centre of trade and attracted craftsmen such as Georg Friedrich Dinglinger, the goldsmith, and his brother, Johann Melchior, Gottfried Silbermann, the organ builder, and the man responsible for introducing porcelain to Europe, Johann Friedrich Böttger. Dresden's rise to real importance occurred during its so-called Augustan Period when the king of Poland, August II, came to rule it as Elector Friedrich August I of Saxony (known as August der Starke or the Strong). He was followed by his son, Friedrich August II,

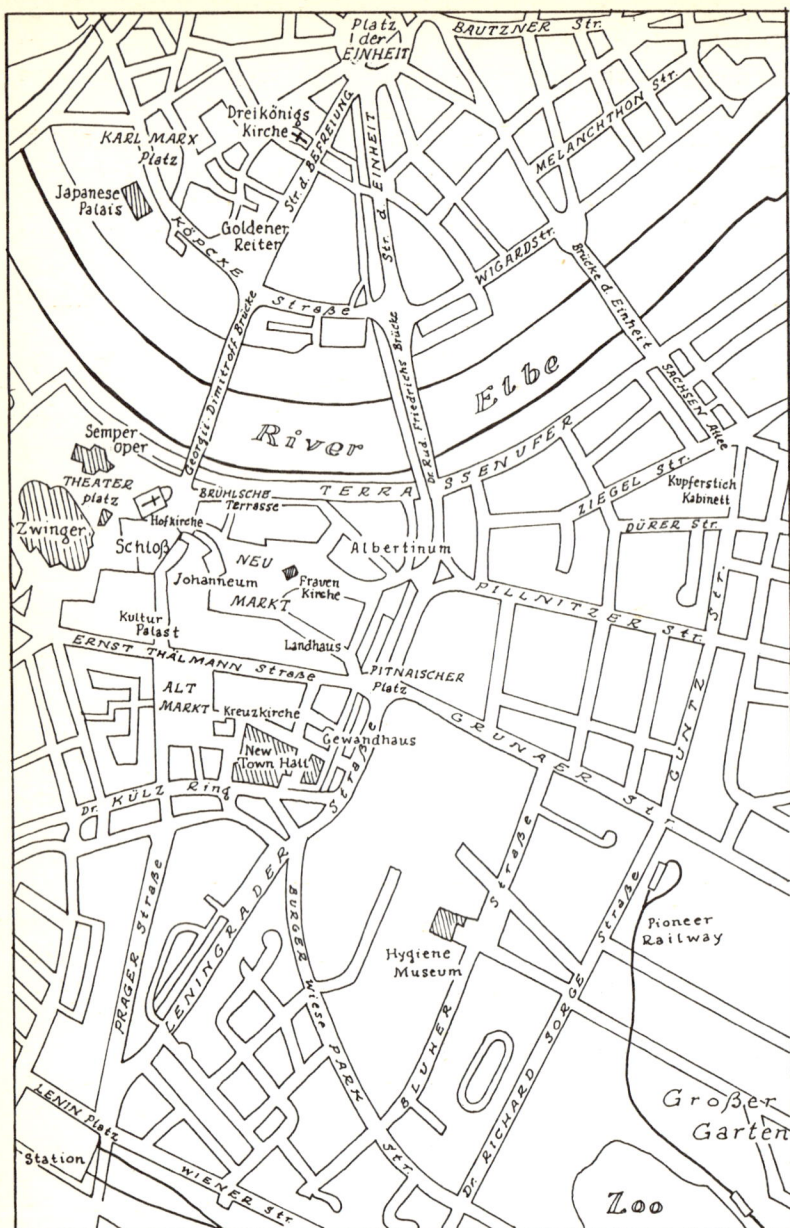

DRESDEN

and between them they dominated the life and history of Dresden from 1694-1783. It was during this period that buildings such as the Zwinger, the Frauenkirche and the Hofkirche came to be built. Under their rule the town became an intellectual and artistic centre, and the population grew to 63,000 in 1755 compared to only 21,000 at the end of the 17th Century.

Yet further expansion occurred in the 19th Century. The town flourished musically under the influence of Weber, who lived here from 1817-1826, and Wagner who stayed for seven years from 1842-1849, and later Richard Strauss.

Dresden has also been one of the focal points of political developments. It played an important part in the 1848-1849 revolution. In May 1849 the people drove the army and ministers of the king from the town and established a provisional government which lasted for about four weeks before being defeated by the armed forces.

The 19th Century also brought industry, dominated initially by the tobacco industry. The first tobacco processing factory in Germany was built here in 1862. By 1880 there were 21. One rather eccentric one remains at the corner of Weißeritzer Straße and Magdeburger Straße on the south bank of the Elbe and is distinctive because of the dome and minaret which give it the appearance of a mosque. The chemical and pharmaceutical trade also established factories and offices here. The Dresdner Bank (which still exists today as a West German bank) was established in 1872 to provide the town with its own financial services.

During the night of February 13-14 1945 Dresden was virtually razed to the ground by British bombers acting directly on orders from Churchill. With the defeat of Hitler already imminent at this time, the justification for the decision is now a matter of doubt, and it is hard to see the military advantage of an attack that destroyed the fabric of an important cultural centre and killed some 35,000 civilians.

The removal of rubble, undertaken largely by women workers, is commemorated in a statue of the rubble lady (Trümmerfrau) opposite the town hall. Reconstruction began in 1946. Work on the historic centre was inaugurated by Walter Ulbricht at a ceremony in 1953. Over 100,000 flats were built. In spite of the skill that has gone into much of the restoration (the most impressive example is the opera house), parts of the town are marred by ugly modern building and by the remains of war damage even now.

Dresden today is a sophisticated and prosperous city of some 500,000 people, important for its art and architecture as well as for its trade and industry, even though large parts of it, notably the palace, still await re-construction.

The historical centre
Altmarkt
The Old Market (Altmarkt) lies at the very centre of Dresden. Documentary mention of the square goes back to 1370. It only became known as the Old Market to distinguish it from the New Market (Neumarkt) when the Sorbs came to settle and in doing so created their own new focal point close to the Frauenkirche.

Apart from its role as a market place, the square was also for centuries the entertainment centre of the town, the site of tournaments, animal baiting, carnivals and festivals. It was also the political centre of the town. It remains the site of the old town hall (Rathaus), a building in the baroque style built between 1741-1745 under Johann Christoph Knöffel. It was the scene of fighting in the 1848 revolution and the seat of the provisional government set up after the revolution in May 1849. Wagner is said to have been the first to appear on the balcony of the town hall to cheer the formation of the new government. That political tradition came to an end when the town administration moved to a new town hall in what is now the Dr-Külz-Ring in 1910.

The whole of the Altmarkt was razed to the ground in the bombing of February 13-14 1945. Only in 1952 did work begin on removing the rubble. At a solemn ceremony on May 31 1953 Walter Ulbricht (the then First Secretary of the Central Committee of the SED) laid the first stone that began the reconstruction work that continued until the late 1950s. At the same time the size of the square was considerably extended in line with the needs of a modern city.

Webergasse
A passage called the Webergasse leads into the market square from the west. The name (Weber is the German for weaver) can be traced back to 1396, and indeed weavers lived and worked here from medieval times, and had their guildhall (Innungshaus) here until 1878. The passage is now entirely modern.

Neues Rathaus
The new town hall is a sandstone building with five courtyards dominated by a massive domed tower on the top of which stands the 5m high figure of the golden man (Goldener Mann). The

golden man, with his outstretched right arm and cornucopia, is the work of Richard Guhr and is the highest point in the town.

The Dr-Külz-Ring, at the end of which the town hall stands, is named after Dr Wilhelm Külz, the mayor of Dresden from 1931-1933 until he was forced from office by the Nazis.

Gewandhaus

The former drapers' house (Gewandhaus) is just behind the town hall in the Kreuzstraße. It was built in 1768-1770 in a late baroque/early classical style by Johann Friedrich Knöbel. Again it was the centre of fighting in 1849 and prison for many captured revolutionaries after the collapse of the revolution. It became a hotel in 1966.

Kulturpalast

The north side of the Altmarkt is the site of the Palace of Culture (Kulturpalast). This modern building (made of stone, concrete, glass and aluminium) was opened to commemorate the 20th anniversary of the founding of the GDR in 1969. It contains a concert hall as well as halls for meetings and conferences, a cinema, a small studio theatre and a number of places to eat. The Dresdner Philharmonie and the Staatskapelle play here.

The front of the building overlooking the Schloßstraße is decorated with a gigantic mural depicting the history of the working class movement. It is the work of an artists' collective directed by the rector of the Dresden School of Arts, Prof. G. Bondzin.

Kreuzkirche

The Kreuzkirche (Church of the Cross) stands on the eastern side of the Altmarkt. It takes its name from a relic, a splinter of the cross on which Christ died, allegedly held in the church. The original church on this site was built in about 1200. It burned down in 1491 and was remodelled. In 1760 it was damaged by canon fire, and in 1765 the famous Renaissance tower (which can be seen in the paintings of Canaletto) collapsed because of the inadequate foundations. It burned down again in 1897, was restored again in 1900, only to be destroyed again in 1945. Restoration and reconstruction began in 1950 following the form the church had taken on in the reconstruction of 1764-1792. The roof is copper covered. The interior is simple, devoid of almost any decoration, allowing the visitor to experience the full effect of the size of the interior pillars.

The tower houses five massive bells weighing almost 30 tonnes. A new organ was installed in 1963. The church is also the home of the famous Kreuzchor choir.

The Kreuzkirche was the setting for the first joint GDR/UK television production, a performance of Benjamin Britten's *War Requiem*.

In November 1989 a joint service of reconciliation took place at the Kruezkirche and Coventry cathedral (Dresden and Coventry are twin towns) to commemorate the end of World War II. A partnership between Dresden and Coventry was established soon after World War II, both towns having suffered devastating bombing, Coventry in 1940 and Dresden in 1945, and the Coventry-Dresden Friendship Society continues to play an important role in promoting peace and understanding between the UK and East Germany.

Landhaus

The Landhaus was built between 1770-1776 in early classical style, destroyed in 1945 and rebuilt in 1963-1965. It is now a museum of the history of Dresden. The principal feature of the Landhaus is the rococo staircase.

The Landhaus is the only historic building on Ernst-Thälmann-Straße, the main road that cuts through the centre of Dresden from east to west. This has always been a main thoroughfare but got its present name only in 1954 when it was dedicated to the memory of Ernst Thälmann on August 18, the 10th anniversary of his death in Buchenwald.

Frauenkirche

The ruins of the Frauenkirche are the principal feature of the Neumarkt. The Frauenkirche (Church of Our Lady) was erected in 1726-1743 to a design by Georg Bähr. The church was almost round, the shape according to the plans looking rather like a turtle. It was designed with the protestant liturgy in mind, the congregation clustering around the preacher. The organ was by Gottfried Silbermann.

Until the bombing of February 1945 the Neumarkt was said to be the most attractive part of the centre of Dresden, and the church was regarded as the symbol of Dresden. The ruins remain as a memorial to those who died in the bombing.

Martin-Luther-Denkmal

In front of the ruins of the Frauenkirche stands the Martin Luther monument by Rietschel and Donndorf (1885), a bronze cast after the original at Worms.

Albertinum

The Albertinum (originally the Arsenal) was built in 1559-1563 but reconstructed in the 18th Century and adapted as a museum and gallery in the 1880s. It is the home of the Gallery of Modern Masters (Gemäldegalerie Neue Meister) and concentrates on paintings of the 19th and 20th Centuries (entrance on Brühlsche Terrasse). Among the painters whose works hang here are Caspar David Friedrich (his paintings *The Cross on the Mountain* and *Two Men Contemplating the Moon* are hung here), Anselm Feuerbach, Max Liebermann, Emil Nolde and Otto Dix; impressionists are represented by Manet, Monet, Renoir, Gaugin, Dégas and Toulouse-Lautrec. Temporarily housed here are a number of Dresden's old masters normally hung in the Zwinger, including Raphael's Sistine Madonna and Canaletto's views of Dresden (see below — Zwinger). The gallery is open Tuesdays to Sundays 9.00am — 5.00pm.

The Albertinum also includes the Green Vault (Grünes Gewölbe), a vast collection of gold, silver and jewellery some of which goes back to the 15th Century (entrance Georg-Treu-Platz). Especially noteworthy is *The Delhi Court on the Birthday of the Great Mogul Aurangzeb* with over a hundred gold and painted enamel figures and over 5,000 diamonds (the work of the Dinglinger brothers between 1701 and 1708), August der Starke's golden coffee service (again by the Dinglingers), ivory statues of the four seasons by Permoser, Ivan the Terrible's drinking cup and glasswork by Giovanni Battista Metellino. The collection represents six centuries of patronage by the Electors of Saxony.

Also in the Albertinum is a sculpture collection begun in the 18th Century, containing works from Egypt, Crete, Greece and Rome as well as sculptures and statues from Italy, Germany and France.

Finally, mention should be made of the coin collection found in the Münzkabinett with over 200,000 coins, medals, bank notes and seals.

These three collections are open Fridays to Wednesdays 9.00am — 5.00pm, with an extra hour until 6.00pm on Tuesdays.

Brühlsche Terrasse

The Brühl Terrace (Brühlsche Terrasse), in the street of the same name, was laid out in 1738 under the direction of Count Brühl, a minister in the court of August III, on the site of the old town ramparts. The ramparts themselves were built by Caspar Voigt von Wierandt in about 1550 and improved and strengthened by Buchner in 1590. The terraced gardens are reached by a flight of 41 steps, but all that now remains of Brühl's original scheme is the dolphin fountain and the ironwork.

Apart from the Terrace, Brühl also had a palace, a library and a gallery built here. However, the Palais Brühl was demolished in 1889 and replaced by the Diet (Landtag), built between 1901-1906, destroyed in World war II and replaced then by a building that now houses a museum of mineralogy and geology. The Brühl library was restored in 1964 but became a restaurant (Gaststätte Sekundogenitur). The picture gallery building was likewise destroyed by bombing, and although it has been partially restored has never housed paintings again.

The gardens still contain the bronze groups of *Night*, *Evening*, *Noon* and *Morning*, the work of Schilling. Also the work of Schilling is the monument to Ernst Rietschel (Rietscheldenkmal), the Dresden sculptor who lived from 1804-1861 and was made a professor at the Dresden Academy of Art in 1832. The monument was erected in 1875 on the site of the sculptor's workshop. At the head of the steps that lead from the Brühlsche Terrasse down to the Albertinum and the Academy of Arts stands a statue of Gottfried Semper, the architect of the opera house.

Johanneum
The Johanneum museum is situated to the west of the Neumarkt. It was erected in 1586-1589 but underwent substantial change in 1872-1875 and was originally the palace stables. It was damaged during the war but re-opened as a transport museum (Verkehrsmuseum). Although the museum deals with all aspects of transport, there is an emphasis on rail travel as the museum was formerly the Saxon Railway Museum (established 1877) and has taken over many of its exhibits including the Muldenthal, a steam locomotive built in Chemnitz in 1861 and the oldest original steam locomotive remaining in East Germany.

It is open from April to September 9.00am — 5.00pm every day except Monday, and October to March 10.00am — 5.00pm.

Langer Gang and Stallhof
The Langer Gang or Long Passage runs the length of Augustusstraße. The work of Paul Buchner, it was built between 1586-1591 for the elector, Christian I. The inside consists of an arcade of 22 columns in Tuscan mode, and the exterior, facing onto the street, depicts a courtly procession of Saxon princes. The original in 'sgraffito' was a work of the Renaissance. It was

restored by the painter and restorer, Walther (1874), but
renewed in porcelain in 1908. Inside, reached by a gate leading
in from the Augustusstraße, are the stables and stableyard. The
stables provided accommodation for 128 horses and various
wagons and carrriages.

Schloß

The Royal Palace (Schloß) was established on its present site in
about 1530 and subject to frequent additions and enlargements
notably by August der Starke after a fire damaged the building
in 1701. The present Renaissance character of the building is
attributable to extensive alterations carried out by Dunger and
Fröhlich between 1890-1901. It is still in ruins, the only section
currently intact being the Georgentor (George Gate) built in the
16th Century under Georg der Bärtige (George the Bearded).
The statue of Georg himself on top of the gate is the work of
Christian Behrens (1901). It was restored in 1967.

Hofkirche

The Hofkirche (Court Cathedral) is the largest church in Saxony
and since 1980 has been the seat of the bishop of Dresden-
Meissen. It is dedicated to the Holy Trinity (and is thus often
referred to as the Kathedrale Sanctissimae Trinitatis). The
catholic community of Dresden decided to have this church
built to counter the influence of the protestant Frauenkirche.
The Roman architect, Chiaveri, was commissioned in 1737, and
construction began in 1738, finishing in 1751. Unusually the
church does not face east, for it was decided that it should be
sited at an angle to the bridge over the Elbe for better effect so
that the high altar is in the south-west of the church. It is one
of the last examples of the Italian baroque style and is thus
important for the history of Italian as well as German
architecture. Built mainly of sandstone, it is badly in need of
cleaning, as are many of Dresden's historic buildings.

Notable features of the cathedral are its main door (of oak)
and the 78 statues of saints on the parapets and at the entrances
(the work of another Italian, Mattielli). The 85.5m tower houses
the bells installed in 1807. A processional aisle runs around the
central nave. This was used for processions that the catholic
minority of Dresden could not hold in the town itself. The
gallery seating was used by members of the royal family and the
nobility and was connected to the palace by a sort of bridge that
can still be seen between the Hofkirche and the ruins of the
Schloß.

The altar-piece depicts the ascension and is the work of Raphael Mengs, one time court painter. At the back of the church a modern altarpiece serves as a war memorial. The organ (installed 1750-1753) was the last and greatest work of the organ builder, Gottfried Silbermann. Luckily it escaped damage as it was removed from the cathedral before Dresden came under attack and was replaced in 1968-1969.

Four vaults contain the bodies of 49 of the Saxon kings and princes, and an urn contains the remains of the heart of August der Starke (the rest of his body was buried in Cracow).

Organ music and prayers (Orgelvesper) take place every Saturday between May and October at 2.00pm, and an organ recital, again between May and October, on Wednesdays between 6.45pm and 7.15pm.

Opera House (Semper Oper)

The Opera House was constructed between 1838-1841. It used to be called the Hoftheater (court theatre), but is now more commonly referred to as the Semperoper, commemorating its architect, Gottfried Semper. The original opera house, a smaller and simpler building where Wagner's *Rienzi*, *Flying Dutchman* and *Tannhäuser* were premièred, burned down in 1869. The second opera house was built in Renaissance style by Manfred Semper, the son of Gottfried, after plans prepared by his father in Vienna. It faces the Hofkirche, and the main entrance is flanked by statues of Goethe and Schiller, both the work of Rietschel. This second opera house saw the première of Strauss's *Der Rosenkavalier* in 1911, conducted by Ernst von Schuch and directed by Max Reinhardt. One of the most frequently performed operas here is Weber's *Der Freischütz*, the score of which was completed by Weber in Dresden on May 13 1820. Even though the first performance actually took place in Berlin (in the Schauspielhaus on June 18 1821) and the first Dresden performance was not until 1822, the opera has become associated with Dresden and the Semperoper.

Like so much of Dresden, the opera house was largely destroyed in 1945. Reconstruction work began in 1970 culminating in a grand re-opening with a performance of *Der Freischütz* on February 13 1985, the 40th anniversary of the bombing. The restoration work has not only preserved the spirit of the original building, but also provides good air conditioning and comfortable seating.

Altstädter Wache

To the south of the Theaterplatz is the Old Town Watch, built between 1830-1831 to a design by Schinkel similar to that of the Neue Wache in Berlin.

Zwinger

The Zwinger (literally translated Zwinger means Keep) is Dresden's best known building. Built by Mathäus Daniel Pöppelmann in co-operation with the sculptor Balthasar Permoser on part of the former town fortifications between 1710-1732, it consists of seven pavilions connected by a one storey gallery, and is considered to be one of Germany's finest baroque buildings. Badly damaged in the war, it was restored in 1964. The whole complex is symmetrical and built around a central courtyard, the Zwingerhof, formerly the site of carnivals and tournaments. The southwestern side is dominated by the Kronentor (Crown Gate), a two storey triumphal arch surmounted by the Polish royal crown, the symbol of the house of August der Starke (built 1710). On the southeastern side is the Glockenspiel pavilion with two rows of bells in its tower.

The galleries house various museums: in the west wing the zoology museum (Museum für Tierkunde), in the north the Mathematisch-Physikalischer Salon with its exhibition of scientific instruments, in the southwest the porcelain collection, and in the east wing the art gallery (see below). Between the mathematical-physical salon and the picture gallery is the Nymphenbad, an elaborate fountain in imitation of a grotto, richly decorated with dolphins, naiads and nymphs.

Gemäldegalerie Alte Meister

The Zwinger is the home of Dresden's most famous art collection, the Gallery of Old Masters. It is regarded as being the most important art collection in East Germany. Although founded by August III (1733-1763), the present building is the work of Semper, built between 1847-1854. The paintings were so highly praised by the art historian Joachim Winckelmann, that Goethe was moved to travel to Dresden from Leipzig in 1768 to see them. In *Dichtung und Wahrheit* (an autobiographical work written between 1811-1831) Goethe relates the impatience with which he waited for the gallery to open, the rich impression made on him by the splendour of the interior, and the atmosphere of silent awe like that of a church. Kleist, Grillparzer, Tolstoy, Dostoevsky, Mme de Staël, Stendhal, Balzac and Cocteau have all admired and written about the gallery.

At the time of writing the gallery is closed and several of the most important pictures are temporarily hung in the Albertinum. It is expected that the Zwinger will re-open with the pictures described here in autumn 1992.

The collection is divided into a number of sections: the old German masters (works of Dürer, Holbein, Cranach and Baldung-Grien), Dutch masters (van Eyck, Rembrandt, Rubens, van Dyck, Vermeer and others), Italian masters (represented by Titian, Veronese, Giorgione) and paintings by members of the French and Spanish schools. Any selection from such a vast collection must be subjective, but Vermeer's *Girl Reading a Letter*, Raphael's *Sistine Madonna*, Dürer's *Portrait of a Young Man* and Cranach's *St Catherine's Altar Piece* are notable.

Historisches Museum
The Historical Museum (temporarily closed) is located in the east wing of the Zwinger on the other side of the entrance that leads to the Theaterplatz. Its exhibits include costumes, clothing and arms (both ceremonial and designed for combat). Current plans are for the museum to re-open in autumn 1992.

Other sites south of the Elbe
All the above are to be found in the old centre of Dresden south of the Elbe. The following are also situated in the south but some way out of the centre.

Palais Marcolini
Built in 1727 for Ludwig of Württemberg-Teck, this palace became the property of Count Brühl and later Count Marcolini. It became a hospital in 1845 and is now the Bezirkskrankenhaus Friedrichstadt. The Neptune Fountain (Neptunbrunnen) in the garden is regarded as the finest fountain in Dresden. Worked in sandstone by Lorenzo Mattielli (1741-1744) to a design by Zacharias Longuelune, it consists of three basins at different levels, the river gods Tiber and Nile at the bottom, and Neptune and Amphitrite above surrounded by winged stallions and other fabulous creatures. It is situated in Friedrichstraße near the Dresden Mitte station.

Catholic Cemetery
Opposite lies the catholic cemetery (Katholischer Friedhof). The minority catholic community of Dresden was permitted to use this site (outside the then town boundary) in 1720. It is full of tombs and gravestones in baroque, rococo and classical style. A

stone sarcophagus marks the grave of Balthasar Permoser, the sculptor (1651-1732). The composer, Carl Maria von Weber (1786-1826), is also buried here. Although he died in London (of consumption) his son had his body brought back to Dresden for interment in the family vault (the work of Semper).

Kupferstichkabinett

The Cabinet of Engravings containing over 200,000 drawings and engravings from the 15th Century onwards is in the east of the town in the Güntzstraße and opens from 10.00am — noon and 2.00pm — 4.00pm on Mondays and Wednesdays (open until 6.00pm on Tuesdays).

Großer Garten

The Great Garden (Großer Garten) is a large park between Stübelallee and Tiergartenstraße. Now a people's park (Volkspark), it was conceived in the 17th Century and laid out under the supervision of Martin Göttler and Johann Georg Starcke for the elector, Johann Georg II. However, it was a battlefield in both the Seven Years' War and at the battle of Dresden in 1813 and was re-designed in French formal style in 1683. In 1873 it was restored and extended by Friedrich Bouché who favoured the English style, and it was he who gave it its present character.

Thousands of Dresden's inhabitants sought refuge here during the bombing of February 13-14 1945, but the second wave of the attack destroyed the garden and its buildings and killed those who wrongly thought they would be safe out of the built-up areas of the town.

In the centre of the park stands the baroque Palais, a pleasure palace built in 1678 for Johann Georg III. Also noteworthy is the marble group sculpture *Time carrying off Beauty*, the work of Pietro Balestra.

Zoo

The Dresden zoo occupies a corner of the Großer Garten. The main entrance is on Tiergartenstraße. It was opened in 1861, destroyed in the 1945 bombing but restored again and restocked by Professor Wolfgang Ullrich who travelled to India and Africa in the 1950s to find new specimens. It now houses over 2,000 animals representing some 500 different species, and boasts the largest collection of primates in East Germany.

Pioneer Railway
The Pioneer Railway (Pioniereisenbahn) is a model railway that runs through the park. Modelled on the real GDR Reichsbahn, it was until recently run by Young Pioneers, a youth group for children aged 10-14. There are 5.6km of track and five stations. It operates from April 1 to the end of October.

Botanical Garden
The Botanical Garden, also part of the Großer Garten, was laid out under Professor Oskar Drude in 1889-1892. Destroyed in the bombing of 1945, it re-opened in 1950 as part of the Technical University of Dresden to which it remains attached.

Hygiene-Museum
The Deutsches Hygiene-Museum in der DDR (Lingnerplatz 1) is not an obvious tourist attraction but is an institution of which Dresden is proud, and is referred to for that reason in all the literature about the town. The neo-classical building that houses the exhibits was built in 1927-1930 and dedicated at the Second International Hygiene Exhibition held in Dresden in 1930. Apart from matters of hygiene and safety at work, the museum also demonstrates the development of the human anatomy and is famous for its glass woman, glass cow and glass horse, see-through anatomical models crafted with considerable skill for the 1930 opening of the museum. (Opening times: Saturdays-Thursdays from 9.00am — 6.00pm.)

Prager Straße
The Prager Straße (Prague Street) leads from the main railway station to the old town (Altstadt). It is a pedestrian zone and the main shopping street, as well as the site of several of Dresden's hotels, many restaurants and a large cinema in an unusual round building. The south end is the site of the Lenin Monument (Lenindenkmal) erected in 1974.

North of the Elbe
On the north side of the Elbe is the Neustadt (New Town) reached by crossing the oldest bridge (in origin if not in its present form), the Georgi-Dimitroff-Brücke. A plaque half way across the bridge commemorates Dimitroff.

Blockhaus
The Blockhaus (also called the Neustädter Wache or guardhouse) is at the northern end of the bridge and is all that remains of a

number of buildings that clustered around the Neustädter Markt. It was begun in 1730 to designs by Longuelune and completed in 1755 by Knöffel. Now it is occupied by the House of German-Soviet Friendship (Haus der Deutsch-Sowjetischen Freundschaft), a sort of club house where meetings are held and films shown about the Soviet Union. There is a restaurant on the top floor.

Goldener Reiter
The Golden Horseman (Goldener Reiter) in the shadow of the Bellevue hotel is a monument to August der Starke and depicts the ruler in classical style on a rearing horse. It was worked on by Ludwig Wiedemann (1732-1734) but the gilding was added in 1965.

Straße der Befreiung
The Street of the Liberation (Straße der Befreiung) leads north out of the Neustädter Markt. It is a pedestrian zone and is perhaps Dresden's most impressive promenade with old and new building styles carefully and effectively blending in some parts and clashing in others. The street contains several pleasing restaurants and wine cellars. No. 11, for example, contains various places to eat and drink; although the house was damaged in a fire in 1685 the vaulting in the Bierkeller goes back to pre-1695. The street is also noted for its Museum of Early Romanticism (Museum der Frühromantik) at number 13. The home of the painter Wilhelm von Kügelgen (1802-1867), the house was visited by Caspar David Friedrich, Kleist, Goethe, Schlegel and Tieck. It bears a blessing: 'An Gottes Segen ist alles gelegen' (With God's blessing, all is well).

Nearby is the Church of the Three Kings (Dreikönigskirche) (1732-1739) begun by Pöppelmann but finished by George Bähr (entrance in Friedrich-Engels-Straße). A little further along on the left, before the Platz der Einheit, is a walled statue of Schiller, surrounded by scenes from his works.

The Straße der Befreiung ends at the Platz der Einheit (Square of Unity), formerly the site of one of the town gates, the Schwarzes Tor (Black Gate). Here on November 7 1945 the Monument to the Soviet Army (Ehrenmal der Sowjetarmee) was dedicated to the Soviet troops who liberated Dresden from fascism, the liberation that caused the name of this street to be changed from its former name, Hauptstraße. The bronze reliefs on the base depict Soviet troops doing battle, and the bronze statue above depicts two soldiers defending the banner of the revolution.

The Japanese Palace
The Japanese Palace (Japanisches Palais) was built between
1727-1735 by Pöppelmann after designs by Longuelune, de
Bodts, Knöffel and Pöppelmann himself. It replaced a so- called
Dutch Palace built by Count Flemming in 1715. Built in a late
baroque/early classical style, the palace consists of four wings
surrounding a courtyard around three sides of which runs a
gallery at second storey level. The gallery is supported by
Chinese busts in conformity with the 18th Century penchant for
chinoiserie (examples of which can also be found at Sanssouci
in Potsdam). The name of the palace, however, comes not from
the oriental elements in the building but from the fact that it
was used to house a priceless collection of Chinese and Japanese
porcelain belonging to August der Starke.
     Since reconstruction (completed in 1952) the palace has been
the home of the Museum of Pre-history and the Museum of
Ethnology.

Schloß Pillnitz
Whatever you may decide to omit from a short visit to Dresden
it must not be Schloß Pillnitz. In fact Pillnitz is a small complex
of palaces set in carefully tended grounds and gardens on the
banks of the Elbe. It can be reached by boat (with the Weiße
Flotte) or by the number 85 bus. The journey itself is pleasant,
with the road between Dresden and Pillnitz passing through
impressive suburbs and vineyards on the hills overlooking the
Elbe.
     The Water Palace (Wasserpalais) facing directly onto the Elbe
and the Mountain Palace (Bergpalais) confront one another on
either side of the pleasure garden (Lustgarten). They are both
the work of Pöppelmann, and the shape of the roofs again
reflects the obsession of the age with oriental shapes and styles.
These two mirror-image edifices are connected by the New
Palace (Neues Palais), added in 1822 by Christian Friedrich
Schuricht in place of an older Renaissance building destroyed by
fire in 1818.
     The Lustgarten is a baroque garden, geometric in shape,
leading to the hedge garden (Heckengarten), again a formal
garden of paths and hedges.
     The English garden, in the northwest of the grounds, with its
pond and round pavilion, is wilder and more relaxed in its
layout. Next to it is the Orangery, which is still used to preserve
palms and orange trees in the winter months, a camellia house

with Japanese varieties over 200 years old, and the conifer wood (Koniferenhain).

The Flora Garden (Floragarten) which begins behind the Orangery is named after the statue of Flora by Wolf von Hoyer (1870). It leads on to the Chinese Garden (Chinesischer Garten), the site of a Chinese style pavilion, another example of 18th Century chinoiserie.

The grounds are open all year round, but the palaces are open only between May and October from Tuesdays to Sundays 9.30am — 4.00pm. The Schloßschänke (bar) at the entrance to the palace is open almost all year round, and the village of Pillnitz itself has a number of places to eat and drink.

Opposite the Wasserpalais out in the Elbe is the Elbinsel or Elbe Island, a nature reserve that is closed to the public.

Dresden Heath
Northeast of Dresden beyond Neustadt is the heath (Dresdner Heide), a large open park and woodland area criss-crossed with marked and unmarked paths.

Where to stay
Dresden has seven Interhotels, including the luxurious Bellevue Hotel on the banks of the Elbe (Köpckestraße 15). Other Interhotels are: Dresdner Hof, Am Neumarkt; Newa, Leningrader Straße; Königstein and Lilienstein, Prager Straße; Astoria, Ernst-Thälmann-Platz 1; Motel Dresden, Münzmeisterstraße. A cheaper alternative is the Gewandhaus, Ringstraße 1.

Where to eat
The Straße der Befreiung is a good place to look for food and drink. On the street itself are several restaurants including the Kügelgenhaus (with a grill, restaurant, Bierkeller and café), the Äberlausitzer Töppl and the Meißener Weinkeller; facing the Platz der Einheit too are several possibilities: Gaststätte am Tor, Piccolo Restaurant, Cocktail Bar and another bar, Der Löwe. Other restaurants include the International, Prager Straße; Am Zwinger, Ernst-Thälmann-Straße (a large self-service restaurant); Ratskeller, Dr-Külz-Ring; Luisenhof, Bergbahnstraße 8; Secundogenitur, Brühlsche Terrasse; Kulturpalast Dresden, Ernst-Thälmann-Straße; Szeged, Ernst-Thälmann-Straße (Hungarian); Haus der Deutsch-Sowjetischen

Freundschaft (in Blockhaus), Köpckestraße; Altmarkt Keller, am Altmarkt on the corner of Ernst-Thälmann-Straße.

Events

The Dresden Music Festival, held in the opera house, the Kulturpalast and theatres, as well as in palaces and gardens in and around Dresden, takes place annually from mid-May to mid-June. Dresden also has an International Dixieland Festival in May and a pop festival in September.

Information

Further information can be obtained from Dresden-Information, Prager-Straße 10/11.

Excursions from Dresden
Radebeul

About 8km northwest of Dresden is the small town of Radebeul. It is in itself an attractive town, with its baroque and Renaissance residences, but is best known as the site of the Indian Museum (Indianer-Museum), also known as the Karl-May-Museum. Karl May (1842-1912) was a famous German writer of adventure stories for children, many of which are set in the days of Red Indian America; his work is popular even today. The museum contains an exhibition devoted to May's life and work, and tools, weapons, trophies, and other objects representative of the culture of the North American Indians.

The museum is open Tuesdays-Sundays from 9.00am — 5.00pm (but closed in January).

Schloß Moritzburg

Schloß Moritzburg, about 14km north-west of Dresden, is a baroque palace reminiscent of some of the Loire châteaux. It was built in the 16th Century for Duke Moritz and used principally as a hunting retreat. The original building was extended considerably by August der Starke between 1723-1730 to plans drawn up by Pöppelmann, Longuelune and Knöffel. Its setting in the middle of an artificial lake adds to its grandeur.

The palace was taken into public ownership in 1946, and from 1947 became a Baroque Museum concentrating on furniture, paintings and other 18th Century objects. The artist Käthe

Kollwitz (1867-1945) fled here in 1944 to escape the Nazis, and a section of the museum is devoted to her memory.

Walking through the park at Moritzburg you come to the Fasanenschlößchen (Pheasant Palace), built between 1769-1782 in rococo style, originally as a summer residence. It now houses an ornithological exhibition. Opening times: April 15 to the end of October, Saturdays to Wednesdays.

Several well-marked walks, ranging in length from 3km to 22km, also start from Moritzburg.

Moritzburg can be reached by road or on the narrow-gauge railway that runs from Radebeul to Radeburg. The palace is open between February and November Wednesdays to Sundays.

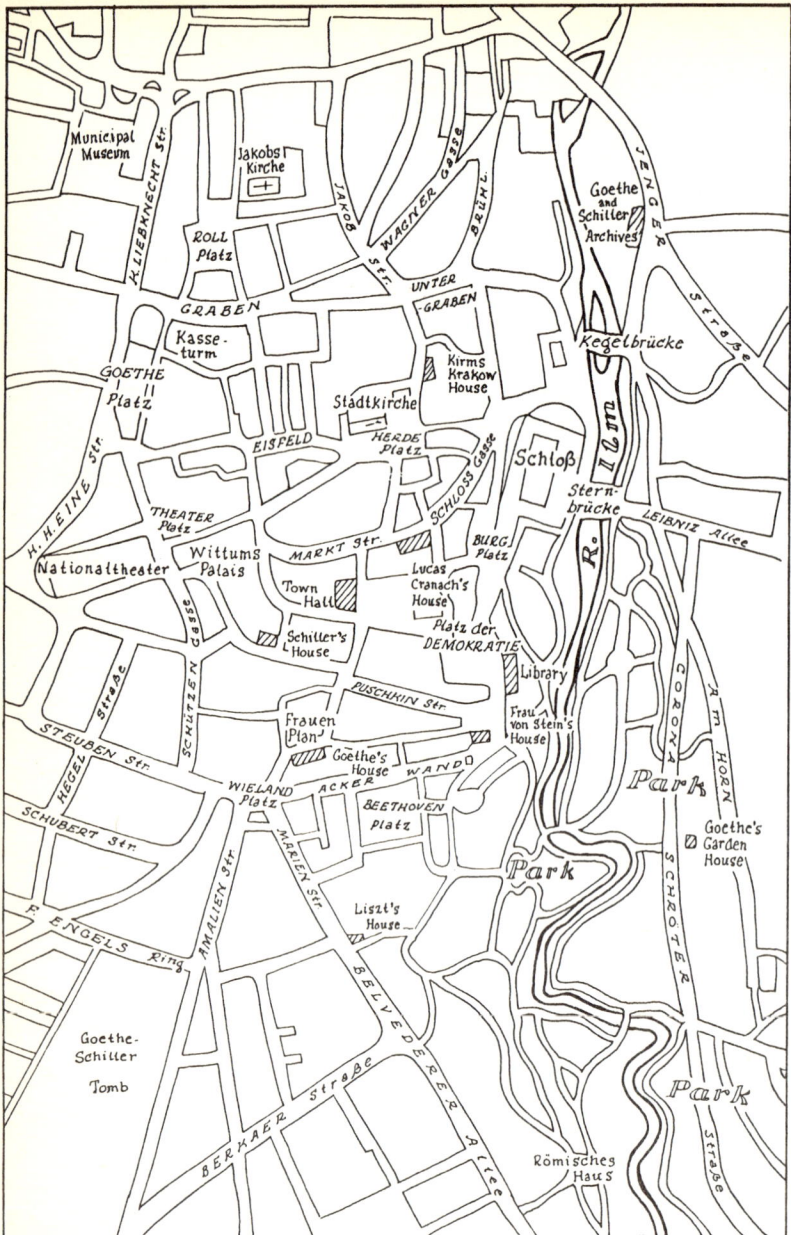

Municipal
Museum

K.LIEBKNECHT Str.

Jakobs
Kirche

JAKOB Str.

WAGNER GASSE

BRUHL.

JENGER Straße

Goethe
and
Schiller
Archives

ROLL
Platz

GRABEN

UNTER
GRABEN

Kegelbrücke

Kasse-
turm

GOETHE
Platz

Kirms
Krakow
House

Stadtkirche

EISFELD

HERDE
Platz

SCHLOSS Gasse

Schloß

H.HEINE Str.

THEATER
Platz

Wittums
Palais

MARKT Str.

BURG
Platz

Stern-
brücke

R. Ilm

LEIBNIZ Allee

Nationaltheater

SCHÜTZEN GASSE

Strasse

Town
Hall

Lucas
Cranach's
House

Schiller's
House

Platz der
DEMOKRATIE

Library

PUSCHKIN Str.

STEUBEN Str.

HEGEL Str.

Frauen
Plan

Goethe's
House

ACKER WAND

Frau
von Stein's
House

CORONA

AM HORN

WIELAND
Platz

BEETHOVEN
Platz

Park

SCHUBERT Str.

F. ENGELS Ring

AMALIEN Str.

MARIEN Str.

Liszt's
House

Park

SCHROTER Straße

Goethe's
Garden
House

Goethe-
Schiller
Tomb

BERKAER Straße

BELVEDERE Allee

Römisches
Haus

Park

WEIMAR

0   150

m

Weimar

Weimar, picturesquely situated on the river Ilm, provides more attractions for those interested in German history and culture than anywhere else in East Germany with the exception of Berlin and Dresden. Its small town atmosphere, coupled with a plethora of well-preserved classical buildings associated with great names from Goethe and Schiller to Liszt, make it both an extremely pleasant and a very rewarding town to explore in depth.

Background
Weimar was established as a town in about 1250, but excavations have shown that the Ilm valley was inhabited at least 135,000 years ago. The place names Weimare and Wimare can be traced back to 975.

The town became the possession of the landgraves of Thuringia then came under the rule of the electors of Saxony, the elector Johann Friedrich making it his residence after his defeat at the battle of Mühlberg in 1547. His successors proclaimed themselves dukes of Weimar, and the town became the capital of the duchy of Saxony-Weimar in the 16th Century and remained such until 1918.

Weimar has undergone two great periods of expansion. The first was in the 16th Century when extensive building work attracted people to settle here including the painter, Lucas Cranach. The second was in the 18th Century.

Bach lived and worked in Weimar from 1708-1717. In 1772 the duchess Anna Amalia appointed the writer Christoph Martin Wieland as tutor to her sons. She was widowed at a young age, and one of her sons, Carl August, became the ruler. At his instigation Germany's greatest literary figure, Goethe, came to Weimar in 1775 and remained here for virtually the rest of his life. His literary reputation was important in the development of the town, but his ability as a politician, administrator and planner also influenced the character and appearance of the place. Weimar became the centre of German culture, drawing to it writers such as Schiller and Herder and in due course composers — Hummel, Liszt and Richard Strauss. It also became an important centre for art. The Free School of Drawing was founded in Weimar in 1776. This century has seen Weimar as the centre of the Weimar School of painters (Rohlfs, Buchholz, Hagen and others) and the first home of Walter Gropius's Bauhaus style.

In 1919 Weimar became the focus of political life in Germany. After the downfall of the monarchy the National Assembly met in Weimar to avoid revolutionary workers in Berlin and formulated the Weimar constitution before returning to Berlin in 1920. Thus the so-called Weimar Republic came into being. However, it experienced severe economic difficulties that paved the way for the rise of National Socialism in the 1930s culminating in the appointment of Hitler as Chancellor in 1933 and the suspension of the Weimar constitution.

Weimar was the capital of Thuringia from 1920 until the reorganization of the administrative regions in the GDR in 1952. Today, with a population of 63,000, it is important partly as an industrial centre (clocks and watches and agricultural machinery) but mainly as a centre of culture and learning.

A walk around the centre of Weimar
Goethehaus
Goethe's house is the obvious place from which to begin sightseeing in Weimar. Goethe first came to Weimar in 1775 and under Duke Carl August became involved in affairs of state as well as maintaining his literary output. The range of his interests expanded into forestry and agriculture, mining and mineralogy. Here he met Charlotte von Stein who, although seven years older and the mother of several children, became much more to him than an intellectual companion: his letters to her evidence a deep love between them, a love that inspired a great deal of Goethe's Weimar period poetry. Except for a journey to Italy in 1786, from which he returned in 1788, he remained here until his death.

Goethe's house is to be found in the Frauenplan. It is a relatively simple, two storey baroque building dating from about 1700 and in which Goethe lived from 1782 until his death in 1832. The house now belongs to the Goethe-Nationalmuseum and is devoted to exhibitions of Goethe's art, mineral and scientific collections. It is possible to walk around the room in which he worked, visit the room where he died and admire his library of 5,400 books. The museum itself is next door and is open from April to October on Tuesdays to Sundays between 9.00am — 1.00pm and 2.00pm-5.00pm. Goethe's visitors often stayed in the inn, Zum Weißen Schwan (The White Swan), opposite the house. A cannon ball forming part of the wall of the inn recalls the shelling of Weimar by Napoleonic troops in 1806.

Next to the White Swan is a house bearing a memorial plaque commemorating the fact that Schiller stayed there on his first visit to Weimar.

Wielandhaus
South of Goethe's house is Wielandplatz, named after another German writer and poet, Christoph Martin Wielands who lived in Weimar almost continuously from 1772 until his death in 1813. Little of Wieland's work is read today other than by serious students of German literature, but his output was prodigious and he earned an important place in European literary history for his translations into German of 22 of Shakespeare's plays. The square is dominated by a statue of Wieland by Gasser (1887).

Haus der Frau von Stein
Turning from the Wielandplatz into the Ackerwand you come to Charlotte von Stein's house at number 25. This was the town residence of the von Stein family. The living quarters on the first floor were redesigned with assistance from Goethe.

Grünes Schloß
Just north of the von Stein house, past Rogge's bust of Pushkin (1949), is the Grünes Schloß (Green Palace), built between 1562-1565 in Renaissance style as the residence for two brothers of the reigning duke. Its interior is one of the most attractive of all Weimar's buildings. In 1766 the duchess Anna Amalia established a library here and between 1761-1766 a large rococo hall of books filling over three storeys was constructed. For a number of years the library was under the control of Goethe (together with Christian Gottlob Voigt) and under his guidance the building was extended (1803-1805). In the early part of the 19th Century a further extension incorporated an old watch tower, part of the old town defences, which provided further library space. Schiller's skull rested inside the pedestal of

Dannecker's bust of him before it was transferred to the Goethe and Schiller vault (see p.110).

The palace is now the Central Library of German Classical Literature and houses an important collection of 17th and 18th Century works as well as collections of maps and globes and antique musical instruments.

Platz der Demokratie

The Platz der Demokratie (Democracy Square), formerly the Fürstenplatz (Princes' Square), is the site of the old Fürstenhaus, a three-storey baroque house built in 1774. It became the temporary residence of the duke, Carl August, after a fire in the palace in 1774; he remained there until 1803. In 1808 Weimar's Freie Zeichenschule (Free School of Drawing) moved in. It is now the home of the Franz Liszt School of Music, named after the composer who lived in Weimar from 1869 to 1886.

The square is dominated by the Carl August monument, a grand scale statue of the duke on horseback depicted as a Roman emperor. Executed by Adolf von Donndorf, it has stood in the square in its position in front of the Fürstenhaus since 1875.

On the western side of the square stands the Rotes Schloß (Red Palace), a long, three-storey Renaissance building (1574-1576) which, however, was subjected to extensive rebuilding in the 19th Century. It was the home of the Free School of Drawing from its foundation in 1776 until it moved to the Fürstenhaus. Nearby is the Gelbes Schloß (Yellow Palace) built in about 1702.

Lucas-Cranach-Haus

Just to the north of the Platz der Demokratie is the Markt (Market). Between the Platz der Demokratie and the Markt you pass by the former Parkhotel. The house next to it bears a plaque commemorating Bach's musical contribution to the life of the city during the nine years he worked here as organist and Hofkonzertmeister (court composer).

The Lucas-Cranach-Haus in the Markt is the house where the painter Cranach the Elder lived after he came to Weimar in 1552 until his death in 1553. Cranach, a former mayor of Wittenberg, was a leading artist of the German Renaissance and Reformation. His many works include portraits of Luther and allegorical paintings expressing the principles of the Reformation, many of which remain in the possession of the Weimar state art collection.

The house itself was built in 1549. It is a three-storey building in Renaissance style and decorated with pillars and columns, arches, tendrils, dolphins and other extravagances. It is marked by its two prominent gables. Cranach had his workshop on the third floor and it was here that he painted the famous altar piece (completed after his death by his son) that is now in the Herderkirche. The house is sometimes referred to as the Brück-Haus since it actually belonged to Dr Brück, Cranach's son-in-law.

After his death Cranach was buried in Weimar's oldest cemetery, the Jakobsfriedhof, but the tombstone was moved to the Herderkirche to protect it from damage and decay.

Hotel Elephant

The Markt is also the site of Weimar's best known hotel. The façade blends in with the historic character of the square it overlooks, but the inside is modern in style. Apart from its obvious practical significance to travellers (it is unquestionably the most attractive hotel for visitors to Weimar) the Hotel Elephant is famous, at least for Germans, for the part it played in Thomas Mann's novel *Lotte in Weimar*. Written in 1939, the novel describes an imaginary meeting in 1816 between Goethe at the pinnacle of his success and Lotte (Charlotte) Kestner, his love of 40 years ago. The opening lines of the book describe Lotte's arrival in Weimar in September 1816 and show her taking up residence in the Gasthof Zum Elephanten am Markte.

Residenzschloß

The Grand Ducal Palace (Residenzschloß) stands on the west bank of the river Ilm. The oldest parts of the palace are those around the tower which are believed to date back to the 15th Century. However the building that stands today dates from 1789-1803. Much of it was constructed under Goethe's supervision. Notable features are the staircase in the east wing, the classical Festsaal and the Goethe room (Goethezimmer) conceived by Schinkel.

Over 70 rooms in the palace are now given over to the art gallery that houses the Weimar Art Collections (Kunstsammlungen zu Weimar). It is an impressive gallery exhibiting a wide range of work by artists as diverse in style and period as Cranach and Baldung-Grien to Veronese and Tintoretto and Rubens and Ostade. The collection of German painting covers the Goethe period to the 20th Century and includes works by members of the Weimar School (Rohlfs, Buchholz and Hagen etc) and artists of the Bauhaus period

(Gropius and Klee). Lovers of German Romantic painting will enjoy the work of Caspar David Friedrich, Runge and Kersting. The palace is also the home of an important collection of Russian icons from the 15th — 19th Centuries. The opening times of the museum are Tuesdays to Sundays 9.00am — 1.00pm and 2.00pm — 5.00pm, but it is not open until 10.00am on Fridays.

Herderkirche

The Herderkirche (Herder Church), also referred to as the Stadtkirche (Town Church) stands in the Herderplatz, west of the Palace. It takes its name from Johann Gottfried Herder, the writer, philosopher and theologian. Herder was born in East Prussia in 1744 and studied medicine at Königsberg but changed to theology and took holy orders. He came to Weimar in 1776 as chief pastor, and it was in Weimar that he wrote his largest work, *Ideen zur Philosophie der Geschichte der Menschheit* (Ideas on the Philosophy of the History of Humanity), which was published between 1784-1791. He died in Weimar in 1803 and was buried in the church that now bears his name. Just in front of the church stands Herder's memorial statue; executed in bronze, it is the work of Schaller and dates 1850.

The Herderkirche itself used to be dedicated to SS. Peter and Paul. The original church goes back to 1498, but was rebuilt between 1735-1745 in baroque style. It has three late Gothic naves and is the home of the Cranach altar piece begun in 1552 by Cranach the Elder and completed by his son. It depicts the crucifixion and incorporates portraits of Luther and of Cranach himself.

In 1945 the church was badly damaged by bombing, only the outer walls remaining. It was restored in 1953. Thomas Mann contributed 20,000 marks awarded to him as a National Prize winner towards the work.

The large tombs in the chancel date mainly from the 16th and 17th Centuries and bear witness to the fact that the church was the burial place of the Ernestine princes between 1547-1825. Herder himself was buried where he worked, in the west chancel under the organ loft. The simple slab tombstone was engraved with his motto, 'Licht, Liebe, Leben' (Light, Love, Life).

The church is open to visitors 10.30am — noon and 2.00pm — 3.30pm on weekdays and from 2.00pm — 3.00pm at the weekend. In summer, organ recitals are given on Sundays at 6.00pm.

The parsonage behind the church is still the residence of Weimar's chief pastor. It is distinguished by its commemorative plaque to Herder.

Kirms-Krackow-Haus

The Herder museum is housed on the second floor of the Kirms-Krackow House which is located in the Jakobstraße to the north of the Herderplatz. It is one of the oldest buildings in Weimar and was documented as early as 1532. It has a simple baroque façade, a yard (Hof) surrounded by a wooden gallery, and living and work rooms in classical style.

The house takes its names from the two families who lived in the house at different times. In Goethe's time it was the home of the Kirms brothers. Franz Kirms (1750-1826) worked with Goethe as a manager of the Hoftheater and assisted Goethe generally in the theatrical affairs of the town. In later years the house was the residence of members of the Krackow family, notably Charlotte Krackow (1825-1915), the niece of the Kirms brothers. She preserved the 18th Century interior intact as a monument to Weimar's classical period. After her death the house became the property of the city, and in 1917 was opened to the public as a museum for the first time.

The Luthergasse runs behind the Kirms-Krackow-Haus. A short, curved and narrow street, it still preserves the atmosphere of classical Weimar. Nearby at Jakobsgasse 4 is another historic house, the home of Christiane Vulpius, Goethe's mistress for many years.

Luthergasse 1 was the home of the poet and writer Martin Wieland who lived here from 1773-1777. Goethe was a frequent visitor. In 1822 the house was purchased by Johann Daniel Falk, a philanthropist who devoted a great deal of time and energy to the care of children orphaned in the war of 1806-1813. He established the Falk Institute of Education and Training here. In recognition of his services the people of Weimar erected a simple monument in his memory which can still be seen on the corner of Teichgasse, on the other side of the Herderplatz.

Jakobskirche

Moving away from the historical centre of Weimar, if you cross the main road (Graben) and follow Jakobstraße north, you come to the Jakobskirche in the street called Am Jakobskirchhof. This splendid baroque church was built in 1712-1713 and is easily recognized by its onion-shaped west tower. It was in the vestry of this church that Goethe married his mistress, Christiane Vulpius, on October 19 1806.

The cemetery has already been mentioned as the oldest in Weimar (records of it as a place of burial go back to 1530) and the site of Cranach's grave. The oldest recorded individual grave is, in fact, that of Cranach. The tomb stone, portraying Cranach's bulky figure, is to be found not in the cemetery itself but on the church wall and is a copy of the original which was removed to the Herderkirche in 1859.

Many leading Weimar figures were buried here. Georg Melchior Kraus (1733-1806) came to Weimar from Frankfurt-am-Main in 1775 and became the first director of the Free School of Drawing. His drawings and paintings hang in many of Weimar's museums and galleries. Ferdinand Jagemann (1780-1820) was the son of Anna Amalia, the founder of the Central Library, and another important artist who also directed the Free School where he had been a student.

'Hier ruht J.J. Bode' (here lies J.J. Bode) is the simple epitaph that identifies the tombstone of Johann Joachim Bode (1730-1793) again attached to the wall of the church. Bode was an important writer and critic, a well respected translator and publisher, a friend of the dramatist, Lessing, and the editor of the *Hamburgische Dramaturgie* (a leading work of the time on dramatic theory).

Close by is the memorial to Carl August Musäus (1735-1787), another writer whose name is now barely known for his original writings but is still remembered for his popular collection of German fairy tales.

Schiller was originally buried here in the so-called Kassengewölbe, but his remains were removed in 1826 to the Goethe-Schiller-Gruft at the instigation of the then mayor of Weimar, Schwabe.

The cemetery is also the site of the grave of Christiane von Goethe (1765-1816) née Vulpius. She was among the last of Weimar's citizens to be buried here before the graveyard was closed in 1818.

Bertuchhaus

On Karl-Liebknecht-Straße west of the church is the Bertuch House which adjoins the school built between 1780-1800 for the publisher, financier and entrepreneur, Friedrich Johann Justus Bertuch, who also acted as secretary and keeper to the Duke's privy purse. Bertuch published a number of leading geographichal works and brought out the first fashion magazine in Europe. Among other manufacturing concerns, he owned an artificial flower factory near the Erfurt Gate (Erfurter Tor) where Christiane Vulpius worked before she met Goethe.

The house is now given over to the Municipal Museum (Stadtmuseum Weimar) devoted to the history of Weimar. It is open Sundays to Thursdays 9.00am — 1.00pm and 2.00pm — 5.00pm.

Goetheplatz

Heading south back towards the centre of the town you reach the Goetheplatz which runs alongside the Heinestraße. The main post office is on the west side of the square. To the right of the post office, but separated from it by a street, is the former Bürgerschule (community school) built in Goethe's time (between 1822-1825) by Clemens Wenzeslaus Coudray. The fountain with its statue of a boy reading, which stands in front of the main gate of the school, is by Rauch.

Also on the Goetheplatz is the Kasseturm, a tower that was part of the medieval town fortifications, now a student club.

Theaterplatz

The Wielandstraße leads south out of Goetheplatz and connects it with the Theaterplatz (Theatre Square).

Wieland spent the last years of his life (1806-1813) at what is now Wielandstraße 1, but the building that now stands there is not the original.

The Theaterplatz is dominated by the Deutsches National-theater (German National Theatre). The building that now stands on the square is in fact the fourth theatre to have been built here. Plays were originally performed in the Palace until the fire of 1774. In 1779 a comedy theatre (Komödienhaus) was built, and Goethe was its manager (Intendant) from 1791 until 1817 during which time a number of Schiller's plays (*The Robbers*, *Wallenstein* and *William Tell*) as well as his own (*Egmont* and *Torquato Tasso*) were premièred here. This theatre burned down in 1825 but it was rebuilt under the direction of Steiner in only five months. The new theatre saw the first performances of Goethe's *Faust* in 1829 and of Wagner's *Lohengrin* (under Liszt) in 1850.

This second building was pulled down in 1907 to be replaced by a bigger and more modern theatre. Only the façade of this survived the bombing of World War II. The fourth structure, the one that still stands today, was opened on August 28 1948 with a production of *Faust*, and was itself completely renovated in 1975 as part of the celebrations of 1000 years of Weimar's existence.

It was in this theatre too that the German National Assembly met in 1919 and the constitution of the Weimar Republic was adopted.

Goethe-Schiller-Denkmal
The Goethe-Schiller Memorial in front of the theatre is the work of the sculptor Ernst Rietschel (1857). It depicts a rather austere figure of Goethe clasping the hand of Schiller in friendship.

Wittumspalais
On the east side of the square stands the Wittumspalais (1767), the palace of Duchess Anna Amalia who resided here from 1774 until her death in 1807. It now serves as a museum containing furniture and other objects from the Weimar classical period and paintings by Graff, Tischbein, Jagemann and others. Especially impressive is the small Festsaal, the room in which Goethe delivered his famous funeral oration in celebration of the life and work of Wieland. The palace also houses the Wieland museum. It is open April — October from Tuesdays — Sundays 9.00am — noon and 1.00pm — 5.00pm.

Schillerhaus
South of the Wittumspalais is the house in the Schillerstraße where Schiller lived from 1802 until his death in 1805. It was here that he wrote three of his last works, *William Tell*, *The Bride of Messina* and *Demetrius*.

Before acquiring the house on his arrival in Weimar from Jena in 1799 he lived in rented accommodation in the nearby Windischenstraße. During the time Schiller lived here the kitchen and domestic rooms were located on the ground floor, the living rooms were on the first floor, and the attic contained Schiller's work room. The house was acquired by the town as a museum as long ago as 1847, so much remains in its original state. Extensive restoration was undertaken in 1986-1987.

On November 10 1984 (the 225th anniversary of Schiller's birth) work began on the construction of a Schiller museum behind the house. The museum was opened on November 13 1988 and exhibits objects and documents relating to Schiller's life.

Gänsemännchenbrunnen
The Goose Man's Fountain in the Schillerstraße is a copy of an original in Nuremburg.

Other places of interest in Weimar
The Park
A long park runs behind the Residenzschloß on both sides of the river Ilm. It is called variously the Park on the Ilm (Park an der Ilm) or the Goethepark (because Goethe supervised its laying out over a 10 year period in the late 18th Century). It is an informal park in the English tradition rather than the tightly structured manner of many European 18th Century parks and gardens.

Goethe had owned a small garden house (Goethe's Gartenhaus) by the Ilm since 1776. It is a small, simple house, built in 1700, and used by Goethe for six years. It was in this house that he worked on his novel *Wilhelm Meister*, his nature poems and his plays, *Iphigenia* and *Torquato Tasso*; it was also the scene of many meetings between Goethe and Christiane Vulpius and Frau von Stein. Some of the rooms still preserve the original furniture and other items actually used by Goethe. The house is open from April to October on Wednesdays — Mondays from 9.00am — noon and 1.00pm — 5.00pm.

Opposite the garden house the Ilm is crossed by a picturesque bridge, the nature bridge (Naturbrücke). It is said that at this point on the Ilm the body was discovered of Christiane von Laßberg, a lady in waiting who, disappointed in love, took her own life in January 1778. She was still clutching a copy of Goethe's epistolary novella of unrequited love and suicide, *Die Leiden des jungen Werthers* (The Sufferings of the Young Werther). Goethe was apparently so affected by the episode that he had a rocky grotto, known as the Eye of the Needle (Nadelohr), built in the girl's memory. It is a typical example of the 18th Century fascination, indeed obsession, with nature. The park is full of similar follies: a thatched wooden hut with moss-covered walls built as a hermitage (Einsiedelei) and artificial ruins.

Close to the Naturbrücke stands the Shakespeare memorial (Shakespearedenkmal); the work of Theodor Lessing, it was erected here in 1904 and is said to be the first memorial to Shakespeare in continental Europe.

In the middle of the park, half way between the Ilm and the Belvederer Allee, is the Soviet Cemetery, the burial place of Soviet soldiers killed in World War II.

Duke Carl August used to use the hermitage in the park as a summer house. He had it extended and roofed in shingle, and it became known as the small bark house (Borkenhäuschen). He abandonned it in due course in favour of a mock classical

Roman House (Römisches Haus) built for him between 1791-
1797 to a design by Goethe.

Schloß Belvedere

The Belvedere, to the south and some way from the town
centre, was built in 1739 and used as a retreat and hunting lodge
and as a summer residence by the dukes of Weimar. The rooms
are decorated in rococo style. The baroque garden laid out
between 1756-1758, again under Goethe's direction, contains a
number of smaller buildings including the Orangery (with a
collection of historic coaches and wagons). It is open
Wednesdays — Sundays 10.00am — 1.00pm and 2.00pm —
6.00pm.

Alter Friedhof

The Old Cemetery (Alter Friedhof) was opened in 1818. Two
buildings dominate the scene. The first is the tiny Russian
Chapel (Russische Kapelle) built in 1862 as a mausoleum for the
Grand Duchess Maria Pavlovna. The other is the Goethe-
Schiller Tomb (Goethe-Schiller-Gruft). Reached by walking
along a broad avenue of linden trees, the mausoleum was built
in 1825-1826 as the last resting place for members of the ducal
family, and many members of the family were buried here
including Carl August. Schiller was buried here in 1827 and
Goethe in 1832.

Many other important figures in the history of Weimar were
buried here. Close to the entrance is the grave of Johann Peter
Eckermann (1792-1854), Goethe's friend and secretary and the
author of Gespräche mit Goethe (Conversations with Goethe).
Many members of the Goethe family also have their graves here:
Ottilie von Goethe (1796-1872), Goethe's daughter-in-law Alma
(1827-1844), and his grandchildren Walter (1818-1885) and
Wolfgang (1820-1883). As both Goethe's grandchildren died
childless the line died out with them. Charlotte von Stein, who
died at the age of 85, also lies here.

Next to the vault of the Falk family is the grave of one of
Weimar's best known mayors (he held office from 1820-1830),
Carl Leberecht Schwabe.

Franz-Liszt-Haus

East of the cemetery and on the edge of the park stands Liszt's
house. The composer lived here from 1869-1886. It is now a
museum (open April to October from Tuesdays to Sundays
between 9.00am — 1.00pm and 2.00pm — 5.00pm) and displays

the pianos Liszt played and pictures, letters and manuscripts relating to his life.

Museum für Ur- und Frühgeschichte Thüringens

The Museum of Pre- and Early History of Thuringia is located in the Poecksche Haus in Amalienstraße. Open Tuesdays to Fridays from 10.00am — 1.00pm and 2.00pm — 5.00pm it has 24 rooms devoted to the early history of the area.

Naturkundemuseum

The natural history museum (Am Herderplatz 14) is housed in a former school, the Gymnasium Wilhelminum Ernestinum (1712-1715).

Schloß Tiefurt

The Tiefurt Palace is some way out of the centre of Weimar at the end of the Tiefurter Allee which leads to it through the wooded Webicht park. It dates back to the end of the 16th Century and acted as the summer residence of Anna Amalia from 1781-1806. Its rooms are decorated variously in rococo, classical and Biedermeier style. It is open from April to October on Tuesdays to Sundays from 9.00am — 1.00pm and 2.00pm — 5.00pm. Behind the palace an attractive park runs along the banks of the Ilm.

Goethe- und Schiller-Archiv

The Goethe and Schiller Archives opposite the western end of the Tiefurter Allee at the junction of Jenaer Straße constitute one of the most important literary collections in the German-speaking world. The archives contain the literary estates of Wieland, Herder, Hebbel and Mörike and 600,000 original documents from the 18th-20th Centuries.

Where to stay

Weimar has two Interhotels: Belvedere, Belvederer Allee; Elephant, Am Markt 19. Other hotels include Einheit, Brennerstraße 42; International, Leninstraße 17; Russischer Hof, Goetheplatz 2.

Where to eat

Restaurants include Weimarhalle, Schwanseestraße; Gastmahl des Meeres (fish), Herderplatz; Ratskeller (in town hall), Markt; Schwanseebad, Herbststraße 2; Schwarzer Bär, Markt; Weißer

Schwan, Frauentorstraße 23; Theaterkasino, Theaterplatz; Alt Weimar, Steubenstraße; Waldschlößchen, Jenaer Straße 56; Zum Siechenbräu, Ferdinand-Freiligrath-Straße 17; Birkenhaus, Leibnizallee; Hainfels, Belvederer Allee; Schloßgaststätte Belvedere, Belvederer Allee.

Special events
Weimar has a number of events and festivals each year associated with its classical traditions. These include a festival at Goethe's house, held on his birthday, August 28. Musical events include the Thuringia Bach Festival (March — April) and an international musical festival in July.

Information
Weimar-Information, Marktstraße 4

Excursions from Weimar
Ettersberg/Buchenwald
The Ettersberg is about 8km outside Weimar. It used to be a favourite excursion for the Weimar nobility but is now remembered as the site of the Buchenwald concentration camp. It was established by the National Socialists in 1937 and held over 240,000 prisoners; more than 56,000 prisoners met their death here, including Ernst Thälmann, the leader of the German communist party.

The site of the camp has been preserved as a national memorial. A bell tower rises up above the mass graves; before it stands a monument by the sculptor Fritz Cremer depicting a group of prisoners fighting for freedom from oppression and racial prejudice. The former changing rooms have been turned into a museum and exhibition dedicated to Ernst Thälmann's life and work.

The museum is open Tuesdays to Sundays 8.45am — 4.30pm. Buchenwald can be reached by bus from a stop near the railway station in Weimar (departures every hour).

Schloß Kochberg
Although Schloß Kochberg is over 30km from Weimar it is convenient to mention it here because it was the family seat of the von Steins, acquired by Baron von Stein in 1733. Goethe was a frequent guest between 1775 and 1786. He visited Kochberg for the last time in 1788 when his friendship with Charlotte

ended, only to resume again in old age. The palace underwent substantial renovation between 1968 and 1975 to preserve the appearance and decoration of Goethe's times here. The rooms on the ground floor are devoted to the history of the palace and castle (first mentioned in 1380); the first floor contains the restored apartments, contemporary documents and Charlotte von Stein's writing table.

The Goethe-Schiller tomb and Russian chapel, Weimar

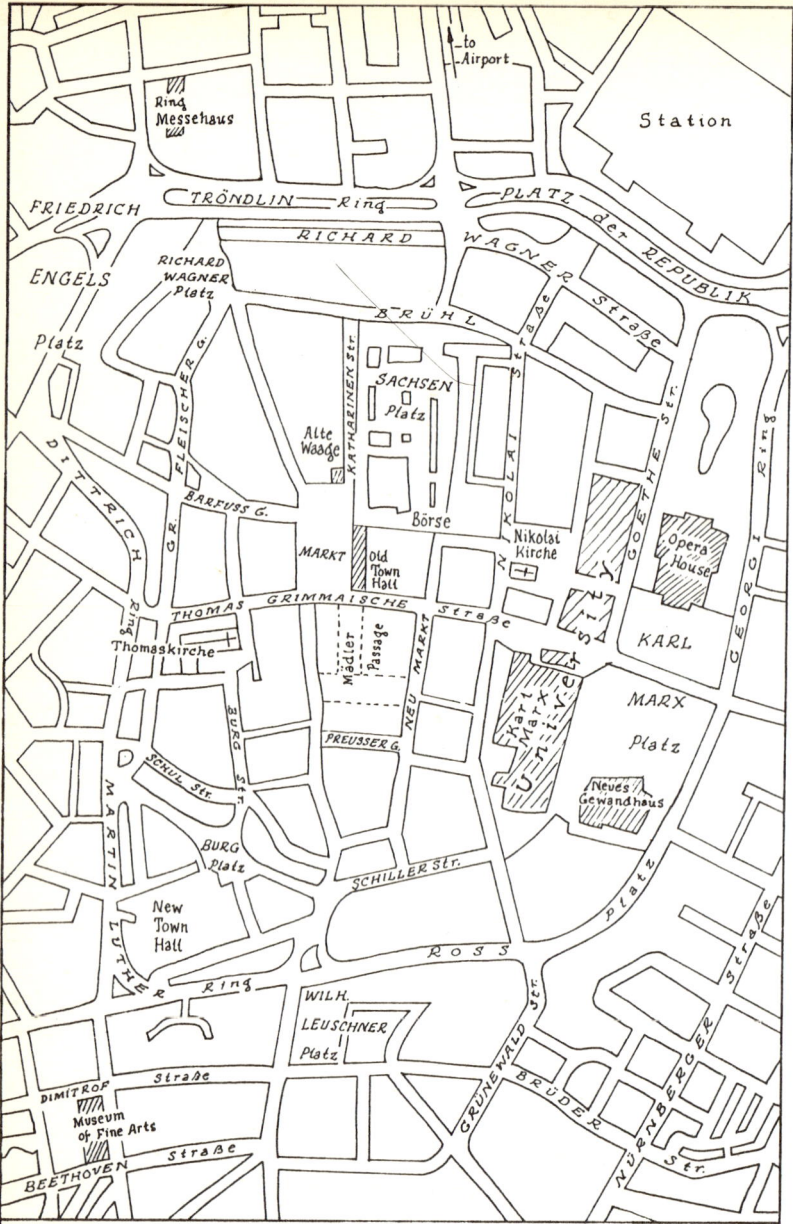

LEIPZIG

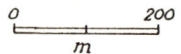

0   200
m

Leipzig

Leipzig (population 560,000), is the second largest city in East Germany, and a centre of interest for business visitors and for tourists. Every year in spring and autumn thousands of people converge on the city for its international fairs, but increasingly Leipzig is also drawing visitors interested in music, books and its historical monuments and sites.

Background

A slavonic settlement known as Lipzi (meaning place of the lime trees) is first mentioned in the 7th Century but the town did not begin to develop significantly until it was granted municipal status by Margrave Otto of Meissen in 1165. Its position at the intersection of the important medieval trade routes, the King's Highway and the Imperial Highway, meant that it expanded rapidly, and as early as 1497 was granted the right to hold an imperial fair by the Emperor Maximilian. In the course of the next 300 years Leipzig grew in stature as a trading centre and became known in the 18th Century as the 'market-place of Europe'. The original imperial fair developed into a sample fair for industrial and consumer goods, and became by the 20th Century, one of the biggest all-round trade fairs (Messen) in the world. The distinctive MM sign (Mustermesse) can be seen all over the city on buildings associated with the trade fair.

Leipzig's traditions as a musical city have developed in parallel with its economic expansion. It has long been known for the St Thomas Choir and the Gewandhaus Orchestra, as well as for its connections with composers including Bach, Mendelssohn and Wagner, and conductors such as Furtwängler and more recently Kurt Masur.

Leipzig is also important as the centre of the book trade in East Germany. From the middle of the 18th Century until 1945 the city dominated publishing in the whole of the German-speaking world, and at the beginning of this century there were as many as 900 publishing houses and booksellers established here. At present some 35 publishers are based in Leipzig, many of them with long traditions, as well as a number of large libraries, including the Deutsche Bücherei (German Library), the Deutsche Zentralbücherei für Blinde (the National Library for the Blind), and a training college for printing and publishing. The internationally-known Peters Verlag (Peters Publishing House) combines the musical and printing traditions of Leipzig as one of the world's largest music publishers.

Historically Leipzig has frequently been at the forefront of movements for change. In 1813, at the Battle of the Nations, one of the bloodiest battles in European history, which took place just outside Leipzig, Napoleon's defeat at the hands of the allied armies meant an end to French plans for foreign domination. Towards the end of the 19th Century the town became a centre for the German working class movement, as August Bebel and Wilhelm Liebknecht both spent several years working here. A little later Lenin stayed in Leipzig on several occasions, and in 1900 the first issue of the Russian Marxist newspaper *Iskra* was printed secretly here. More recently, the Monday evening marches in Leipzig in autumn 1989 were the first major signs of unrest in the GDR prior to the overthrow of the Honecker government.

The market and the old town

The massive (10,000m²) market place was badly destroyed during World War II but has been partially restored in its original style. On the east side stands the Altes Rathaus (Old Town Hall), originally built by the Leipzig mayor Hieronymus Lotter in the Renaissance style, but practically rebuilt in 1907 and again in 1950. The latest restoration was completed at the beginning of 1990 to mark 825 years of the city's existence. The tower in the centre of the long colonnaded building includes a covered balcony from which the town pipers, dressed in traditional costumes, still give short performances at the weekend. The town pipers (Stadtpfeifer) have been an institution since 1479 when they were first invited to play to entertain the people of the town, and stayed thanks to the ample supply of beer. The town hall now houses the Museum of Local History (Museum für Geschichte der Stadt Leipzig), which in addition to civic treasures and exhibits relating to the working class movement, also contains a Mendelssohn room; the composer worked from 1835 until his death in 1847 as the conductor of the Leipzig Gewandhaus orchestra.

On the north side of the market is the Alte Waage (Old Weigh House), built in 1555 again by Lotter, where imported goods were weighed and duties levied. Nearby, at the corner of Hainstraße, stands Barthels Hof, 1523, the only remaining trading area dating from the 16th Century Leipzig fairs. A little further north, at Hainstraße 9, the Adler Apotheke (Eagle Dispensary) has a plaque commemorating the time Theodor Fontane spent working here between 1841-1842.

At Kleine Fleischergasse 4 the Kaffeebaum (Coffee Tree), one of Europe's oldest cafés, is to be found. During the 18th and 19th Centuries it was a favourite haunt of writers and musicians, including Goethe, Lessing, Liszt, Wagner and Schumann. It is here that Schumann developed the idea of the Davidsbund (League of David), an imaginary society dedicated to criticism of philistinism, and which found musical expression in his *Davidsbündlertänze*, a series of short piano pieces composed in 1837. Today it has a Gaststätte and Bierstube.

On the south side of the market square a narrow passage, the Mädler-Passage, leads off the Grimmaische Straße, and it is here that the entrance to Auerbach's Keller (Auerbach's cellar), marked by two large statues of Faust and Mephistopheles, is located. The wine cellar was built between 1530 and 1538 by Heinrich Stromer von Auerbach but became famous only much later when Goethe set a scene of *Faust* here. Mephistopheles brings Faust here to show him the pleasures of convivial company and sings the well-known *Song of the Flea*. One of the revellers in the cellar, Frosch, expresses his love of Leipzig: 'Mein Leipzig lob ich mir! Es ist ein klein Paris und bildet seine Leute,' (My Leipzig, I praise you. You are a second Paris and nurture your people). The cellar has a Goethe room, with many reminders of the author's life, paintings depicting scenes from *Faust*, and in the inner room a wooden statue of Dr Faust. The cellar is still a popular eating and drinking place and tends to be extremely crowded both at lunchtimes and in the evening.

The Mädler-Passage leads into a number of shopping malls characteristic of old Leipzig. A wide variety of shops and cafés have sprung up on the sites of the old trading houses, and in the central passage is a glockenspiel made from Meissen porcelain.

The Naschmarkt (Food Market), off Grimmaische Straße, houses the Alte Börse (Old Exchange), an early baroque building (1678-1687) by J.G. Starcke which has been elegantly restored since being burnt down in 1943. In front of it is a statue of Goethe as a student in Leipzig (Seffner 1903). At the side of the

Naschmarkt, the attractive gabled windows and the ornate biblical texts are part of the rear side of the Rathaus.

Around this whole central area are scattered 17 Messehäuser (trade exhibit houses) dating back to the beginning of this century and representing mostly more traditional trades and crafts than the pavilions at the Fair site in the south of Leipzig. They include the Brühlzentrum on the east side of the Sachsenplatz, the centre for fur; the Hansahaus on Nikolaistraße, the centre for jewellery; the Untergrund-Messehaus (underground trade exhibit house) below the market, the centre for food, and, along the Mädler-Passage, the centre for glass and ceramic products.

Thomaskirche

For devotees of Johann Sebastian Bach, the first visit in Leipzig should be to the Thomaskirche (Church of St Thomas), where Bach worked as organist and choirmaster of the Thomas school between 1723-1750. It was here that Bach wrote much of his sacred music, including the *St Matthew Passion* which was first performed here in 1729.

A statue of Bach by Seffner has been erected outside the Thomaskirche (1908) and in 1950 Bach's tomb was also moved to the interior of the church. Organ recitals are a regular feature of church life and the St Thomas choir also gives regular performances of motets and cantatas at 6pm on Fridays, as well as at Sunday, Easter and Christmas services.

The church itself, though of more note for its musical traditions than its architectural prowess, has some distinctive features. Built on the site of a 13th Century Augustinian church, the present building dates from the 14th and 15th Centuries and contains a number of items worth seeing, including the font (1614) and the altar cross (1720).

Opposite the church, at the Bosehaus, where Bach lived for a time (Thomaskirchhof 16), it is possible to visit the Bach archives and a display of various Bach memorabilia. Opening times are Tuesdays to Sundays 9.00am — 4.30pm.

Sachsenplatz

The Sachsenplatz (Saxony Square) lies north of the market place, and is notable for a number of baroque houses on the west side. Amongst these the so-called Romanus-Haus stands out as a particularly attractive example. Originally built between 1701 and 1704 by the architect G. Fuchss for the mayor of Leipzig, Dr Romanus, the house was reconstructed in the mid-1960s and is now the headquarters of the Leipzig artists' and journalists' associations. Nearby, a modern feature of the square is a totem-pole-like structure depicting incidents from the history of Leipzig.

Nikolaikirche

Between the Sachsenplatz and the Karl-Marx-Platz on Nikolaistraße is the Nikolaikirche (Church of St Nicholas), architecturally perhaps Leipzig's most interesting church, and the church from which the demonstrating crowds left for Monday evening rallies in the autumn of 1989. The white walls and pews of the church and the green plant designs at the top of the pillars give an unusually unified and fresh impression. Although founded in 1165, the Gothic choir dates from the 14th Century and the nave from the 16th Century. At the end of the 18th Century the interior was fully reconstructed in classical style and a number of trompe-l'oeil paintings added by the artist A.F. Oeser. The alabaster reliefs depicting scenes from the passion, also in the choir, are by Felix Pfeifer and date from 1905. The Luther pulpit dating from 1521 is impressive for its detailed reliefs, although it is by no means sure that Luther ever preached from it. The church is open for visitors Mondays to Thursdays 10.00am — 6.00pm, Fridays noon — 6.00pm and Saturdays 10.00am — 4.00pm.

Karl-Marx-Platz

The Karl-Marx-Platz (Karl Marx Square), in contrast to the Market Square and the Sachsenplatz to its north, is entirely modern. It is dominated by the 34-storey Karl Marx University, often referred to as the jagged tooth (steiler Zahn), erected in 1967-1968 and since 1973 the home of around 1,500 academics and researchers. The Panorama-Café, 110m above ground level, is a good place for a snack and a view of the centre of Leipzig, and can be reached by express lift from the base of the tower, after buying a ticket near the entrance on the ground floor. On the main university building next door, a huge bronze relief entitled *Leninismus-Marxismus unserer Epoche* (Leninism and Marxism in our Time) contrasts sharply with the 1836 entrance to the university designed by Schinkel standing at the back of the main building.

Next to the university stands the Neues Gewandhaus (New Drapers' Hall), built in 1981 by R. Skoda, and home of the world famous Leipzig Gewandhaus orchestra. The building includes two concert halls, the largest organ in East Germany, built by Schuke and with 6,638 pipes, a massive painting on the foyer ceiling and an impressive range of pictures and sculptures by contemporary artists. In front of the opera house stands the Mendebrunnen, a fountain constructed around a tall obelisk and originally erected in 1886.

The opera house occupies the north side of the Karl-Marx-Platz. This was the first new theatre to be built in the GDR, the opening performance taking place in 1960. Looking north from the opera it is impossible to miss the Leipzig Hauptbahnhof (main railway station), built between 1901 and 1915, and which claims to be the largest rail terminus in central Europe. Every day 265 long-distance trains leave from one of its 31 platforms. Railway enthusiasts may also be interested in the Bayerische Bahnhof (Bavarian Station) at the Bayerische Platz (Bavarian Square) south of the old town, which was built in the early 1840s and is the oldest railway station still functioning in Europe.

Just east of the Karl-Marx-Platz on the Johannisplatz the Grassi Museum houses museums of ethnology, crafts and musical instruments. It is open 9.30am — 6.00pm Tuesdays to Fridays, 10.00am — 4.00pm on Saturdays and 9.00am — 1.00pm on Sundays, and visitors may be lucky enough to hear a concert performed on historic instruments.

The south-west

The area south of the Thomaskirche contains several places of interest, including the Neues Rathaus (New Town Hall), the Georgi-Dimitroff-Museum and the Museum der Bildenden Künste (Museum of Fine Arts). All are within walking distance of the city centre.

The Neues Rathaus is a large building, constructed between 1899-1905 by H. Licht on the foundations of the 13th Century Pleißenburg, a castle pulled down in 1897-1898. The base of the old tower has been incorporated in the central tower of the new building. The clock, to the right of the façade, with the Latin inscription 'Mors certa hora incerta' (Death is certain, the hour is uncertain), is a well-known part of Leipzig life. The inscription is now often humourously translated as 'Certain of death, the clock is always wrong'! On the next block to the east, a plaque commemorates the dispute between Martin Luther and opponents including Dr Eck and Andreas Bodenstein which took place in the Pleißenburg in 1519, and in which Luther propounded his belief that the Bible, not the pope, was the only true revelation of God's will.

Both the Georgi-Dimitroff-Museum and the Museum der Bildenden Künste are housed in the former Imperial Court building (Reichsgericht — built 1888-1895). The former celebrates the life of the Bulgarian workers' leader, Georgi Dimitroff, who successfully defended himself against Goering in the Reichstag Fire Trial in 1933 and subsequently became prime minister of Bulgaria. Opening times are Tuesdays to Fridays 9.00am — 5.00pm and Saturdays and Sundays 9.00am — 2.00pm. On the ground floor the Museum der Bildenden Künste offers one of East Germany's most significant art collections. It is strong particularly in early German and Dutch painting, although it also covers German painting of later periods, Italian Renaissance works and 19th and 20th Century sculpture. Lucas Cranach the Elder (including *Adoration of the Magi*), Pieter de Hooch (*The Music Party*), Rembrandt, and modern German painters including Max Liebermann (*Self-Portrait*), Menzel, Klinger and Feuerbach, are all well represented. The museum is open Tuesdays to Sundays, excluding Wednesdays, 9.00am — 5.00pm, and Wednesdays 1.00pm — 9.30pm. The museum also has a pleasant café.

Outside the centre: north

A 10 minute ride on the no. 20 tram north from the main station will take you to the Zoologischer Garten (zoo), well-known for its expertise in breeding large cats and its collection of lions, Siberian tigers and black panthers. A little further north, and accessible by bus from the city centre, is the Gohliser Schlößchen (Gohlis Château) at Menckestraße 23. This charming rococo palace was built in 1756 by Seltendorff for the Leipzig councillor C. Richter, and has many interesting features including a wrought-iron rococo tower and a painting on the first floor ceiling by A.F. Oeser, entitled *Lebensweg der Psyche* (Psyche's Path through Life — 1779). A little further along the same street (Menckestraße 42) is the Schillerhäuschen (Schiller's House), where the author lived in 1785 while working on the play *Don Carlos* and a first version of his poem *An die Freude* (Ode to Joy), later set to music by Beethoven in his 9th Symphony.

Outside the centre: south

A trip to the south of the city could take in the Deutsche Bücherei (German Library), the Russische Gedächtniskirche (Russian Memorial Church), the Völkerschlachtdenkmal (Battle of the Nations Monument), the Iskra Denkmal (Iskra Monument) and the site of the Leipzig Fair (Leipziger Messe).

The Deutsche Bücherei (open Mondays to Saturdays 9.00am — 4.00pm) on Deutscher Platz is the largest library in the German-speaking world and since its completion in 1915 has collected all books in German published inside and outside the country — to date around 8.2 million volumes. Not far away on Semmelweißstraße is the Russische Gedächtniskirche, also called the Church of St Alexi, built by W.A. Pokrowski in 1912-1913 in the style of 16th Century Novogorod churches to commemorate the 22,000 Russians who gave their lives in the Battle of the Nations outside Leipzig 100 years earlier. The battle, in which 140,000-150,000 French troops under Napoleon fought for four days in October 1813 against an allied army of 300,000 Prussians, Russians, Austrians and Swedes and were finally defeated against a background of total estimated losses of 100,000 men, is further commemorated by a monument in the park to the south of the Fair site (the Völkerschlachtdenkmal). Erected between 1898 and 1913 by B. Schmitz and C. Thieme, the monument dominates the surrounding area. A viewing platform, 91m above the ground, provides a good vantage point, on a clear day, for coming to grips with the city and surrounding area. Choral concerts are given here most Sundays at 10.30am.

The Fair site, opened in 1920, is easily reached from the city centre by trams 15, 21 and 25. A large number of pavilions and exhibition halls cover all aspects of industrial and technological progress from metallurgy to food processing and packaging. Fairs are held here every spring and autumn.

Even further to the southeast, and accessible by bus from the town centre, is the Iskra Denkmal, Russenstraße 48. At a small printing press on this site the first five issues of the Bolshevik newspaper *Iskra* (The Spark) were produced between December 1900 and May 1901. Lenin himself came to Leipzig in order to edit the first issue. Opening times are Tuesdays to Saturdays 9.00am — 5.00pm and Sundays 9.00am to 1.00pm.

Where to stay

Because of its importance as a trade centre, Leipzig has a large choice of top quality hotels, including one 5-star Interhotel, Hotel Merkur on Gerberstraße. 4-star Interhotels are Hotel Astoria , Platz der Republik; Hotel am Ring, Karl-Marx-Platz; and Hotel Stadt Leipzig, Richard-Wagner-Straße. Both the Hotel International, Tröndlinring, and the Hotel zum Löwen, Rudolf-Breitscheid-Straße, are 3-star Interhotels. Other hotels include

The cathedral and church of St Severus, Erfurt

The Wartburg, Eisenach

The pulpits, Freiberg cathedral

Moritzburg near Dresden

Saxon Switzerland

the Parkhotel, Richard-Wagner-Straße 7, and Vier Jahreszeiten, Rudolf-Breitscheid-Straße 23.

Where to eat

Leipzig offers the opportunity to eat in historic as well as modern surroundings. Both Auerbachs Keller, Grimmaische Straße 2-4, and the Kaffeebaum, Kleine Fleischergasse 4 (see p.117) serve meals in pleasant traditional surroundings, but reservations are essential. Other restaurants serving traditional German food include the Ratskeller (cellar of the Neues Rathaus) on Burgplatz; the Burgkeller, Naschmarkt 1/3; Thüringer Hof, Burgstraße 17-19; Stadtpfeifer next to the Gewandhaus; Stadt Kiew, on Petersstraße opposite St Thomas's Church; Plovdiv wine restaurant and the Café Fregehaus both on Katharinestraße; Bierstube Zills Tunnel and wine restaurant both at Barfußgässchen 9; Restaurant Paulaner on Klostergasse. A pleasant place for a drink is the Kümmel Apotheke on Grimmaischer Straße. Possibilities for eating other types of food are Gastmahl des Meeres, Dr.-Kurt-Fischer-Straße 1, which concentrates on fish dishes, a Vietnamese restaurant in the Hotel Bürgerhof, Große Fleischergasse 4, a Cuban restaurant, Varadero, at Barfußgässchen 8, and an expensive Japanese restaurant, Sakura, in the Hotel Merkur, Gerberstraße 15.

Special events

Every four years an International Bach Competition, drawing young musicians from all over the world, takes place in Leipzig; the next will be in summer 1992. In tandem with this runs the International Bach Festival, a series of concerts given by musicians performing well in the Competition, and held the following September; the next Festival is therefore planned for September 1993.

Every year in October the Gewandhaus Festival takes place at the New Gewandhaus. Concerts draw on the classical as well as contemporary musical repertoire. In November an international documentary and short films festival is held, and in May there is a cabaret festival.

Information

Further information can be obtained from Leipzig-Information, Sachsenplatz 1. Details of trade fairs and other matters connected with the Leipzig Fairs can be obtained from the Messeamt (Fair Office), Markt 11-15.

Excursions from Leipzig
Colditz
The village of Colditz lies about 22km southeast of Leipzig, and its infamous castle needs little introduction to British visitors. It is here, in the castle described by Reichsmarschall Hermann Goering as escape-proof, that British, French, Dutch, Polish and Belgian officers who were persistent escapers were imprisoned from 1939 until the castle's liberation by the US First Army on April 15 1945. Although in theory the high granite walls, the moat and the castle's position towering above a small village, coupled with extra tight security, made escape almost impossible, in practice the vastness of the castle, and the array of expert skills from all over Europe, meant that success was not ruled out. In total, 300 prisoners were caught while trying to escape; 130 prisoners succeeded in getting away from the castle but were subsequently recaptured within German territory, and 30 managed to regain their homelands.

Among those who escaped were 14 French prisoners, and nine British prisoners, including Airey Neave, who later became a Conservative MP and was killed in 1979 by an IRA bomb in the House of Commons car park. His escape, like many others, reads like a work of fiction: he and a Dutch colleague, disguised as German officers, escaped one snowy January night in 1942, by walking boldly through the security gate and through the German officers' married quarters before finally scrambling over the 12 foot stone wall, covered in ice, that separated the castle garden from the outside world. Neave arrived in England in May, after travelling through France and Spain with the help of resistance workers and boarding a troop ship from Gibraltar to the Clyde.

Although there has been a castle at Colditz since 1014, the present building dates from 1578-1591. After being captured several times by the Swedes, it became an official residence of the dukes of Saxony, and after 1800 became first a prison and then an asylum for the insane. After the German army swept through Poland in October 1939, it became a prisoner-of-war camp for Polish officers, and later, as a Sonderlager (a maximum security camp), housed many Allied officers.

The castle is now used as a hospital, but a museum has been constructed in the basement. Known as the Museum of Escapes, it contains exhibits dating from World War II, including a hand-made sewing machine used to manufacture German civilian and military outfits to be worn by escapers. The exhibits are imaginatively displayed around the entrance to a 42 yard escape tunnel built by prisoners in eight months but discovered by the German authorities before it was completed. The castle also has a room with a mural by a nephew of Winston Churchill. As the castle is not yet regularly open to the public, it is advisable to contact the East German tourist office before planning a visit. A rather different attraction is the local beer, brewed in Colditz village, generally considered among the best in East Germany.

The Stallhof in Dresden; In the background, the Hofkirche

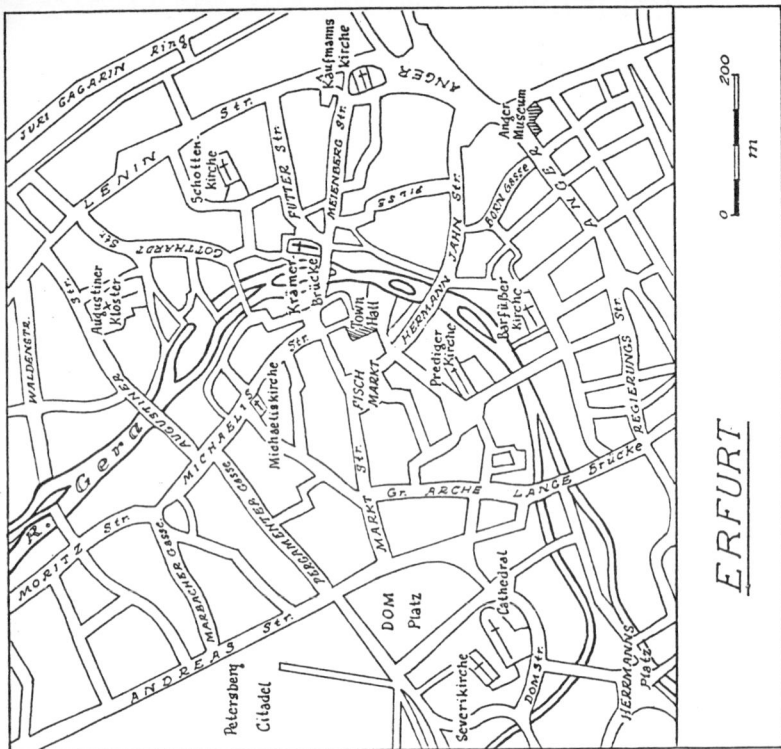

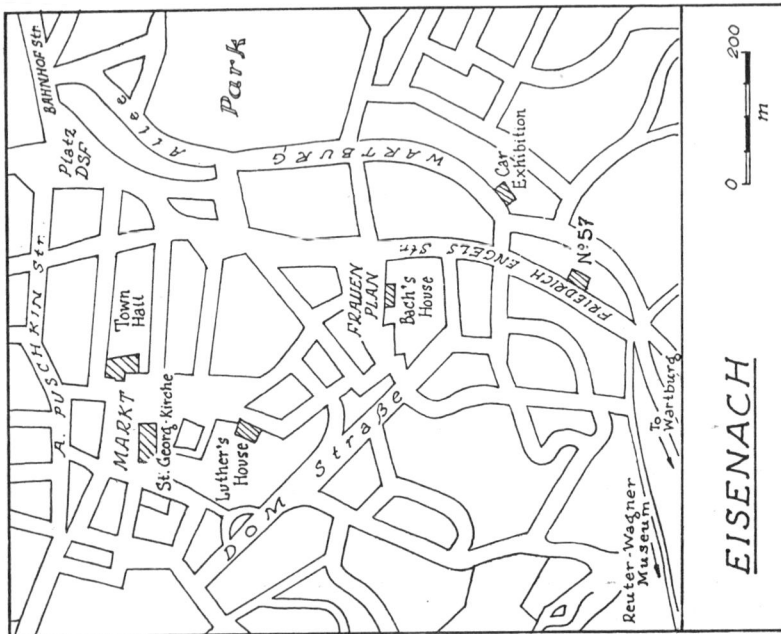

The South-West

ERFURT

Erfurt is one of the oldest towns in East Germany. In itself it offers a wide range of attractions from historical monuments, including a cathedral and a large number of colourful patrician mansions from the Gothic, Renaissance and baroque periods, to an international horticultural exhibition; it is also a convenient base for exploring the surrounding area of Thuringia.

Background

Erfurt first appears in records in 742 when the English monk Boniface (later canonised), sent by the Pope to convert the Germanic tribes, founded a bishopric here at a ford ('Furt') over the river Gera. During the middle ages the town became an increasingly important centre for trade thanks to its position on the King's Highway (Königstraße), the route which led from the Rhine to Russia. With the opening in 1392 of a university, after Prague the second largest in central Europe, it also became a major centre of learning; among its students was Martin Luther, who studied here between 1501 and 1505. Although the university was closed in 1816, many institutes and colleges have been set up, including a horticultural college, and several thousand students still study here.

By the 17th Century Erfurt's traditional trading commodity, woad, had been supplanted by cheaper supplies of indigo while at the same time Leipzig had become a more powerful trading centre. As a result a weakened Erfurt fell in 1664 to the Electorate of Mainz, and remained under control from Mainz until becoming Prussian in 1802. During this period the town expanded as an agricultural and horticultural centre, laying the foundations for what remains one of its major economic activities today.

Erfurt has also been at the centre of the stage for two major political events: the Erfurt Congress in 1808, when Napoleon met Tsar Alexander I behind closed doors and tried, without success, to win him over to his side; and the Erfurt Party Congress in 1891 at which the German Social Democratic Party issued its Erfurt Programme, a blue-print for socialist policy, heavily influenced by Engels, which was used for a number of years as a model for socialists in much of Europe.

During the 20th Century metal working and a range of light industries have been established in and around the town, and, most recently, Erfurt has become an important producer of microelectronics. As the capital of the Thuringian region it is also a major cultural and administrative centre.

The Cathedral and the Church of St Severus

Visitors to Erfurt can hardly fail to be impressed by the twin sights of the cathedral (Dom) and the Church of St Severus (Severikirche) standing side by side at the top of a flight of 70 steps on a hill looking down over the old town. The Cathedral, with its tall Gothic choir leading the eye back to three towers which in turn mirror the three spires of the neighbouring church, presents with St Severus an ensemble which is unique in central Europe.

The older of the buildings is the cathedral, which was begun in around 1154 and was erected on a huge substructure, the 'Cavaten'. The choir, in pure Gothic style, was built between 1347 and 1370, while the nave and aisles are later additions (1456-1472). The fine stained glass windows in the choir date from the 15th Century. Also of note in the interior are the choir stalls (14th Century), a bronze candelabrum with the figure known as 'Wolfram' (1160), on the south wall a picture of St Christopher (1499) and, in the middle tower the largest bell in East Germany and one of the largest in the world, the 'Gloriosa'.

St Severus (built 1278-1400) is widely acknowledged as one of the leading examples of German 14th Century architecture. Its five aisles and three spires are of a quality and size rarely encountered. A figure of Severus as a bishop can be seen above the south door (1365), while the panels of a sarcophagus in the interior of the church depict scenes from the bishop's life. A font with an elaborate pierced canopy (1467) should also not be missed.

The large Cathedral Square (Domplatz) in front of the churches is frequently used as a site for fairs and markets. It also has some of the most attractive Renaissance houses in

Erfurt, including the Tall Lily (Zur Hohen Lilie) built in 1538, for many years Erfurt's most prestigious inn and now functioning as a restaurant.

The old town
The old town, which extends east from the Cathedral, has been extensively restored and is a pleasant area for a two or three hour walk. A route beginning in the Fish Market (Fischmarkt), across the Krämer Bridge (Krämerbrücke), north to the Augustinian monastery (Augustinerkloster) and back to the Anger would include many of the most picturesque and historically interesting sights.

The Fish Market was the centre of trading activities during the middle ages, although most of the buildings now remaining date from the 16th and 19th Centuries. The house known as the Red Ox (Zum Roten Ochsen) was built by a woad dealer in 1562, but now houses the town's art gallery. Another Renaissance building on the north side of the square, the Wide Hearth (Zum Breiten Herd), dating from 1584, preserves the original spirit of the square as it is now the headquarters of the Erfurt Trades' Council. The Fish Market is, however, dominated by the neo-gothic town hall (Rathaus) (1879-1875). It is worth peeping inside the entrance hall to have a look at the paintings depicting scenes from Thuringian history, German fables, including Faust and Tannhäuser, and the life of Martin Luther.

Just to the north of the Fish Market is the Krämer Bridge (Krämer means shopkeeper) across the river Gera, the only bridge north of the Alps to be lined on both sides by timbered houses. A total of 32 houses (originally there were 62 tiny shops) now mostly sell antiques and works of art.

After studying at Erfurt University (on the site of what is now 39 Michaelis-Straße), Martin Luther spent six years (1505-1511 with a one year break 1508-1509) at the Augustinian Monastery (founded in 1277). The monastery and adjoining church were badly damaged in World War II but parts have been restored, including Luther's cell. The Augustinian church on the same site (1290-1350) is also notable for its connections with Luther, as well as for three 13th Century stained glass windows in the choir.

The Anger (meaning village green), now a pedestrianised shopping street running through the centre of the town, was first mentioned as early as 1196 and was in medieval times a major woad trading area. Several old buildings remain, and a glance above the shop and restaurant fronts will often reveal unexpected architectural features. Note particularly no. 18, a baroque building which in 1883 became the Anger museum and which contains a collection of medieval art; no. 28/29, known as Swan Keeper and Paradise (Schwantreiber und Paradies), with well preserved baroque façades; no.37/38 the Dacheröden's House, named after its owners the von Dachenrödens, and one of the finest Renaissance houses in Erfurt.

The old town is a continuing source of pleasure for anyone interested in architecture and in medieval and Renaissance life. Those wishing to explore further could visit some of the following addresses, although the list is by no means exhaustive: the Petersberg citadel, a preserved building and, with its eight bastions, the largest city fortification in East Germany; the 13th Century Merchant's Church (Kaufmannskirche) with a fine Renaissance altar and a statue of Martin Luther (1889) outside; the Scottish Church of St. James (Schottenkirche St. Jakob), originally built in 1136 but subsequently largely re-built, one of the few indications of the missionary activities of Scottish and Irish monks in this area in the 12th Century; the Bare Foot Church (Barfüßerkirche), a Gothic basilica with Erfurt's oldest stained glass windows (13th Century), now a museum of medieval art; Renaissance houses on the Market Street (Marktstraße), particularly no.38, and Lenin Street (Leninstraße), including no.178 the Green Canary (Zum grünen Sittich) and no.169 the Dried Cod (Zum Stockfisch).

The International Horticultural Exhibition

Signposted as 'iga' (Internationale Gartenbauaustellung), this permanent exhibition will be interesting to garden lovers whatever the season. As well as 16 exhibition halls, the site, which spreads over 100 hectares to the west of the centre, includes a museum, library and public observatory. It is a pleasant place for walking, as is the Steigerwald to the south of the city, a wooded area with 20km of rambling paths, and the Thuringian zoo in the north.

Where to stay

Erfurt has two Interhotels: the Hotel Kosmos on the Juri-Gagarin-Ring and the Erfurter Hof, just in front of the main railway station. When on March 19 1970 Willy Brandt, the West German chancellor, initiating a policy of closer relations with the GDR, came to Erfurt to meet Willi Stoph, the chairman of the GDR Council of Ministers, it was from the balcony of this

hotel that the two politicians addressed a large crowd of East
Germans, all ambiguously cheering for 'Willy/i'.

Where to eat

Both the Interhotels have restaurants, but they tend to be busy
and should be booked in advance. A more traditional ambiance
can be found at the Hohe Lilie, Domplatz 31, and the Gildehaus
on the Fish Market: again bookings should be made in advance.
It is generally possible to find seats at the Wilbret game
restaurant at Anger 8; the restaurant serves a good variety of
hare and other game dishes and you can help yourself to as
much salad and pickled vegetables as you like. Typical East
German cuisine in a new-town setting can be sampled at the
Stadt Vilnius restaurant, Straße der Völkerfreundschaft in the
north of the city; this is a no-frills eating and drinking place,
which is both clean (starched white table-cloths) and friendly.

Events

On most Sundays throughout the year, organ recitals are given
at the Angermuseum (Anger 18), and on Sundays at 2.00pm the
bells are rung from the Bartholomäusturm on the Anger. Annual
events include the Krämerbrücke festival in September/October,
the Thuringian Bach festival in March/April and auctions in
May/June.

Information

Information is available from the Information Office at 27
Bahnhofstraße. A 1½ to 2 hour tour of the old town also starts
regularly from this office.

MÜHLHAUSEN

The town of Mühlhausen, northwest of Erfurt, has been called
Thomas-Müntzer-Stadt Mühlhausen since 1975 in honour of the
revolutionary theologian, Thomas Müntzer, who worked as
parish priest here in 1525. It is an old town, known at various
times as a wool weaving and textile centre, a royal residence, a
Hanseatic town and a free imperial city in the Holy Roman
Empire, but most of all perhaps for the role it played in the
Peasants' Revolt (1524-1525).

Historians have judged Thomas Müntzer quite variously. Born around 1489 in Stolberg in the Harz Mountains, he studied classics and theology in Leipzig, and was for a time a firm supporter of Luther before dismissing him as a Schriftgelehrter (scribe) and soft-liver. In his twenties, he became increasingly involved in spiritualist movements and made an attempt to rouse the Bohemians in Prague to revolution, before finding a hospitable base at Allstedt, west of Halle. There he attracted increasing attention by his reforms of the Mass, including conducting services in German rather than Latin so the peasants could understand. After delivering a blood-curdling sermon in 1524 he was forced to move on, and became deeply involved in the Peasants' Revolt. In the early months of 1525 he worked as a priest at the Marienkirche in Mühlhausen, but with the collapse of the revolt in May he was captured, tortured and killed.

For the GDR, Müntzer was an early hero of the struggle of the oppressed masses for a better life with social equality and security, and the 500th anniversary of his birth was widely celebrated in 1989. Mühlhausen celebrates this vision of Müntzer in several ways: the Barfüßerklosterkirche is now a museum devoted to the Peasants' Revolt, the 14th Century Pfarrkirche St Marien (Parish Church of St Mary) is also a museum, containing exhibits relating to Müntzer and explaining his significance, and in front of the Rabenturm (Raven Tower), part of the old town wall, is a statue of Müntzer (1956). In the town hall is the room where in March 1525, at Müntzer's instigation, the so-called Eternal Council (Ewiger Rat), a citizens' body committed to serving both the word of God and the common good of the citizens, was established.

Also of interest in the town is the Pfarrkirche Divi Blasii (Parish Church of St Blasius), dating mainly from the 13th Century, the remaining parts of the old town wall, and a large number of burgher houses, including at Herrenstraße 1 the house where Müntzer lived.

Where to stay and eat
Accommodation is available at the Stadt Mühlhausen, Wilhelm-Pieck-Platz. Restaurants include Thuringia, Steinweg 5; Hubertusklause, Wanfriedstraße 43; Breitsülze, An der Breitsülze.

Information
Tourist information is available at Görmarstraße 57.

Other places associated with Thomas Müntzer

For anyone interested in Müntzer a trip northeast to Bad
Frankenhausen and Allstedt is recommended. Above the town
of **Bad Frankenhausen** near the Schlachtberg (Battle Hill),
where the struggle began in 1525, a round building houses a
huge panoramic mural depicting scenes from the Peasants'
Revolt and Müntzer's part in it. The wonderfully detailed
painting is the work of Werner Tübke and was only completed
in 1987.

A short way to the east at **Allstedt** it is possible to visit the
palace where in 1524 Müntzer gave a rousing sermon
encouraging Duke John of Saxony to rise in armed revolt against
supporters of the Pope. A small museum has been set up here;
a further exhibition can be seen in the Pfarrkirche St Wiperti
(Parish Church of St Wipertius), where Müntzer regularly gave
crowd-pulling sermons.

To the south both of Allstedt and Bad Frankenhausen lies
Heldrungen, where Müntzer was held prisoner after being
captured at the battle of Frankenhausen. A tower in the castle
is popularly known as the Müntzerturm, although it is not
proved that Müntzer was really held here. The castle also
contains a small museum dedicated to Müntzer, and in the
grounds is a striking monument showing Müntzer as a prisoner
(1976).

Further to the north in the Harz mountains is **Stolberg**, the
town where Müntzer was born, probably in 1489. Here it is
possible to visit the house where he was born (Thomas-
Müntzer-Gasse 2), although the original building burnt down in
1851. On the same street at no. 19 is Stolberg's Heimatsmuseum,
which in rooms 5 and 6 contains exhibits relating to the
Peasants' Revolt and to Thomas Müntzer. Opposite the station
a large monument showing Müntzer carrying a flag and dressed,
with the exception of his priestly headgear, as a peasant, was
erected in 1975.

HEILBAD HEILIGENSTADT
Northwest of Mühlhausen and almost on the West German
border lies Heiligenstadt, for centuries an important centre for
the archbishops of Mainz. In addition, the well-known

woodcarver Tilman Riemenschneider was born here, and the poet and short story writer Theodor Storm worked here as a judge between 1856 and 1864, completing in that time 11 of his short stories.

As well as many well preserved timber-framed houses and a baroque townhall, Heiligenstadt has two churches well worth seeing: the Stiftskirche St Martin and the Propsteikirche St Marien. Several parts of St Martin's church, including the north portal, date from the early 14th Century; much later, however, the Jewish poet Heinrich Heine had himself baptised here (1825), believing that 'the baptismal certificate is the entrance ticket to European culture'. St Mary's church is a Gothic hall church dating from the second half of the 14th Century. In the interior note a bronze font (1492) and wall paintings (1507).

THE THÜRINGER WALD

The Thüringer Wald (Thuringian Forest), with its small traditional towns, woods, hills and rivers, is one of the most picturesque areas of East Germany and an ideal place for walking holidays, as well as for other outdoor and cultural activities. It covers an area over 100km in length across the southwest corner of East Germany. The Thuringian Forest proper extends from Eisenach in the west to around Katzhütte, but including the Thüringer Schiefergebirge (Thuringian Slate Mountains) continues further east to around Schleiz. The area is hilly, rather than mountainous; Grosser Beerberg (Great Berry Mountain), the highest point, is a relatively modest 982m above sea level.

The largest towns in the area, Eisenach, Gotha, Suhl and Ilmenau, lie on the edges, and all offer interesting cultural and historical sites, as well as easy access to the forest. It is also possible to stay at some of the villages in the forest itself, many of which are spas. Pleasant accommodation is available, for example in Friedrichroda, including the Schloß Reinhardsbrunn (a former palace now a hotel), south of Gotha, an attractive village with large parks, an open-air swimming pool and excellent hiking routes.

Sporting facilities are many and various throughout the region. The most famous hiking route, the Rennsteig (Border Way), extends for 160km along the top of the hills. For real enthusiasts, a route is also marked out from the Wartburg in Eisenach as far as Budapest! There are, however, many shorter, and well-marked routes criss-crossing the whole area. Many villages also have swimming pools and facilities for bowling, rowing and fishing.

For winter sports enthusiasts, Oberhof near Suhl provides facilities for skiing, ski jump, bob-sleighing, skating etc. It also has a large Interhotel, the Panorama. Other centres for winter sports include Finsterbergen, Pappenheim, Steinbach, Tambach-Dietharz and Winterstein.

Another of the pleasures of a stay in the Thuringian Forest is taking a cure. The main season is from May 1 to September 30, but many resorts are open all the year round. Special stays can be arranged, with medical care and laboratory tests provided as part of the package. The major health resorts in the area are Bad Salzungen, Bad Liebenstein and Bad Langensalza.

In addition to its natural attractions, Thuringia is well-known for its arts and crafts. Traditional gunsmiths' crafts have long been a speciality of Suhl, while not far away in Lauscha glass blowing techniques have been developed over the centuries. Though not as famous as Meissen, porcelain made in Thuringia also has a good reputation, and factories still exist in eight towns in the region, including Volkstedt, Unterweissbach, Lichte and Sitzendorf.

EISENACH (map p.126)

Eisenach, close to the West German border at the northwest edge of the Thuringian Forest, has a special place in the hearts of many Germans because of its close associations with both Bach and Luther. The Wartburg, one of the finest early medieval secular buildings in Europe, dominates the town and has been involved in many important events in German history; more recently, it has given its name to the second most popular make of car in the GDR.

The Wartburg

The Wartburg castle is thought to have been founded around 1067 by Ludwig der Springer and was for many years the residence of the Landgraves of Thuringia. During the 12th and 13th Centuries the castle became an important cultural centre for the whole area and it is here that the traditional Sängerkrieg, a contest between minstrels, is said to have taken place in 1207. The story of this contest between famous medieval poets, including Wolfram von Eschenbach, Heinrich von Ofterdingen and Walter von der Vogelweide, has reached opera audiences world-wide since Richard Wagner, who stayed at the Wartburg in 1842, made it the subject of *Tannhäuser*.

Around the same period Elisabeth (1207-1231), daughter of Andreas II of Hungary and wife of Ludwig IV of Thuringia, took the poor and the sick into the Wartburg, and was canonised four years after her death.

Another famous resident of the Wartburg was Martin Luther, who between May 4 1521 and March 6 1522 worked here on his translation of the New Testament from the original Greek text into German. Disguised as the Junker Jörg, Luther was able to enjoy almost a year of peace, protected from the Emperor's sheriffs by the Elector Friedrich der Weise.

The New Testament was published in 1522 and the whole Bible in 1534. It was not an academic's translation but was written in the ordinary German of the common people. It was important not just for theological reasons but also for the development of the German language, for it went a good way to standardising a written and to some extent spoken language out of the many dialects. As Luther himself said in his *Tischreden*, he aimed to write a language understandable to the Low and High German speaker.

The castle is constructed around two courtyards and consists of a large number of buildings dating from the 11th to the 16th Centuries, most of which had, however, fallen into decay by the end of that period. Major renovation work was undertaken between 1838 and 1867, with the object of presenting, according to a contemporary account, 'a faithful picture of the condition of the castle in the 12th Century, its most glorious era'. Further work, particularly on the interior, took place between 1978 and 1983.

The first courtyard, with its restored 15th and 16th Century half-timbered buildings, leads through to the older and more imposing inner, or second, courtyard. On the left is the late Romanesque Landgrafenhaus (apartments of the Landgraves) or Palas, which contains, on the ground floor, a Romanesque vaulted Rittersaal (Knights' Hall), a Speisesaal (Dining Hall) with attractive pillars and a room called the Elisabeth Kemenate (bower) decorated with mosaics from Oetken's designs (1902-1906). On the first floor, the Elisabeth Galerie contains frescoes by Moritz von Schwinds, depicting the life of St Elisabeth and the Seven Works of Mercy. The Landgrafenzimmer (Landgraves' room) and the Sängersaal (Minstrels' Hall) are also decorated with frescoes and painting by Schwinds. The whole of the second floor is taken up by the enormous Festsaal (Banqueting Hall); although the interior decorations, the ceiling and the woodwork date from the 19th Century, the arcades and columns in the side gallery are original.

The Wartburg also contains an excellent collection of works of art, including paintings by Lucas Cranach the Elder, a cupboard from a design by Albrecht Dürer and many tapestries. These, as well as an exhibition of the history of the castle, can be seen in the Neue Kemenate and Dirnitz buildings to the north of the Palas.

Luther's residence in the castle is commemorated in the Lutherstube (Luther's room) located near the entrance to the castle. The room itself is preserved much as Luther would have known it, and contains articles such as his table, bookcase, letters, portrait and the Bible he used.

The Wartburg can be reached on foot by following the picturesque wooded path which starts near Fritz Reuter's villa, or by road. From the Eselstation (donkey station) a little before the summit, it is possible to ride part of the way to the castle. Opening times for the castle are daily 8.30am — 4.00pm.

Bach

Johann Sebastian Bach was born at Eisenach in 1685, and the Bachhaus at Am Frauenplan 21 contains a collection of articles relating to the life and works of the whole Bach family. An exhibition of historic musical instruments, sometimes used for concerts of Bach's music, is also on show. The house is open Mondays, Tuesdays, Thursdays and Fridays 9.00am — 5.00pm, and Saturdays and Sundays 9.00 — noon and 1.30pm — 5.00pm.

In the market place stands a bronze statue of Bach, designed by Donndorf. Also in the market place is the Pfarrkirche St Georg (parish church of St George) where Bach was baptised on March 23 1685 and where Bach's works are now frequently performed.

Luther

Luther's visit to the Wartburg in 1521-1522 was not his first stay in Eisenach. Between 1498 and 1501 he lived here with Ursula von Cotta while attending the Latin School. The house, originally 15th Century but destroyed in World War II and since fully restored, stands at Lutherplatz 8 and contains a collection of Luther's works and family-related articles. Opening times are daily 9.00am — 1.00pm and 2.00pm — 5.00pm.

A statue of Luther, also by Donndorf (1895), stands in the Platz der Deutsch-Sowjetischen Freundschaft. Like Bach, Luther also had connections with the church of St George.

Despite being subject to an imperial ban, he preached here on May 2 1521.

In the south of Eisenach
At Friedrich-Engels-Straße 57, the site of the inn Zum Löwen (the Lion), a monument commemorates the founding of the Social Democratic Party by August Bebel and Wilhelm Liebknecht at the Eisenach Party Conference in 1869.

At Reuterweg 2, on the way to the Wartburg, the Fritz-Reuter-und-Richard-Wagner-Museum houses documents about the Low German poet Fritz Reuter, who lived here between 1863 and 1874, and a Richard Wagner Library, the largest outside Bayreuth.

Eisenach is not only a historic town, however. Wartburg cars, now with Volkswagen engines, are manufactured at the VEB Automobilwerk, and a display of cars, including several rare vintage models, can be seen at the Automobil-Ausstellungspavillon (car exhibition) on the Wartburgallee.

Where to stay and eat
There are several hotels in Eisenach, including Stadt Eisenach (Luisenstraße 11-13), Parkhotel (Wartburgallee 2) and Thüringer Hof (Platz der Deutsch-Sowjetischen Freundschaft 11).

Restaurants include Berghof (Göpelskuppe); Phantasie (Mariental 33); Stadt Leipzig (Puschkinstraße 50).

Events
The Thuringian Bach Festival is held in Eisenach, as well as other locations in the area, in late March every year. Every summer the GDR radio station, Stimme der DDR, broadcasts concerts from the Wartburg.

Information
Information can be obtained from Bahnhofstraße 3/5.

ARNSTADT
Often referred to as the 'Gateway to the Thuringian Forest', Arnstadt is most frequently visited either as a base for exploring the area, or because of its connections with the Bach family.

Johann Sebastian Bach was organist at the Neue Kirche (New Church), now renamed the Bachkirche (Bach Church), between 1703 and 1707. His time there is also commemorated by a small museum close to the town hall, known as the Haus zum Palmbaum (The Palm-tree House), by some articles in the local museum, and by a recent statue of the young Bach, completed in 1985 by Bernd Göbel and erected in front of the Bachkirche. Some concerts given as part of the Thuringian Bach Festival are held here in late March each year.

A large collection of dolls, known as 'Mon Plaisir' (My Pleasure), can be seen in the Neues Palais (New Palace). The 400 exhibits were made locally at the instigation of Princess Augusta Dorothea at the beginning of the 18th Century, and are faithful representations of court and everyday working and living conditions of that era. Opening times during the summer are Tuesdays to Sundays 8.30am — noon and 1.00pm — 4.30pm.

GOTHA

Gotha is both a pleasant and a lively town and one where there is plenty for visitors to see. It is also a convenient point of entry into the Thuringian Forest for visitors without a car, as it is from here that the Waldbahn (forest tram) starts on its route to villages such as Friedrichroda in the heart of the forest, terminating at Tabarz or Waltershausen.

Gotha has a very attractive and well-restored centre with a free-standing town hall built in Renaissance style (1567-1577) and a large number of colour-washed houses, including a Lucas Cranach House, mostly dating from the 17th and 18th Centuries, and many decorated with family coats of arms. The Hospital Maria Magdalena, on Brühl close to the market place, is an attractive 18th Century baroque building, and both the Augustinerkloster (Augustinian monastery) with its 14th Century cloisters (on the Klosterplatz), and the 17th and 18th Century Margaretenkirche (Church of St Margaret) at the Neumarkt, are well worth a visit.

The house at Cosmarstraße 10 commemorates the Gotha Party Conference of 1875 when the Eisenach and Lassalle factions joined the Socialist Workers Party, although Karl Marx's critique of the Gotha Programme, which exerted an important influence on the development of the international workers' movement, is perhaps better known than the conference itself. The congress room has been restored in its original state.

Schloß Friedenstein (Friedenstein palace) and its extensive grounds dominate the southern part of the town centre. The white palace with its large tiled roof is an early baroque construction (1643-1654), but the interior has baroque, rococo and classical features. It houses a theatre, with an original 1683 stage, the oldest in East Germany; a gallery, which includes the well-known picture entitled *Das Gothaer Liebespaar* (The Gotha Lovers) by the Meister des Hausbuchs (1484), the first German double portrait; one of East Germany's most important libraries; a very well-stocked cartographic museum, and various other specialist displays.

Close to Friedrichroda, one of the most popular holiday resorts in the area and accessible on the Waldbahn from Gotha, is the Marienglashöhle, a large grotto with rare transparent crystal formations.

Where to stay and eat
Hotels in Gotha include Waldbahn (Bahnhofstraße 16); and Slovan (Hauptmarkt/Jüdenstraße).

Restaurants include the Ratskeller and Gockelgrill, both on the Hauptmarkt; Fischerstube (Schwabhäuser Straße 47); Thüringer Hof (Huttenstraße 8).

Events
Gotha hosts several of the concerts which take place every year as part of the Thuringian Bach Festival. In addition, the Gotha Culture Festival is held annually in September/October.

Information
Information can be obtained from Hauptmarkt 2.

ILMENAU
An attractive town on the river Ilm, with well-known glass and porcelain factories dating from the 18th and 19th Centuries, Ilmenau is a tourist destination largely because of its associations with Goethe. While working as a minister at Weimar, Goethe was a frequent visitor to Ilmenau, where he supervised economic and administrative development, undertook several of his scientific studies and wrote some of his literary works.

In the Amtshaus (Administrative House) in the market place are two rooms, Goethe's work room and his living room, furnished as they were in his lifetime, and maintained to commemorate his life in Ilmenau. The Jagdhaus Gabelbach (Gabelbach hunting lodge), where Goethe stayed when the Duke of Weimar went hunting, is also now a small museum, and contains, among many documents and memorabilia, a record of Goethe's scientific research in the Thuringian Forest. Just north of the lodge is the Goethehäuschen auf dem Kickelhahn (Goethe's house on the Kickelhahn) where Goethe wrote, on September 6 1780, one of his most famous poems, *The Wayfarer's Night Song II*: 'Über allen Gipfeln ist Ruh...' (Over all the hilltops it is still, in all the tree tops you can hardly feel a breath stirring. The little birds are silent in the forest. Wait! soon you too will be still.)

Between Ilmenau and Stützerbach via Gabelbach a hiking route has been marked out, called 'Auf Goethes Spuren' (In Goethe's footsteps) and clearly signposted with the letter 'G'. The whole route is 18km long, and includes all the poet's favourite haunts in the area, but it is also possible to walk shorter sections.

Between Ilmenau and Saalfeld, it is worth leaving the main road to visit the Klosterruine Paulinzella, the ruins of a Benedictine monastery, founded in 1112. The style of building employed here foreshadowed later developments in ecclesiastical architecture.

MEININGEN

The town of Meinigen, to the west of Suhl, has long been a cultural centre for the surrounding area. Conductors including Richard Strauss (1885-1886) and Max Reger (1911-1914) worked at the court at Meinigen, while the theatre ensemble, Die Meiniger, became famous throughout Europe and influenced the dramatic theory of Stanislawski and Max Reinhardt. The town is also closely associated with Schiller, who took refuge in nearby Bauerbach in 1782, while fleeing from the Württemberg rulers.

Prettily situated on the river Werra, Meinigen offers two sites of interest: the Goethe-Park, once known as the English Garden, and Schloß Elisabethenburg, formerly the Ducal Palace, which dates largely from the period 1682-1692, and now houses a number of museums. The picture gallery contains a fine collection of Dutch and Italian works, and the theatre museum contains documents relating to the Meiningen theatre movement. At Bauerbach, 10km south of Meiningen, a Schiller museum has brought together a number of documents and articles relating to the author's early life.

SAALFELD

The Feengrotten (fairy grottos) 1km southwest of the town attract thousands of visitors every year. These colourful caves, previously a slate mine, are filled with stalactites and depict various fairy stories.

The centre of Saalfeld itself contains a number of historic buildings worth seeing, although the town is now an important industrial centre. The Stadtkirche St Johannis (Church of St John), built 1389-1456, is one of Thuringia's most beautiful churches, and the town hall, constructed straight after the great town fire of 1517, is a good example of the late baroque style, with Renaissance additions. The Hoher Schwarm castle, the ancient symbol of the town dating from the 13th Century and modelled on Thun castle in Switzerland, although partially ruined, is still an impressive sight.

SUHL

Suhl, the capital of the GDR's smallest Bezirk (administrative district), has managed to harmonise a well-restored old town area with modern buildings and is attractively situated, surrounded by the Thuringian Forest. It has been known for many centuries for its manufacture of firearms and, apart from its overall pleasant appearance, its main attraction is the Waffenmuseum (Firearms Museum) housed, on Herrenteich, in one of the oldest (1663) half-timbered houses in the town.

Where to stay and eat

Two hotels are available in Suhl: Thüringen-Tourist, an Interhotel at Ernst-Thälmann-Platz 2, and Stadt Suhl at Straße am Bahnhof,

Restaurants include Gaststättenkomplex Kaluga (Wilhelm-Pieck-Straße); Gastmahl des Meeres (Steinweg 15); Waffenschmied mit Japanrestaurant Fuji (Gothaer Straße 8); Zum Goldenen Hirsch (Suhl Neundorf).

Information
Information is available at Steinweg 1.

GERA
Gera was badly damaged in 1945, but a large part of the old town has been reconstructed in its original style, with modern buildings mainly confined to the outer parts. It is an important industrial centre for textiles, mechanical engineering and electronics but also has a number of historic buildings and cultural centres of interest.

The market place in Gera is among the most attractive in the south of East Germany. It is impressive both because of its completeness and because of outstanding buildings such as the Rathaus (town hall) dating mainly from 1573-1576, and the 1606 Stadtapotheke (town dispensary). The Salvatorkirche (Church of the Saviour) near the market place, is largely baroque (1717-1720) but is noteworthy for the double galleries in the aisles which were added at the turn of this century.

Gera has an active theatrical and musical life, and the main theatre, which also houses a concert hall, is an attractive Jugendstil construction (1902). The Orangery, an imitation of the Zwinger in Dresden, contains the Gera Art Gallery and also a permanent exhibition of the works of the painter Otto Dix (1891-1969), who was born in Gera.

Where to stay and eat
Gera has an Interhotel (Gera — Straße der Republik); more basic accommodation is available at Stadt Gera (Franz-Petrich-Straße).

Restaurants include Ratskeller (Markt); Theaterrestaurant (Dimitroffallee); Jagdhof (Auf dem Hainberg); Sliven (Kornmarkt).

Events
Gera hosts a number of musical events, including the Gera Organ Week (July), Thuringian Music Days (April) and a festival of workers' choirs (May). Other events include a dahlia festival in September and the Gera culture festival in October.

Information
Tourist information is at Dr-Rudolf-Breitschied-Straße 1.

JENA
Jena is known throughout Europe for its university, founded in 1548, and, more recently, for the optical instruments firm, Carl Zeiss. In the late 18th and early 19th Centuries Jena was a centre for German philosphy, and memorials to figures such as Schiller, Goethe, Hegel and many others are scattered throughout the town.

Since 1972 Jena has been physically, as well as intellectually, dominated by the university. A 120m tall circular building in the centre is now used for many academic activities; on the 26th floor is a café, offering fine views over the town. The university campus, completed by Theodor Fischer in 1906, occupies the site of the palace of the Dukes of Saxe-Jena, and is located on the Goethe Allee, northwest of the market place. About 6,000 students study here. Because of Friedrich von Schiller's work as a professor at Jena from 1789, the university has long been known as the Friedrich-Schiller University.

Jena's connections with the optical industry go back to 1846 when Carl Zeiss set up a workshop in Jena. By 1866 the workshop was making microscopes, and in 1880 production of lenses and optical instruments began in a new factory. After World War II there was a great deal of litigation between the Carl-Zeiss-Stiftung of Jena and Carl Zeiss of West Germany over the right to use the name, including one case that came before the House of Lords in London in 1966, where the whole question of the legal standing of the GDR was in issue.

In the botanical garden north of the Goethe Allee is the Zeiss Planetarium, the oldest functioning planetarium in the world. The original cupola was built in 1926, but substantial work between 1983 and 1985 has resulted in fully-computerised operation. On the Carl-Zeiss-Platz in the southwest of the town stands the Optisches Museum der DDR (Optical Museum), which contains over 12,000 exhibits from historical items to recent articles used in space exploration. The museum is open Tuesdays to Fridays 9.00am — 5.30pm and Saturdays 9.00am — 4.00pm.

Other buildings of interest include the Collegium Jenense, the original university, where famous thinkers including Leibniz, Hegel and Fichte worked, and where Karl Marx took his doctorate; the late Gothic town hall and the market place, the

Stadtkirche St Michael (town church of St Michael — 1390); the Frommansches Haus at Goethe Allee 18, a burgher house that was at the centre of intellectual life in Jena at the time of Goethe, and the remains of the medieval town fortifications, including the Pulverturm (Powder Tower) and the Johannistor (St John's Gate) dating from 1305.

Where to stay and eat
Jena has an Interhotel, the Hotel International on Ernst-Thälmann-Ring.

Restaurants include Zur Sonne, Markt 22; Ratszeise, Markt 1; Forelle, Holzmarkt 14.

Information
Information can be obtained from Neugasse 7.

SAALETAL
The river Saale extends from the southern border of East Germany until it joins the Elbe northwest of Dessau. In the southern stretches in particular, the Saale Valley is both scenically and historically interesting. In the Thüringer Wald area the river passes close to the late Gothic castle of Burgk, a popular destination in summer for its exhibitions and concerts, and through Bad Blankenburg and Saalfeld. On the edge of the forest it passes through Rudolstadt, and further north through Jena, past the Dornburg palaces and close to Naumburg.

Rudolstadt
Rudolstadt is well-known for the Schloß Heidecksburg (1737), the palace which dominates both the town and the river below. Wilhelm von Humboldt, coming to this district, described it as 'one of the most beautiful areas of Germany'. Today the castle houses several museums, including collections of furniture, painting and weapons. Between April and September recitals of baroque music are given once or twice a week in the castle. Opening times are Tuesdays to Sundays 9.00am to 4.00pm in summer, and 9.00am — 3.00pm in winter.

The town was also known in the 18th and 19th Centuries as a second Weimar: literary and musical figures, including Schiller, Goethe, Richard Wagner, Liszt and Paganini all spent time here.

Schiller in particular was closely associated with Rudolstadt, and the town has several reminders of this connection. At Schillerstraße 25 (the house formerly belonging to the Lengefeld family) Schiller first met his future wife Charlotte von Lengefeld, and during her childhood Charlotte lived at Lengefeldstraße 1. A small memorial to Schiller can also be found on the Eichberg, including a copy of Dannecker's bust of the poet and playwright.

Dornburg

Further north between Jena and Naumburg are the Dornburg palaces, now memorials to Goethe. The poet first visited the palaces in 1777 but later returned frequently, writing here works including *Iphigenie* and *Egmont*. His final stay in Dornburg was in 1828, after the death of the Grand Duke Carl August, when he claimed the landscape along the river Saale revived his creativity.

The three palaces, built on steep limestone cliffs, are in different styles. The Altes Schloß (Old Palace — 1521) is now a social centre (Feierabendheim); the southernmost Palace, known as the Goetheschloß (Goethe Palace — 1539), where Goethe lived for a time from 1828, now contains rooms dedicated to Goethe's memory; between these two buildings is a rococo palace (1736-1747) in which Goethe also sometimes stayed.

NAUMBURG

The Dom St. Peter und Paul (Cathedral of St Peter and St Paul) and the late Gothic town hall make Naumburg a popular destination for German tourists, although its attractions are not well-known outside Germany. This is a pity as the cathedral ranks among the most interesting in Europe.

The building of the cathedral began at the end of the 12th Century, and the bulk was completed in the late Romanesque style by 1249, although there was substantial renovation work in the 19th Century. The oldest remaining section is the spacious crypt under the east choir, which dates from around 1170. The northwest tower is original (1249) but the matching southwest tower was erected only in 1894.

The west choir is decorated with 12 life-size figures of founders of the cathedral, the work of the unknown Master of Naumburg (1250). They are strikingly life-like representations in contemporary costume. The best known couple are Ekkehard and Uta. Also of interest are the screens which separate the nave from the choirs and which are decorated with scenes from the Passion. Medieval stained glass remains in several of the cathedral's windows and a number of altars and tombstones are also worth a closer look. The cathedral is open to visitors Mondays to Saturdays 8.00am — 6.00pm and Sundays noon — 6.00pm.

In addition to the cathedral, several buildings in the centre of the town should not be missed. Chief among these is the Rathaus (town hall), built between 1517 and 1528, with an imposing exterior and a richly decorative interior, including a spiral staircase and stucco ceilings.

Behind the Wilhelm-Pieck-Platz, on which the Rathaus stands, is the late Gothic Stadtkirche St. Wenzel (Church of St. Wenceslaus), constructed between 1218 and 1523. It has a Hildebrand organ on which Bach played, and a painting by Cranach the Elder (*Jesus als Kinderfreund* — Suffer little children to come unto me).

Of the original town fortifications, only the Marientor (Mary's Gate), so-called because of the statue of Mary and Jesus on the outside, remains. This large and solid gate stands at the end of the Marienstraße and is now used for performances by the Naumburg puppet theatre.

Where to eat

Restaurants include Stadt Naumburg, Maxim-Gorki-Ring; Ratskeller, Wilhelm-Pieck-Platz; Drushba, Wilhelm-Pieck-Platz; Goldener Hahn, Am Salztor; Café Prokop, Marienstraße.

Information

Tourist information is available at Lindenring 38.

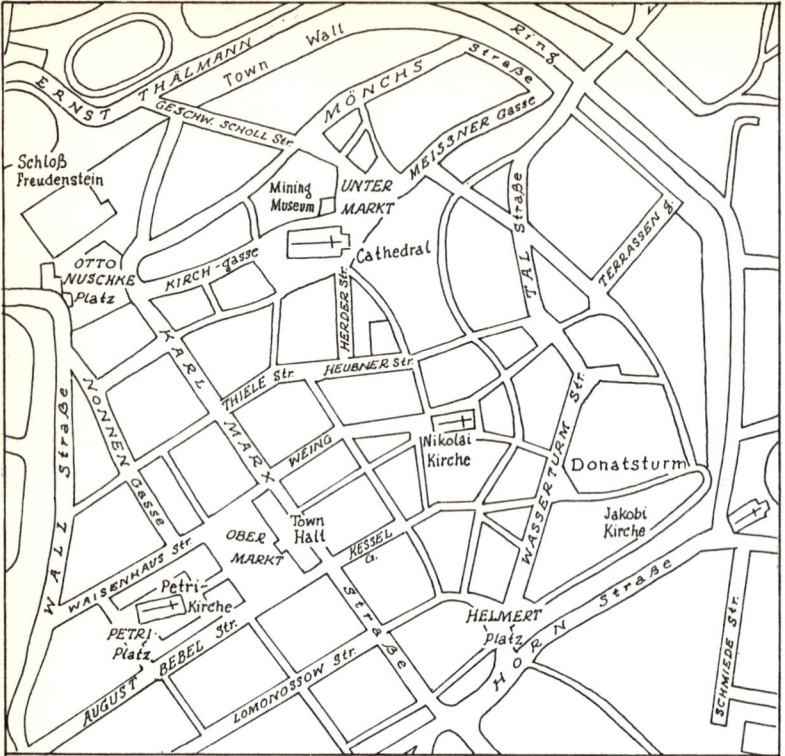

FREIBERG

0 ————— 150
m

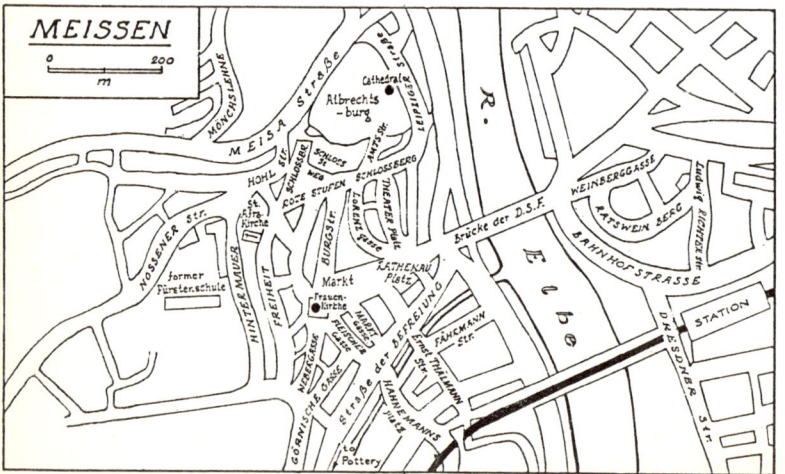

MEISSEN

0 ————— 200
m

The South East

CHEMNITZ/KARL-MARX-STADT

Between 1953 and April 1990, when it was decided by plebiscite
to revert to the original name, Chemnitz (pronounced Kemnitz)
was known as Karl-Marx-Stadt. It is a large, mostly modern,
industrial town important for the manufacture of textile
machinery and machine tools, although it has a number of
reconstructed historical buildings in the centre. It is also a
convenient starting point for excursions into the Erzgebirge.

The Karl-Marx-Monument in the Karl-Marx-Platz is the
focus of the new town centre. The huge image of Marx's head
by the Soviet sculptor Lev Kerbel (1971) stands in front of a
wall on which the final words of the Communist Party
Manifesto ('Proletarier aller Länder vereinigt Euch!', translated
on the monument as 'Working Men of all Countries Unite!') is
engraved in several languages. It is rumoured that the town is
now intent on selling the monument.

Among the older buildings of interest are the Roter Turm
(Red Tower), the lower part of which dates from the 12th
Century, the Altes Rathaus (Old Town Hall) with its intricate
Renaissance entrance (1559) and vault dating from 1469, the
baroque façades on the Marktplatz (Market Place) including the
old Press Café (now called the Café am Markt), and the
Schloßkirche (Castle Church), the church previously attached to
the Benedictine Monastery on the same site, founded in 1136
and with late Gothic interior decorations. The Stadtkirche St
Jakobi (Church of St James), also near the market place, was
founded in 1165, but counts among its more interesting features
an unusual Jugendstil façade on the west side.

The Theaterplatz (Theatre Square), a collection of buildings
mainly dating from the start of the 20th Century, offers some
contrast to the ugliness of the modern building around it. The
museum here includes a number of well-known paintings by
German impressionists and expressionists, several of whom had

links with the town. Three of the founders of the expressionist artists' group known as Die Brücke (The Bridge), Schmidt-Rottluff, Heckel and Nolde, studied together at Chemnitz High School from 1901 before going to Dresden and issuing their manifesto there in 1906. In front of the museum the versteinerte Wald (petrified forest), silicified tree stumps 250 million years old, is a remarkable sight. Further examples and a description of how the trees were first found in 1743 and used originally as jewellery can be found inside the museum. Opening hours: Saturdays to Wednesdays 9.00am — 6.00pm, Thursdays 9.00am — 9.00pm.

Students of German literature may be interested to know that the contemporary writer, and author of *The King David Report*, Stefan Heym, was born here in 1913.

Where to stay
Chemnitz has three Interhotels: Hotel Kongreß on Karl-Marx-Allee, Hotel Chemnitzer Hof on the Theaterplatz, Hotel Moskau on Straße der Nationen, and other hotels near the main railway station.

Where to eat
Both the town hall (Ratskeller on the market place) and the theatre (on Theaterplatz) have restaurants. In addition several restaurants are located in the Industriezentrum building on Straße der Nationen. Other restaurants include Zum güldenen Bock, Rosenhof 2, the Irkutsk close to the Kongreß Hotel, and the Restaurant Baikal at Alfred-Neubert-Straße 17 (take the no. 49 bus to the Arno-Schreiter-Straße stop).

Events
The Robert Schumann Music Days, originally held only in Zwickau, have now spread to Chemnitz, and take place every year in May/June. An annual festival in honour of the Saxon organ builder, Gottfried Silbermann, is held every September in around 20 locations in the Chemnitz district. A festival of Erzgebirge folklore takes place at the end of November; throughout the year, however, wooden toys, lace and other handicrafts made in the Erzgebirge can be bought from a shop just behind the Karl Marx monument.

Information
Information can be obtained at Straße der Nationen 3.

ALTENBURG

The town of Altenburg, south of Leipzig, is best known in Germany as the home of the card game, skat. Thought to have originated among the local Slav peasantry several hundred years ago, the game gradually grew in popularity throughout the country but Altenburg has remained the seat of the Skatgericht (international skat tribunal), and is even referred to as the Skatstadt (Skat Town). A fountain in the oldest square, known as the Brühl, is dedicated to the card game, and the castle museum has an extensive collection of playing cards and a workshop which dates back to 1600.

In addition to this interest, Altenburg has several buildings of note, including an 18th Century castle imposingly built on a porphyry rock above the town, the Schloßkirche (Castle Church) with a Trost organ on which Bach played in 1739, one year after its construction, and the Lindenau Museum at the end of the castle park, which houses significant collections of medieval German and Renaissance Italian sculpture, as well as Italian paintings from the 13th to 15th Centuries.

The Rathaus (Town Hall) is often cited as a good example of Renaissance building. Built between 1562-1564, it dominates the large market square and the burgher houses which surround it. The two towers known as the Rote Spitzen (Red Spikes) are the remains of an Augustinian monastery founded here in the 12th Century, but today contain exhibitions of medieval wood carvings.

Where to stay and eat

The main hotel in Altenburg is the Zum Wenzel, Karl-Liebknecht-Straße 21. In addition to the Ratskeller (Markt), restaurants include Skatgaststätte Grand, Sporenstraße, and the Theatercafé on Rosa-Luxemburg-Platz.

Information

Tourist information is located on the market place at the corner of Weibermarkt 17.

THE ERZGEBIRGE

The region some 130km long and 40km wide which runs along the border with Czechoslovakia from south of Chemnitz to Dresden is known as the Erzgebirge (Ore Mountains) and is, like the Thüringer Wald to the west, a popular holiday destination.

Although the highest mountain in the Erzgebirge range lies over the border in Czechoslovakia, the nearby Fichtelberg, rising to a height of 1,214m, is East Germany's highest peak. The area takes its name from the rich ore deposits, in particular silver, that have been found in the mountains. Despite considerable industrialisation, mainly in the west, the area contains a number of interesting towns and a wealth of natural beauty.

Among the towns worth visiting in the area are Freiberg, at the foot of the Eastern Erzgebirge, Augustusburg, Annaberg (Annaberg-Buchholz), Seiffen, and Zwickau in the west.

For those interested in exploring the natural beauty of the region more closely, there is a large choice of attractive mountain resorts. The largest of these is Oberwiesenthal, which has extensive winter sports facilities, but other possibilities include Altenberg and Geising in the Eastern Erzgebirge, and, in summer, the areas near the dams in the Western Erzgebirge, including for example the Flöha Valley. The area also offers a number of spas, such as Bad Gottleuba and Berggiesshübel.

FREIBERG (map p.148)

Founded in 1170 with the discovery of silver mines, Freiberg remains an important centre of mining research as well as an established university town. Reminders of its connections with mining can be seen all over the town: the statue of the miner behind the Rathaus, the decorations on the door of Obermarkt 17 depicting mining scenes, and the Miners' Pulpit in the cathedral, to name but a few. The whole of the centre of Freiberg is well preserved and it is a pleasure to walk through its narrow pedestrianised streets.

The highlight of a visit here is the cathedral. The main body is late Gothic dating from 1484-1501, but the famous Goldene Pforte (Golden Portal) is a relic from a former Romanesque church on the same site, and its magnificent sculptures, among the best of medieval German work, are thought to date from around 1230. Not to be missed are the Tulpenkanzel (Tulip Pulpit) of 1508-1510, a richly decorated stone pulpit in the form of a tulip with steps supported by figures of the sculptor and his pupils, the Bergmannkanzel (Miner's Pulpit) of 1638, supported by a stone figure of a miner, the altar picture, probably from the Cranach school, and the Pietà in which Christ has been given a wig made from horse-hair. The cathedral has two organs by Gottfried Silbermann, a native of Freiberg, one of which was built between 1711-1714 and is the oldest and largest of the 31

Silbermann organs still in existence. Notably missing from the cathedral is stained glass: it is said that the miners, condemned to working long hours in the dark, appreciated as much light as possible in church.

The cathedral can be visited only on guided tours. These take place Tuesdays to Sundays at 11.00am and 2.30pm, although additional tours may be arranged during holiday periods.

At Otto-Nuschke-Platz 6, west of the cathedral, the house where Silbermann had his workshop between 1711 and 1751 can be seen.

Near the cathedral on the Untermarkt (Lower Market) a patrician house has been converted into a mining museum. (Opening hours Tuesdays to Sundays 9.00am — 5.00pm). The tiny but well-preserved miners' houses in the crooked alleyways also give a clear picture of earlier conditions. In the Obermarkt (Upper Market) there are many old patrician houses dating from the 16th Century, and a late Gothic town hall (1470-1474, but later reconstructed). In the centre of the square is a statue of Otto der Reiche (Otto the Rich), who, it is claimed, founded Freiberg to protect and develop the mining industry. The nearby Petrikirche (Church of St Peter) is also late Gothic and, like the cathedral, contains a Silbermann organ. The Nikolaikirche (Church of St Nicholas) between the two market places dates from the 14th and 15th Centuries and has a richly decorated interior.

A walk round the Ring, the road following the line of the old town wall, takes about an hour and passes a number of interesting sights, including in the east the Donatsturm (Donat Tower), a remnant of the city fortifications, and, almost opposite, the Jakobikirche (Church of St James) built 1890-1892 but incorporating a Silbermann organ, and to the west the Schloß Freudenstein (Freudenstein Castle), a 16th Century building, used until recently as a grain store.

Where to eat
Freiberg has a large choice of eating places including Brauhof, Körnerstraße; Ratskeller , Obermarkt 16; Gastmahl des Meeres, Karl-Marx-Straße 3; Stadt Dresden, Dresdner Straße 4; SächsischerHof, Berthelsdorfer Straße 23; Café Erbisches Tor, Karl-Marx-Straße 14.

Events
During the summer, there are regular concerts in the cathedral.

Information
The tourist information centre is at Weingasse 9.

AUGUSTUSBURG
This picturesque small town, around 13km east of Chemnitz, is
well-known for its Renaissance castle (1567-1573), built as a
hunting lodge for the Electors of Saxony but today a museum
(exhibitions of hunting and gamekeeping, and motorcycles) and
youth hostel. The Schloßkapelle (Castle Chapel) has a gilded
altar over which hangs a painting by Lucas Cranach the
Younger depicting the Elector Augustus with his family before
the crucified Christ. The castle can be visited on guided tours
only; these are available daily between 8.00am — 4.00pm, with
frequency varying according to demand. The museums are also
open daily, from 9.00am — 4.30pm.

Augustusburg can be reached by road, or by taking a train to
Erdmannsdorf in the valley and then an eight minute cable car
ride up to the castle. Erdmannsdorf is also a good place to
explore the countryside on foot. Several paths are marked from
the station, including three routes (3-4km) to Augustusburg and
a 2km walk to Kunnerstein.

ANNABERG
Annaberg, amalgamated in 1945 with a neighbouring town to
form Annaberg-Buchholz, originally developed, like Freiberg,
as a result of silver mining, but with the decline of this industry
towards the end of the 16th Century became important as a
centre of lace-making. This tradition continues today, as does
wooden toy-making, originally a hobby among miners in the
area.

The old centre of the town is well preserved and contains,
among other monuments largely from the 16th Century, the St-
Annen-Kirche (Church of St Anne) built in 1499-1525 of local
gneiss (a coarse-grained rock composed mainly of quartz,
felspar and mica) and the largest hall church in Saxony. Among
its noteworthy features are the sculptures on the Schöne Tür
(literally Beautiful Door) and the Bergaltar (Miners' Altar),
which depicts miners working in the local silver mines (1521).
The church is open June to September 10.30am — 11.30am and
2.30pm — 3.30pm on weekdays, to 4.00pm on Saturdays, and on

Sundays 2.00pm — 3.30pm; during the rest of the year it closes at 3.00pm.

Just north of Buchholz at Frohnau in the Sehma Valley is the Frohnauer Hammer, originally a corn mill which was used from the 17th Century to 1904 as a forge. It is now a technology museum, while the nearby former owner's timber-framed house is a Museum of Folklore and a restaurant.

SEIFFEN

The village of Seiffen lies around 40km southeast of Chemnitz and is well-known both as the centre of the traditional wooden toy industry and, because of its beautiful setting and pleasant climate, also as a health resort.

At the Erzgebirger Spielzeugmuseum (Toy Museum), at Ernst-Thälmann-Straße 73, the development of the wooden toy industry from a local hobby to a major export industry for East Germany is recorded. Best-known are the hand-carved Christmas pyramids and nut-crackers in the form of characters in traditional dress, which sell for large sums outside East Germany but, due to demand outstripping supply, are frequently unobtainable locally. At a nearby factory (Bahnhofstraße 12) it is possible to see turners, carvers and painters at work.

Seiffen also contains a small village church representative of many in the region. It is an octagonal baroque building (1779) with a steep tiled roof surmounted by a typical South German tower, and has an attractive interior with a gallery running right round.

ZWICKAU

Zwickau lies on the Mulde at the extreme west of the Erzgebirge and is mainly known as an industrial town, the home now, for example, of the small East German car, the Trabant. It was also a major coal-mining town until its pits were closed in 1977.

It is at Zwickau that the composer Robert Schumann was born in 1810, and since 1956 his house (Hauptmarkt 5) has been a museum. Furniture from the period, various keyboard instruments and other items relating to his work, principally piano compositions and Lieder, are on display.

Also of interest are the Gewandhaus (1522-1525), built as a drapers' hall but now a theatre, and the Dom St Marien (St Mary's Cathedral), founded in 1206 but rebuilt in the second half of the 15th Century. The cathedral possesses a fine high altar in carved wood, with paintings by the Nuremberg painter Wolgemut (1479), an early Renaissance pulpit and an interesting Pietà.

Where to stay and eat
Visitors can stay at the Stadt Zwickau at Bahnhofstraße 67. Eating places include Parkgaststätte, Bahnhofstraße 1; Lindenhof, Marienthaler Straße 3; Windberghaus, Werdauer Straße 152; and the historical Weinstube, Neuberinplatz.

Events
The Robert Schumann Days, held annually in June, are concentrated on Zwickau, although concerts are also held in surrounding towns, including Chemnitz.

Information
The tourist information office is at Hauptstraße 4.

OBERWIESENTHAL
The resort of Oberwiesenthal is a border crossing to Czechoslovakia and one of East Germany's most popular sporting areas. The town is surrounded by a large number of ski runs, many reached by ski lifts, and nearby there is a major toboggan run. Numerous walks are also signposted throughout the area, and the unusual flora is well worth seeing, particularly in spring and summer.

For the less energetic a Schwebebahn (cable car) operates from close to the railway station to the Fichtelberg. The view from the platform of the Fichtelberghaus at the top of the mountain can be over 100km on a clear day.

A further attraction is the Erzgebirgebahn, a narrow-gauge railway built in 1887, which runs from Oberwiesenthal to Cranzahl, 17km away. The journey itself is a pleasure; a bonus is the dam at Cranzahl, the first dam built in the GDR (1948-1951).

VOGTLAND

The area in the extreme west of the Erzgebirge, centred around Plauen and the river Weisser Elster, is known as Vogtland, a name deriving from the fact that imperial governors (Vögte) used to control the important north-south trade routes passing through the countryside. It is a hilly region with several dams and lakes, popular for sailing, and, like the rest of the south, also good for walking.

Places of note within Vogtland include the small town of Markneukirchen, picturesquely situated in the woods but known principally for its tradition, continued today, of making musical instruments (a museum of musical instruments is situated in the east wing of the Paulusschlössel — Paul Palace); the picturesque town of Klingenthal right on the Czech border; spas such as Bad Brambach, East Germany's only radon spa, and Bad Elster; dams and lakes at Talsperre Pöhl and Talsperre Pirk; picturesque villages with timber-framed houses such as Raun near Bad Elster; the capital of the region, Plauen, with its strange Altes und Neues Rathaus (Old and New Town Hall), the original 1508 late Gothic construction built into the 1912 neo-baroque town hall; and the town of Greiz with its palace (Oberes Schloß), summer palace in the Lenin Park and classical parish church.

SÄCHSISCHE SCHWEIZ

East of the Erzgebirge and southeast of Dresden, lies one of East Germany's most beautiful areas, known since the time of the German Romantics as Sächsische Schweiz (Saxon Switzerland), but known to earlier travellers as the Meissen Highlands. It is a favourite holiday destination for East German tourists, largely because of its rich possibilities for walking and climbing, but also because its strange shaped rock formations, deep valleys and rushing streams provide plenty of interest for those who only wish to look.

The sandstone mountains through which the river Elbe runs have long been subject to erosion, and many unusual shapes have been formed. The area near Rathen, known as the Bastei, is a kind of rock labyrinth; a path through the rocks and over a dramatic stone bridge leads up to viewing point, from where there is an excellent panorama of Sächsische Schweiz. Near the viewing point there is a restaurant, and lower down the slopes towards Rathen is the Felsenbühne, an open-air theatre among the rocks where there are performances in the summer months.

A path also leads to the Amselsee (Lake Amsel) north of Rathen, where it is possible to hire boats.

Another popular centre in the area is Bad Schandau, a spa prettily situated on the Elbe, from where there is easy access into the surrounding mountains. Enjoyable excursions from Bad Schandau include the Lichterhainer Wasserfall (waterfall), an 8km trip on the Kirnitzschtalbahn tram line, or the Schrammsteine (rocks), 3km to the southeast, one of the most impressive rock formations in Sächsische Schweiz.

Also of interest is the fort at Königstein. Towering 360m above the Elbe, the fort was designed as an impregnable bastion, first for the kings of Bohemia and later for the rulers of Meissen. For many years it served as a prison; it counts among its inmates such well-known figures as August Bebel (1874) and the dramatist Frank Wedekind (1899). Today, however, the fort is a museum; many of the buildings, dating mostly from the 16th and 17th Centuries, are original, and several weapon collections, as well as a memorial to August Bebel, can also be seen.

Close to Königstein is the Lilienstein (Lily Stone), an outcrop a little higher than Königstein on the opposite bank of the Elbe, It can only be reached on foot, but the view from the top, the picturesque ruins of a medieval castle, and a welcoming restaurant, combine to make the effort worthwhile. The Pfaffenstein (Priest's Stone) to the east of Königstein is also a popular destination because of its strange weather-beaten shapes.

Pirna, closer to Dresden, is a pleasant town on the Elbe, sometimes known as the Gateway to Saxon Switzerland. In the town itself, the late Gothic Stadtkirche St Marien (Town Church of St Mary) and the free-standing Rathaus, dating in parts from 1485, as well as many well-maintained burgher houses in and around the market place, are of interest. 4km to the south, Bad Gottleuba is a major health resort offering a range of treatments, from mudbaths to baths with iron-enriched water.

A pleasant way to view Sächsische Schweiz is from one of the boats belonging to the Weiße Flotte, including vintage paddle steamers, which travel along the Elbe between Dresden and Bad Schandau calling at a number of towns and villages en route.

Where to stay
The Elbhotel at Bad Schandau is in the heart of Sächsische Schweiz. Otherwise it is possible to stay in Dresden and make a day trip along the Elbe.

Where to eat
Restaurants in Bad Schandau include Am Stadtpark, Otto-Buchwitz-Straße 7; Sigl's Gaststätten, August-Bebel-Straße 17; and Waldhäus'l, Kirnitzschtal 89.

ZITTAU
In the far southeastern corner of East Germany, beyond the Lausitzer Bergland, lies Zittau and the Zittauer Gebirge (Zittau Mountains), a gentle hilly area rising to 800m and dotted with village resorts. The narrow-gauge steam railway called the Zittauer Bimmelbahn, which runs from Zittau to Oybin or Jonsdorf, offers a leisurely way to see the countryside.

In Zittau itself the market place, known as the Platz der Jugend (Young People's Square), is the focus of interest. The Rathaus (Town Hall) was rebuilt in 1840-1845 following plans by Schinkel and is in Italian Renaissance style, although other buildings, including the Noaksches Haus, a patrician house (1689), and the Rolandbrunnen (Roland Fountain), built in 1585, date from earlier times. The Johanniskirche (Church of St John), close to the main square, was also built to designs by Schinkel (1837); those climbing the tower will be rewarded with a good view of the Zittau area.

Where to stay and eat
The principal hotel in Zwickau is the Volkshaus, Äußere Weberstraße 6. Restaurants include Stadtkrug, Platz der Jugend; Dreiländereck, Bautzner Straße 9; Zum Broiler, Frauenstraße 11.

Events
A folk festival is held annually in June.

Information
Tourist information can be obtained at Rathausplatz 6.

MEISSEN (map p.148)
Among East Germany's many attractive small towns, Meissen is unique in offering a picturesque setting on the banks of the Elbe, a historic town centre, virtually unscathed by World War

II, and a variety of specialities from its world-famous porcelain to local wine. It is also one of the south's oldest towns, mentioned as early as 929 and a thriving trading centre throughout the middle ages. Subsequently the town's fortunes have risen and fallen several times, suffering under Swedish occupation during the Thirty Years' War when it was badly destroyed by fire (1637), and again under French occupation during the Napoleonic Wars, but gaining ground with the foundation of the porcelain factory (1710) and its popularity among the German Romantics at the beginning of the 19th Century.

The imposing skyline is dominated by two buildings, the cathedral and the Albrechtsburg, both of which are worth closer inspection. The cathedral was begun in 1270 and the naves and aisles completed around 1380. The two west towers, 91m high, were destroyed in a fire caused by lightening in 1547 and not re-erected until 1903-1908. The interior contains a number of statues of benefactors, dating from around 1260, by master-craftsmen from Naumburg, monuments to most of the ancestors of the royal family of Saxony in the 15th and 16th Centuries, most of whom are buried here — including a particularly striking bronze monument to Friedrich der Streitbare (Frederick the Warlike, died 1428) — two altar paintings, one from the school of Cranach depicting the crucifixion, and marble reliefs.

Alongside the cathedral, and included in the tour, are a small cloister and a 13th Century side chapel now used to shelter statues and monuments suffering from severe weathering. The cathedral can only be visited on guided tours. These take place April to September daily 9.00am —5.00pm and October to March 9.00am — 4.00pm.

The nearby Albrechtsburg was erected in 1471-1485 by two brothers, the Elector Ernst and Duke Albrecht, and is one of the most complete secular buildings of that period. Between 1710 and 1864 it served as a factory for the manufacture of porcelain but it is now used for local historical and cultural exhibitions. A spiral staircase, known as the Großer Wendelstein and made out of a single stone, is its most unusual feature. Opening times are Tuesdays to Sundays 9.00am — 4.00pm.

Southwest of the cathedral stands the Kirche St Afra (Church of St Afra), dating from around 1300 and previously part of the monastery founded in Meissen in 1205. Several sections date from the 14th and 15th Centuries, although the church has been considerably altered over the years; it also contains an unusual baroque pulpit by Valentin Otte. The former Fürstenschule St Afra, a well-known school which prepared students for university and which counts the dramatist Lessing among its former students, is just opposite, although since 1953 it has been a college for agricultural production co-operatives. St Afra was, according to legend, a prostitute, martyred in Augsburg in the reign of Diocletian in about 304.

In and around the market place are a number of well-preserved buildings, including the late Gothic town hall (around 1472), the 15th Century Frauenkirche with its porcelain bells (1929), and the former Franciscan church, now the civic museum.

Perhaps the high spot of a trip to Meissen, however, is a visit to the porcelain factory. This is located on Leninstraße approximately 1.5km to the south of the town centre and can be reached on foot, taking in on the way the Monument to the Victims of Fascism on Kerstingstraße (1958), and the monument on Philipp-Müller-Straße to Samuel Hahnemann (1755-1843) who was born in Meissen and is acclaimed as the founder of homeopathy. Alternatively buses and trains (Meißen-Triebischtal station) are available. Visitors can see pottery being made in an exhibition hall, as well as displays of Meissen pottery, with its distinctive blue crossed swords emblem. Opening times are April to October Tuesdays to Sundays between 8.00am — 4.00pm (demonstrations between 8.00am — 12 noon, and 1.00pm — 3.30pm).

One of the best places to see and sample the local wine is in the Spaargebirge hills, on the east bank of the Elbe a little over 1.5km from the town centre. The area can be reached on foot or by taking a bus from the station and getting off at the Bauernhäusel stop. The 17th/18th Century building nearby, the Bauernhäusel, is an historic wine restaurant serving local wine, as well as food.

Where to stay and eat

Accommodation and food is available at the Goldener Löwe, Rathenauplatz 6 and at the Hamburger Hof, Dresdner Straße 9. Restaurants include the historical Weinstube Vincenz Richter, An der Frauenkirche; the Ratskeller on the market; Domkeller, Domplatz 9; Burgkeller, Domplatz 11; Am Burgberg, Meisastraße 1; and Meißner Hof, Lorenzgasse 7. A pleasant café is the Café Wehnert in the Theaterplatz.

Events
A wine and harvest festival is held every other September; concerts are given in the municipal museum and regular organ recitals in the cathedral.

Information
Tourist information can be obtained from Willy-Anker-Straße 32.

NOSSEN
Between Meissen and Freiberg lies Nossen, a typical small East German town. It is dominated by an imposing white palace dating from the 16th and 17th Centuries, and on the main street, has an unusual town hall with tiled turrets. The Klosterpark close to the palace was laid out in the 19th Century, and is open to the public daily, except Mondays, from April to October. From Nossen it is possible to enter the attractive valley of the river Mulde.

BAUTZEN
Bautzen (in Wendish Budysin) is the centre of Sorbian culture and politics (see p.11) in Upper Lausitz and is attractively situated on the river Spree.

In the centre of the town the Petridom (Cathedral of St Peter), a Gothic building dating from 1213-1497, has been used since the 16th Century by Catholics and Protestants alike. The catholic section contains a noteworthy high altar by G. Fossati (1722-1724). Also of interest is the Hauptmarkt (Main Market), a square with several patrician houses, a 19th Century Gewandhaus with a 15th Century cellar, the town hall, which contains an imposing staircase, and the slightly leaning Reichenturm tower.

The original walls remain around much of the town, and are particularly complete on the northern side. A walk around the walls takes in several places of interest, including in the south the Deutsch-Sorbisches Volkstheater (German-Sorbian Theatre), the only theatre in East Germany to perform regularly in two languages, and the Haus der Sorben or Serbski Dom (Sorbian House) in which the Domowina ('Homeland'), the Sorbian national political organisation, has its headquarters (Postplatz);

in the northwest the Museum für Geschichte und Kultur der
Sorben/ Serbski Muzej (Museum for Sorbian History and
Culture — open daily 9.30am — 12.30pm and 1.30pm — 4.00pm,
and until 5.00pm on Tuesdays and Thursdays; closed on the first
Monday of each month) in the Schloß Ortenburg, and the
romantic ruins of the Nikolaikirche, from which splendid views
down to the Spree and over the surrounding countryside can be
had; and in the west the Alte Wasserkunst (Old Waterworks),
built in 1588 and now the symbol of the town, and the
Michaeliskirche (Church of St Michael), the Sorbian protestant
church completed in 1498.

Where to stay and eat

The main hotel in Bautzen is the Lubin, Wendischer Graben.
Restaurants include Weißes Roß, Äußere Lauenstraße 11; Zum
Echten, Lauengraben 11; Gastmahl des Meeres, Steinstraße 19a;
Gaststätte zum Gerber, Taschenberg 2; Café Stadtwaage in the
old Gewandhaus, and Café Budysin on Reichenstraße.

Events

Various events connected with Sorbian culture take place in and
around Bautzen, including a major festival of Sorbian culture
every four years, and the Sorbian Music Days every April/May.

Information

The tourist information office is at Hauptmarkt 5.

GÖRLITZ

Görlitz (Zhorjelc in Wendish) lies on the river Neisse and is an
important border crossing into Poland. What was previously the
eastern part of Görlitz, since the signing of the Treaty
recognising the Oder-Neisse border in 1952, has been a separate
town in Poland, Zgorzelec.
  The main sights in the town are grouped around three squares.
Platz der Befreiung (Liberation Square), the southernmost, dates
mainly from the end of the 19th Century, but the Frauenkirche
is late Gothic, completed in 1486; the Centrum department store
near the church is the oldest department store still operating in
East Germany and dates from 1913.

To the north in the Demianiplatz (Demiani Square, named
after a 19th Century mayor) is the Kaisertrutz (literally
Emperor's Defiance), a large round tower dating from 1490 and
now housing a museum of civic history, and the Reichenbacher
Turm (Reichenbach Tower), started in 1376 but with later
additions, and today again a museum.

Northeast of the Demianiplatz is the Untermarkt (Lower
Market), the medieval town centre, which is still surrounded by
late Gothic, Renaissance and baroque houses, with the town hall
on the south side. Many of the houses have individual features
worth looking at, including the former Ratapotheke (dispensary)
with its double sun-dial on the north side, the Renaissance
house at no. 23, and the Brauner Hirsch (Brown Stag) on the
east side, the intellectual centre of the town in the 17th Century.
The town hall has expanded over the centuries, but the oldest
section dates from the end of the 14th Century. The steps, the
statue of Justice on a sculptured column and the portal are all
good examples of the German Renaissance building style.

Further to the north the Pfarrkirche St Peter und Paul (Parish
Church of SS Peter and Paul) was originally erected in 1423-
1497 but largely re-built after a fire at the end of the 17th
Century; the towers are also a later addition (1889-1891). The
church itself, as well as the crypt, is often cited as among the
best examples of late Gothic building in the southeast of the
country.

Where to stay and eat
Accommodation is available at the Monopol, Platz der Befreiung
9. Restaurants include the Burghof, Straße der Roten Armee 96;
Gastmahl des Meeres, Struvestraße 2; Goldener Baum,
Untermarkt 4/5.

Information
Tourist information can be obtained at Leninplatz 29.

The West

WITTENBERG

Wittenberg is indissolubly linked with the name of Martin Luther, one of the major figures of the Reformation, and in recent years has been given the formal name of Lutherstadt Wittenberg. The town first came to prominence, however, in the 15th Century after becoming the seat of the Elector of Saxony in 1422, and from 1486 under the Elector Friedrich der Weise (Frederick the Wise) the castle, castle church and Elbe bridge were constructed.

Shortly after the founding of the university in 1502 Luther came to Wittenberg as an Augustinian monk (1508) and in 1512 became professor of theology at the university. Increasingly disillusioned with many of the practices of the contemporary church, Luther decided to make a personal statement of his views and on October 31 1517 nailed 95 theses protesting, amongst other things, against the abuse of the sale of indulgences by the church, to the door of the Schloßkirche at Wittenberg. The theses, originally written in Latin, were quickly translated into German, and Luther's views found ready favour among ordinary people, tired of the Church's abuses, and among many German princes, who saw a political opportunity to rid themselves of the irksome yoke of Rome.

As the movement against Rome grew, Luther was joined in Wittenberg by many like-minded people, including Philipp Melanchthon and Lucas Cranach the Elder. Luther's increasingly explicit rejection of papal authority and the rising tide of feeling against the Pope which Luther's words were helping create led in mid 1520 to the publication of a papal bull 'against the errors of Martin Luther and his followers' and a threat to excommunicate Luther. When the threat was acted on in 1521 Luther was forced into hiding and spent some time at the Wartburg in Eisenach, before returning to Wittenberg in 1522.

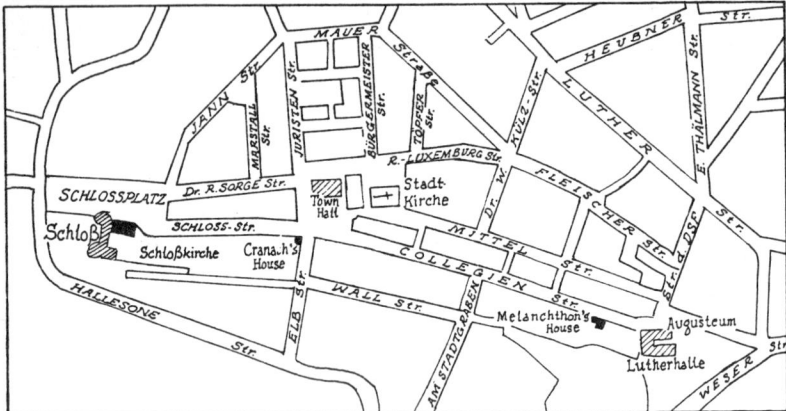

Lutherstadt WITTENBERG

0   500
m

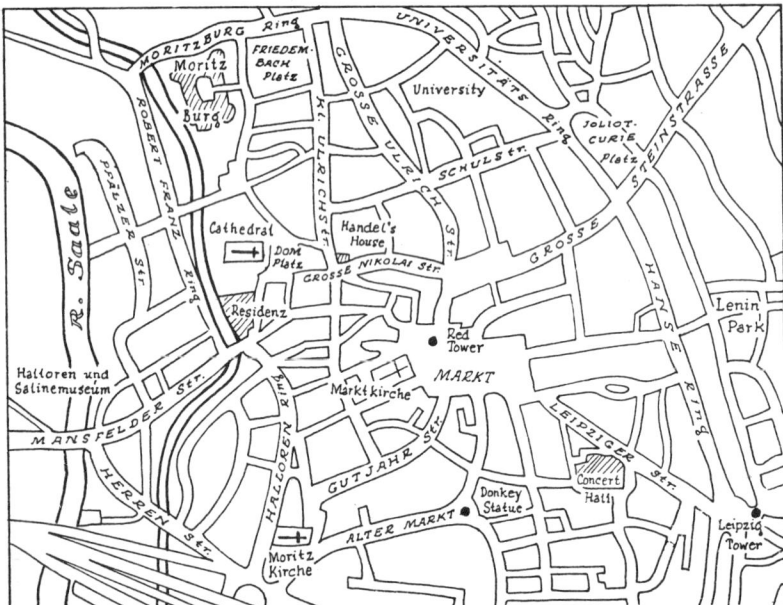

HALLE

0   200
m

Throughout the 1520s, and particularly at the time of the
Peasants' Revolt, which he firmly opposed, Luther travelled
widely, preaching his doctrine that people would be saved 'by
faith alone' rather than by the performance of good works or of
ritual acts of worship. Most of the rest of his life was, however,
spent in Wittenberg; his marriage was celebrated here in 1525
and his children brought up here.

By the middle of the 16th Century, with the death of Luther
and the removal of the Saxon residence to Dresden, Wittenberg's
influence waned. In the Seven Years' War the town was badly
damaged (1760) and in 1817 the once famous university was
combined with the larger university at Halle. Not until the
coming of the railway at the end of the 19th Century did the
town's fortunes revive, as it gradually became an important
centre for industry, including agro-chemicals and machinery.

In the steps of Luther

Much of the town's interest now lies in its various connections
with Luther. One of the more unusual sights is the Luthereiche
(Luther's Oak Tree) on the eastern edge of the old town. The
oak marks the spot where Luther burnt the papal bull on
December 10 1520, although the present tree dates only from
1830, the original one having been destroyed when Napoleon's
armies invaded in 1813.

Also in the east of the old town is the Augusteum, a building
which was used by the university in the mid-16th Century but
which was re-built to conform to the prevailing baroque fashion
in the 18th Century. Contained within the Augusteum is the
house the Augustinian monks (who settled in Wittenberg with
the founding of the university) gave to Luther as a place in
which to live and work. The house (Lutherhaus) was converted
into a museum in the second half of the 19th Century and is
now widely acknowledged as the world's most important
collection of the history of the Reformation. The museum,
known as the Staatliche Lutherhalle, includes the room where
Luther lived from 1524 with its original benches and chair, the
largest collection of Luther's work in its original editions, early
translations of the Bible into German (18 translations appeared
between 1466 and Luther's work in 1522), paintings, including
several of Luther and his parents by Cranach, and furniture
such as Luther's pulpit, which was brought here from the
Stadtkirche St Marien. Opening times are Tuesdays to Sundays
9.00am — 5.00pm (last entrance 4.00pm).

Close to the Lutherhaus, at Collegienstraße 60, the Melanchthonhaus (Melanchthon's House) also contains documents and articles relating to the Reformation. Philipp Melanchthon (1497-1560), who came to Wittenberg as a professor of Greek in 1518, was an enthusiastic supporter of Luther, though in later years with some qualifications, and a major thinker of the Reformation; he is frequently referred to as the Praeceptor Germaniae (Germany's teacher) because of his scholarly writings. The 16th Century house where he lived and died survives very much in its original condition, as do parts of the small garden belonging to it. Here stone items including a table dating from 1551 and parts of the old town wall, as well as 400 year-old yew trees and a herb and spice garden originally planted in the 16th Century, can be seen. Opening times are Mondays to Thursdays 9.00am — 5.00pm; Saturdays, Sundays and public holidays 10.00am — 12 noon and 2.00pm — 5.00pm.

The two church towers which dominate Wittenberg's skyline belong to the oldest building in the town, the Stadtkirche St Marien (Church of St. Mary), where Luther frequently preached. The double-naved choir is the only part of the original 13th Century building still standing; the distinctive octagonal towers date from much later (1558). The interior contains many notable works of art, including a triptych by Lucas Cranach the Elder, representing in the centre the eucharist and on the wings baptism and confession, and including a portrait of Melanchthon, with below a picture of Luther preaching; other paintings by Cranach the Elder and some also by Cranach the Younger, including on the wall behind the altar an elaborate allegory of the Catholic Church and the Reformed Church — Der Weinberg des Herrn; and a bronze font cast by Hermann Vischer (1457). It was in this church in 1522 that holy communion was administered for the first time in both kinds. Martin Luther married Katharina von Bora in the church on June 13 1525, and their children were baptised here.

In front of the Rathaus (town hall), a very attractive Renaissance building (1522-49), statues of Luther and of Melanchthon have been erected under Gothic canopies. Luther's statue is the work of Gottfried Schadow (1821) while Melanchthon's was completed some time later (1860) by Friedrich Drake.

Martin Luther is buried in one of the churches most closely associated with him during his lifetime, the Schloßkirche (Castle Church) which is part of the castle in the extreme west of the old town. It was to the wooden doors of this church (north side) that in October 1517 Luther nailed his 95 theses, although it will not escape visitors' attention that the 'wooden doors' are now bronze; the original doors were burnt down in the Seven Years' War (1760) and replaced in 1858 by more durable bronze ones bearing the original Latin text of the theses.

Inside the church the Reformation is commemorated by a number of statues and coats of arms. The graves of Luther, who died at Eisleben in 1546, and of Melanchthon, who died at Wittenberg in 1560, are marked by Latin inscriptions on raised plaques just in front of the pulpit, and bronze reliefs can be seen on the wall nearby. Also of interest in the church is the grave of Friedrich der Weise (1527), the Saxon prince who acted as a protector to Luther, and a font by Schinkel (1832).

Other points of interest
Wittenberg also offers a number of points of interest not connected with Luther. These include the ethnology and local history museums in the Schloß; the Kapelle zum Heiligen Leichnam (Corpus Christi Chapel), a small church next to the Stadtkirche St Marien now known as the Kinderkirche as children's services take place here, but originally the chapel for a cemetry on this site; the Cranachhaus (Schloßstraße 1), a memorial to the time Cranach the Elder lived in Wittenberg, working as a painter, court painter, mayor and owner of a dispensary (1505-1547), and the Markt (market) which contains several 16th Century houses including no. 3/4 where Cranach the Younger was born in 1515, and no. 6, the Beyer-Hof.

The streets between the market and the castle are full of plaques to notable visitors to Wittenberg, including Tsar Peter the Great, who stayed opposite the castle in 1712, Napoleon who stayed here in October 1806, and Maxim Gorky who lived in the town during 1903.

The Elbe-Elster Theater is based in a modern building close to the castle and, in addition to a traditional theatre, houses a cabaret (Brett'l Keller) and a puppet theatre. During the summer months the company — East Germany's largest travelling theatre — performs at the Musenschänke on the nearby Bergwitzsee.

Where to stay and eat
Wittenberg has two relatively basic hotels: Goldener Adler (Golden Eagle) at Markt 7, and Wittenberger Hof, at Collegienstraße 56. Restaurants include Schwarzer Bär (Black Bear) at Schloßstraße 2, Ratsschenke, Markt 14, Schloßfreiheit

at 24 Dr-Richard-Sorge-Straße, and the Schloßkeller at the castle.

Information

Tourist information is located at Collegienstraße 8.

EISLEBEN

Since 1946 known as Lutherstadt Eisleben as it is the place where Martin Luther was born and died, the town has a number of monuments connected with the reformer. The most informative of these is the Luther Geburtshaus (the house where Luther was born) at Lutherstraße 16, where exhibitions document his life and work. (Opening times: Tuesdays to Sundays 9.00am — noon and 1.00pm — 5.00pm) A little way from the marketplace at Andreaskirchplatz 7 is the Luther Sterbehaus (the house where Luther died) which is furnished as it would have been in Luther's own time, and contains several copies of Cranach paintings and a copy of Luther's deathmask. (Opening times: Tuesdays to Saturdays 9.00am — noon and 1.00pm — 5.00pm, and Sundays 11.15am — noon and 1.00pm — 5.00pm) Finally, a monument to Luther, completed in 1882 by R. Siemering, stands in front of the town hall.

   Almost opposite the Luther Sterbehaus is the Andreaskirche (St Andrew's Church), a late Gothic hall church, where Luther preached the last four sermons of his life in February 1546. The interior contains several notable works of art, including an altar triptych dating from 1500, the so-called Luther pulpit and graves of several of the counts of Mansfeld.

Other places connected with Luther in the Halle area

For anyone interested in the life of Luther and the events of the Reformation, several other towns in the Halle district will be of interest. These include **Mansfeld**, north of Eisleben, where Luther went to school between 1488-1497, and where his parents' house can still be seen; the Stadtkirche St Georgi also contains a portrait of Luther (1540) and a painting from Cranach's workshop; **Stolberg**, northeast of Nordhausen, where Luther preached at the parish church in 1522 and, in opposition to the Peasants' Revolt, in 1525; two life-size pictures of Luther and Melanchthon can be seen inside the church; and the castle at **Pretzsch**, southeast of Wittenberg, where Luther frequently

The market place, Wittenberg

Harz narrow-gauge railway

A traditional boat in the Spreewald

The cathedral and Albrechtsburg, Meissen

The Minster, Bad Doberan

stayed with his friend Hans von Löser, an influential supporter
of the Reformation.

HALBERSTADT

Often referred to as the Gateway to the Harz and famous for its
sausages, Halberstadt lies on the plain north of the Harz
mountains. Although almost completely destroyed in World War
II many of the most important buildings have been restored.
This includes notably the Dom St Stephanus (St. Stephen's
Cathedral), a Gothic building (1239 onwards) with a particularly
splendid west façade, some excellent examples of stained glass,
and a famous treasury containing tapestries, sculptures and
liturgical items. The nearby Liebfrauenkirche (Church of Our
Lady), a 12th Century basilica, is also worth a visit.

An unusual aspect of Halberstadt is the Heineanum (Domplatz
37), a museum of ornithology founded by Ferdinand Heine in
the middle of the 19th Century. Its massive collection includes
over 16,000 stuffed birds and 5,000 eggs.

Where to stay and eat
Accommodation is available at St Florian Hotel, Gerberstraße
10. Restaurants include the Jagdschloß, Spiegelberge; Haus des
Friedens, Thomas-Müntzer-Straße, and Bullerberg, Am
Bullerberg.

Information
Tourist information is available from Spiegelstraße 12.

HARZ MOUNTAINS
The Harz mountains are Germany's northernmost mountain
range and extend for an area some 90km long and 30km wide
along the western border of East Germany. Like the Thuringian
forest to the south, the Harz is a favourite holiday area and
offers a wide range of attractions from varied scenery, including
heavily forested peaks, picturesque streams, valleys and villages,
and unusual and abundant wild life, to historical sites and a
magnificent, functioning steam railway. The highest peak, the
Brocken (1142m above sea level), was for many years out-of-
bounds because of military activities, but in early 1990 all

restrictions were lifted and the climb to the top is once again a popular route.

For walkers the Harz mountains are an ideal area. Many paths are clearly marked, leading in the northern part mostly through evergreen forests and in the south through mixed deciduous and evergreen woods. Wild flowers are particularly abundant in this region, including for example lilies of the valley and woodruff, and many species are subject to nature preservation orders. In the less frequented parts the fauna is also unusually rich. The Harz is known, for example, for its wealth of insect life, its abundance of birds, including many types of owl, and animals such as elks, bison, bears, wolves, lynx, deer and, a peculiarity of this area, the mouflon — a kind of wild sheep with horns, originally found only in Corsica and Sardinia, but introduced into a few areas of central Europe.

The relatively wild nature of the Harz mountains has traditionally made them a favourite place for travel, particularly for the Romantics. Goethe travelled here in November and December 1777 and, inspired by the Brocken, wrote one of his best-known poems *Harzreise im Winter* (Journey to the Harz in Winter). Some fifty years later the poet Heinrich Heine — known outside Germany mainly as the author of many of the poems set to music by Schubert — also made an excursion through the area and wrote a cycle of poems entitled *Die Harzreise* (The Harz Journey — 1826).

One of the most picturesque parts is the Bodetal (Bode Valley), just south of the town of Thale. From Thale a chair lift leads up to the rocky cliffs known as the Roßtrappe and a cable car to the heights of the Hexentanzplatz (Witches' Dancing Floor), the setting for one of the best-known scenes in Goethe's *Faust*. To the west of Thale, still in the Bode Valley, are the remarkable caves at Rübeland. The two best known, Baumannshöhle and Hermannshöhle, named after the men who discovered them, are filled with variously shaped stalactites and stalagmites. The Baumannshöhle is even large enough to house a theatre, the Goethesaal (Goethe Room). Only a few kilometres away lies one of East Germany's major reservoirs, formed by the Rappbodetalsperre dam. The view from here is extremely good; it is also possible to hire boats.

A convenient and pleasant way of exploring the Harz is to take the Harzquerbahn, a narrow-gauge steam railway which runs from Wernigerode in the north to Nordhausen in the south, a trip of around 61km. The railway has been in use since 1899, and in summer there are special tours along the line using a veteran locomotive. The route passes through some of the most beautiful scenery in the area and stops at several spas and resorts. The Steinerne Renne station just south of Wernigerode is close to the Holtemme waterfalls.

The Harz mountains are not only rich in natural beauty, however; they also contain some of East Germany's most attractive and traditional small towns, among which Quedlinburg and Wernigerode are particularly worth a visit.

Quedlinburg

The centre of the town with its tiny winding streets and timber-framed houses has remained virtually intact since the middle ages. The oldest house, dating from the 14th Century, stands at Wordgasse 3 and is now a museum devoted to timber-framed buildings. Within the old town too is the Rathaus (town hall), a Renaissance building with a particularly attractive entrance and a stone figure of Roland on the southwest corner.

Slightly to the south, and dominating the skyline, is the Schloßberg (Castle Mountain) or Burgberg. The castle — which has an interesting interior as well as exterior — was constructed in the 16th and 17th Centuries but the Stiftskirche (Collegiate Church) attached to it is a 12th Century basilica. The crypt, which is built into the sandstone of the mountain, is said to be able to preserve bodies from decay and contains, among others, the tombs of the Saxon emperor Henry I who died in 936 and his wife Mathilda. Immediately below the castle is the Klopstockhaus, a literary museum commemorating the work of Friedrich Gottlieb Klopstock, the first of the great German classicists, who was born here in 1724.

A short walk to the southwest of the castle leads to the Klosterkirche St Wiperti (Monastery Church of St Wipertus), dating from the 10th Century but again with an older, and beautifully vaulted, crypt (840).

Wernigerode

Like Quedlinburg, Wernigerode has managed to preserve its medieval town centre, and a walk round the streets near the Marktplatz (Market Place) will uncover many interesting examples of timber-framed houses: the Waaghaus (House of Scales) next to the town hall, decorated with carnival and religious figures, the Krummelsche Haus (Krummel House) at Breite Staße 72, with rich baroque wood carving, the Kleinstes Haus (Smallest House) at Kochstraße 43, which is only 3m wide, to name but a few. The town hall itself, dating in its present

form from 1543, is one of the most attractive in the area and
perhaps the most notable example of timber-framing in
Wernigerode.

The fairy-tale castle on the wooded hill overlooking the old
town, despite appearance, dates only from 1881 and is now
called a museum of feudal history, although many of its exhibits
date from the 18th and 19th Centuries. (Opening times:
Tuesdays to Sundays 9.00am to 5.30pm — last entrance 4.30pm)

Excursions from Wernigerode include the narrow-gauge
railway (see p.172), the Steinerne Renne, and the Ottofelsen
(Otto Rocks) which are climbed by means of metal ladders and
which offer a spectacular view from the top.

Other towns in the Harz
Also worth visiting if time permits are Querfurt (the castle is
one of the largest and oldest in East Germany), Stolberg (a
medieval town with 15th Century town hall), Aschersleben
(well-preserved medieval town wall) and the old towns of
Nordhausen, the home of one of East Germany's most important
distilleries, and Blankenburg.

Where to stay
The Harz area has a wide choice of accommodation, including
Quedlingburger Hof (Leninstraße 1), Zum Bär (Markt 8) and
the Motel (Wipertistraße) in Quedlinburg; Weisser Hirsch (Markt
5) and Zur Post (Marktstraße 17) in Wernigerode; Handelshof
(Karl-Marx-Straße 12) in Nordhausen; and the Kurhotel
(Mauerstraße 9) in Blankenburg.

Where to eat
Quedlinburg: Am Münzenberg, Weststraße 11-13; Schloßkrug,
Schloßberg 1; Magdeburger Hof, Magdeburger Straße 1.

Wernigerode: Ratskeller, Markt 1; Gothisches Haus, Markt 2;
Wernigeröder Krug, Breite Straße 15; Zum Nico, Nicolaiplatz.

Nordhausen: Stadtterrasse, Rautenstraße; Stadtparkrestaurant,
Wilhelm-Pieck-Straße; Alte Mühle, Darrweg.

KYFFHÄUSER
South of the Harz mountains is a small range of hills, only 19km
west to east, known as the Kyffhäuser. On the peak is a ruined

castle, once occupied by the Hohenstaufen. According to folklore, the Emperor Frederick Barbarossa still sleeps below the castle, ready to burst out and bring better times to Germany. Near the castle is a huge monument, erected at the end of the 19th Century and incorporating a statue of the Emperor Barbarossa, from which there is a fine view over the surrounding countryside.

MERSEBURG

The town of Merseburg, between Halle and Leipzig, prettily situated at the point where the Geisel meets the Saale, is worth visiting for its cathedral and castle. The cathedral was originally commenced in 1015 but much of what remains today is 16th Century. Particularly noteworthy are the late Gothic pulpit, the 12th Century font, the baroque altar and many of the tombs. The cathedral archives contain a rich collection of medieval manuscripts, including an illuminated Bible from around 1200 and the so-called Merseburger Zaubersprüche (Merseburg Spells).

Although the castle (15th — 17th Century) is now used for administration, it houses a museum of local history in the east wing, and has a very attractive garden, including an orangery.

HALLE (map p.166)

Halle has been an important centre for over a thousand years, rising first to prominence because of its salt-works (in fact the name is derived from halla, an indo-germanic word for salt), later because of its strong academic tradition and more recently through industries such as agricultural machinery and chemicals. Although not as badly destroyed as many German towns, Halle nevertheless suffered significant damage during World War II and was later rebuilt partly in the traditional style and partly as an example of socialist construction.

The clearest example of the new style is the Thälmannplatz (Thälmann Square) near the main railway station, which in addition to the Hotel Stadt Halle and a complex traffic system includes a monument to the revolutionary working class movement.

The old town to the northwest of Thälmannplatz contains many sights of interest. In the large market place stands a monument to Georg Friedrich Händel, who was born in Halle in 1685 and later studied law at the university here (1702-1703) while working at the same time as organist at the cathedral. The statue was erected in 1859 by the composer's admirers in England as well as Germany. On the west side of the market place is the Marktkirche St Marien (Market Church of St Mary), a late Gothic hall church with four towers dating from around 1529. It was here that Martin Luther's body lay in state on the way from Eisleben to Wittenberg; a deathmask and impressions of his hands were taken, and remain in the possession of the church. Opening times are currently restricted to 4.00pm — 5.00pm Mondays to Saturdays; organ recitals take place at 4.30pm on Tuesdays. In front of the church is an unusual Roter Turm (Red Tower) which has acted since the 15th Century as a free-standing bell-tower, but which has been marred by the recent addition of a metal gallery at first floor level, used for art exhibitions. The stone statue of Roland on the east side of the tower is a 1719 copy of an earlier wooden statue, and here, as elsewhere in central Germany, was originally a symbol of the freedom and strength of the burghers of the town.

At the end of the Alter Markt, the oldest part of the town, a fountain surmounted by a statue of *Der Esel, der auf Rosen geht* (The Donkey walking on Roses) can be seen. Although this particular fountain is less than a hundred years old, the image of the boy and donkey has been used as a symbol of Halle for many centuries. The story goes back to a time when the people of Halle decided to greet a visiting prince by spreading the ground inside the town gate with roses. In the event the prince entered by a different gate and a miller and his donkey had the benefit of the roses. It is also worth walking to the other end of the Alter Markt to see the Moritzkirche (Church of St Maurice), constructed between 1388 and 1511. The tower was built into the remains of the old town wall and the interior contains sculptures by Konrad von Einbeck.

Northwest of the market place at Große Nikolaistraße 5 is the Händelhaus (Handel's house), where the composer was born and which is now a museum with over 500 musical instruments spanning the last five centuries. The house is open Tuesdays, Wednesdays, Fridays and Saturdays from 9.00am — 5.30pm and Thursdays 9.30am — 7.00pm. It is possible to accompany a tour of the exhibition of Handel's life and works with a free taped voice/musical commentary in English.

The only early Gothic building in Halle, the Dom (Cathedral), is now part of a complex including the Neue Residenz, and has been taken over by various departments of the university

(Martin-Luther-Universität). Particularly attractive features of the cathedral are the larger than life-size figures on the pillars inside. North of the cathedral and surrounded on three sides by cemetries is the 15th Century Moritzburg, which was erected by the archbishops of Magdeburg as a defence against the people of Halle, who tried for many years to free themselves from the archbishops' domination but only succeeded in 1541 in the wake of the Reformation. The castle is now a museum and houses a collection of 19th and 20th Century German paintings. Opening times are Wednesdays to Sundays 2.00pm — 6.00pm and Tuesdays 2.00pm — 9.00pm.

The Halloren- und Salinemuseum, an attractive half-timbered building in a generally run-down area, lies to the west of the old town and across the Schieferbrücke on an island in the river Saale. The museum is on the site of the former salt works and shows the history of the industry up to 1964 when the works became unprofitable and were closed. Opening times: Tuesdays to Sundays 10.00am — 4.00pm.

In the extreme north of the town the Burg Giebichenstein (Giebichenstein castle) has been preserved as a picturesque ruin on the banks of the Saale. The original 10th Century building, lived in for many years by the archbishops of Magdeburg, was destoyed in the Thirty Years' War and never fully restored.

Where to stay and eat
Halle has an Interhotel, Stadt Halle (Thälmannplatz 17); accommodation is also available at the Rotes Roß in the Leipziger Straße.

Restaurants include the Ratsgaststätte at Marktplatz 2; Am Leipzigerturm, Waisenhausring 16; Am Reileck, Reilstraße 132; Tallinn, Rigaer Straße; Panorama, Große Ulrichstraße 6-8; Gaststätte zum Roland, Marktplatz, restaurant and bar Mönchshof, Talamtstraße 5-9 and Bechershof restaurant in Schmeerstraße.

Events
Halle has a strong musical tradition, and concerts are regularly held in a converted church, the Konzerthalle am Boulevard (Leipziger Straße/Kleine Brauhausstraße), and in the small (127 seater) concert hall in the Handel House. A Handel Festival is held in Halle every year in the first half of June.

Other events include a lantern festival on the last weekend in August, the Halle Bazaar in October, and a festival in the Pestalozzi park every September.

Information
Tourist information is available at Kleinschmieden 6.

DESSAU
For anyone interested in 20th Century architecture a visit to Dessau is a must. It is here that Walter Gropius's Bauhaus was constructed in 1925-1926 and here too that the Bauhaus-Siedlung (Bauhaus Settlement — 1926-1928) at Dessau-Törten can be seen. With the exception of the Bauhaus and of the Georgium and Mosigkau palaces, however, the town retains little of its pre-war attraction.

The Bauhaus was formed in 1916 by the fusion of two existing Weimar institutions: the well-established Academy of Fine Arts and the School of Applied Arts founded in 1906. Under the direction of Walter Gropius the school aimed to create a new style of architecture and design that would unite aesthetic sensibility and utilitarian demands. In the increasingly troubled Twenties, criticism of the school by influential citizens in Weimar became intolerable, and in 1925, encouraged by the mayor of Dessau who showed sympathy for Bauhaus aims, Gropius and his school moved north to Dessau.

In designing the new school, Gropius strove to create a modern building which would synthesise the philosophy of the school. The new Bauhaus which emerged from his designs is remarkable for its 1400m² glass façade, its Bauhaus-Brücke (bridge) at the entrance and its overall unity of design, based on a series of rectangular volumes of various sizes linked by intermediary oblongs. Interesting internal features include the window-opening mechanisms, the lighting and, in the theatre, the original seating.

Not surprisingly the building was considered revolutionary at the time, and although it was used as a college for some years it was forced to close in 1933, largely as a result of Nazi criticism of art considered un-German. In 1977 the Bauhaus opened again as a cultural centre for the town, and today contains exhibition halls and a theatre. The Bauhaus is open to visitors Wednesdays to Fridays 10.00am — 5.00pm and Saturdays and Sundays 10.00am — 12.30pm and 2.00pm — 5.00pm.

The Bauhaus-Siedlung in Dessau-Törten south of the centre of the town was an attempt by Walter Gropius to create buildings adapted to the mechanised world of the 20th Century while at the same time making use of the increasing strength of new materials, such as steel, concrete and glass, and new engineering techniques. The 316 villas on the site therefore include many innovations. The Stahlhaus (Steel House), for example, is built on steel supports and has an exterior covered with steel sheeting.

Other Bauhaus buildings in Dessau include the almost circular Arbeitsamt on the corner of August-Bebel-Straße and Willy-Lohmann-Straße, several houses where the Bauhaus teachers lived, close to the school on Ebert-Allee, and the Kornhaus on the river Elbe.

In contrast, the Georgengarten (1780), is a well-preserved example of classical garden design. The palace in the grounds, dating from the same period, houses a good collection of Dutch, Flemish and German paintings, including works by Cranach the Elder, Albrecht Dürer and Tischbein. The house is open Tuesdays to Sundays 10.00am — 6.00pm, and has a pleasant café.

Around 9km southwest of the town centre is Schloß Mosigkau, a late baroque palace, now a museum of furniture, porcelain and paintings. The extensive park contains many rare plants, a maze and an oriental tea house. Every summer exhibitions are held in the orangery.

Where to stay and eat
Accommodation is available at the Stadt Dessau, Wilhelm-Pieck-Straße 35. Restaurants include the Ratskeller (Am Markt 1), Restaurant am Museum, Wilhelm-Pieck-Straße 90, and Jägerklause, Alte Leipziger Straße 76.

WÖRLITZ
The Wörlitzer Park, about 10km east of Dessau, was the first English-style park in Germany (1765-1810). Its lakes, woods, open land and monuments cover an extensive area, and require a good half day to explore thoroughly. At the centre of the park is the Wörlitzer See (lake) and this leads via a series of canals into other smaller lakes. Most of the grounds consist of parkland, but there are also some flower gardens, including the Roseninsel (Rose Island), reached by ferry, which has a large collection of different types of roses.

Among the many buildings in the park, of particular interest may be: Schloß Wörlitz (Wörlitz Palace — 1769-1773), which is an imitation of Claremont Castle in England and which now houses a collection of porcelain and glass; the Gotisches Haus (1773-1813) in which a collection of Dutch painting can be seen; the Villa Hamilton (1791-1794), named after the English archaeologist Sir William Hamilton; the Venus Temple, the statue to the French philosopher Jean-Jacques Rousseau on the Rousseau-Insel (Island) and the Eiserne Brücke (Iron Bridge) based on the iron bridge over the river Severn at Coalbrookdale in England. Most of the buildings are open only between April and October.

TORGAU

Southeast of Wittenberg, and still on the Elbe, lies Torgau, once a residence of the electors of Saxony. The most remarkable building in the town is Schloß Hartenfels (Hartenfels palace), an early Renaissance palace (1483-1622) which has survived intact in its original condition. The spiral staircase in the courtyard is one of the major works of Conrad Krebs (1523-1534).

The town centre contains several buildings of interest, including a number of burgher houses, and the Marienkirche (St Mary's Church), in which Katharina von Bora, Luther's wife, is buried.

KÖTHEN

To the southwest of Dessau, the town of Köthen, once a residence of the princes of Anhalt-Köthen, has a pleasant town centre with several patrician houses, a 15th Century church, a Renaissance palace and a neo-Renaissance town hall. It is most frequently visited, however, because of its connections with J.S. Bach, who worked at the royal court between 1717 and 1723. Two small museums dedicated to Bach can be visited; one in the Ludwigsbau section of the palace, and one in the historical museum in Museumgasse.

BERNBURG

Like Köthen, Bernburg was for many years a royal residence, this time for the princes of Anhalt-Bernburg. The Renaissance palace on the banks of the river Saale is particularly attractive. Also of note are several patrician houses on Thälmannplatz and on Breite Straße, the relatively complete town walls, and a number of churches, including the 13th Century Pfarrkirche St Marien (Parish Church of St Mary).

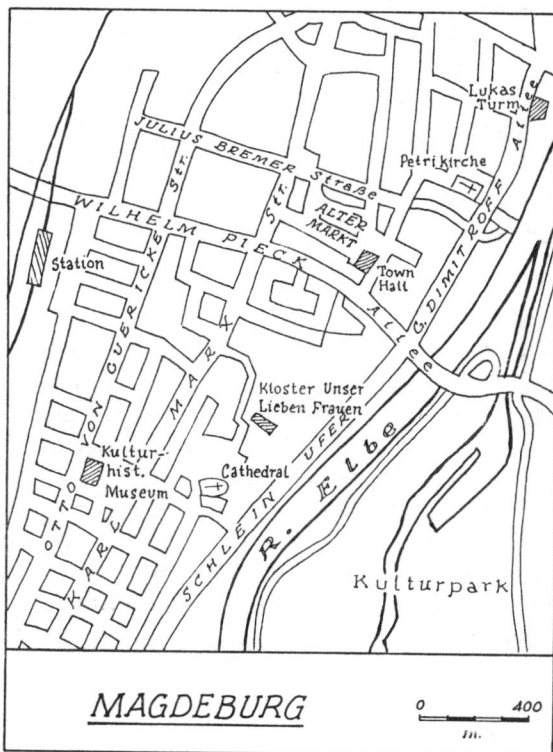

MAGDEBURG

MAGDEBURG

Despite being almost totally destroyed in the Thirty Years' War and again 90% reduced to rubble by bombing in World War II, Magdeburg is today a thriving industrial and cultural centre and capital of the Magdeburg region. Although the outskirts are completely modern, some of the centre, including some of the most notable pre-1945 buildings, have been restored with great attention to historical authenticity. Despite this work, the centre retains a rather desolate impression, fostered by large open spaces.

For many people Magdeburg means only one thing: the Magdeburg hemispheres, two hollow hemispheres developed by Otto von Guericke to illustrate the effects of air pressure and vacuum. As well as being a scientist Guericke (1602-1686) was also mayor of Magdeburg and represented the town at the

Osnabrück Peace Congress at the end of the Thirty Years' War.
He is commemorated in Magdeburg by a statue near the town
hall and by exhibits in the Kulturhistorisches Museum situated
on the street named after him, Otto-von-Guericke-Straße 68-
73 (previously the Kaiserstraße). Several of the exhibits,
including Guericke's air thermometer and various electrical
experiments, can be activated by visitors. The museum also
contains a monoplane and other items connected with Hans
Grade, a pioneer aviator who flew in Magdeburg for 13 minutes
in 1909. Opening times are Tuesdays to Sundays 10.00am —
6.00pm.

During the middle ages Magdeburg was divided into two
halves, one the domain of the clergy and the other of the
merchants. Despite considerable changes, this division can still
be observed: the area southeast of the station contains the two
major ecclesiastical buildings, the Dom (cathedral) and the
Kloster Unser Lieben Frauen (Monastery of Our Lady), while
northeast of the station are the market and town hall.

The Dom St Mauritius und Katharina (Cathedral of SS.
Maurice and Catherine), founded in 1209, is the earliest Gothic
church in Germany. While its external appearance is simple, its
interior contains many details of interest, including alabaster
figures of St Maurice and of the risen Christ (1467), a 16th
Century pulpit and Gothic pews which date from around 1340.
Also of note is Ernst Barlach's memorial to those who died in
World War I. Originally placed in the cathedral in 1929, it was
removed by the National Socialists in 1933 because of its
pacifist message but was re-instated in 1956. The cathedral is
open Mondays to Saturdays 10.00am — noon and 2.00pm —
4.00pm, and Sundays 2.00pm — 4.00pm.

The large Domplatz (Cathedral Square) contains several
attractive baroque buildings, but has one side of modern flats
completely out of character with the rest of the square.

Several monuments near the cathedral are further reminders
of the earlier Magdeburg. These include the medieval fountain
in the otherwise largely re-built and modern Karl-Marx-
Straße, and the 'Kiek in de Köken' watchtower on the
embankment between the cathedral and the river Elbe, although
this is a copy rather than the original.

Just north of the cathedral stands the Kloster Unser Lieben
Frauen. The Klosterkirche (Monastery church), built between
1064 and 1230, has been re-named the Georg Philipp Telemann
Concert Hall, after the prolific composer who during his lifetime overshadowed Bach and who was born in Magdeburg in
1681. As well as the concert hall, the building houses a museum

of sculpture, and many sculptures can also be seen in the grounds around the Kloster. The museum and concert hall can be visited Tuesdays to Sundays 10.00am — 6.00pm. The Alter Markt (Old Market) was the centre of the medieval merchants' quarter and has been pleasantly restored. On the east side the baroque Rathaus (town hall, 1691-98) dominates the square, and in front of it stands a copy, protected by an elaborate canopy, of the Magdeburger Reiter (Magdeburg Horseman), probably depicting Otto the Great, dating from around 1240 and thought to be the earliest (post-classical) free-standing equestrian statue in Germany. The original can be seen in the Kulturhistorisches Museum. Also of note in the square is the Weinkeller Buttergasse (Butter Alley wine cellar). Thought to date from the 12/13th Century but only rediscovered as recently as 1947, the cellar was used in the middle ages as a meeting place, probably for the tanners' guild, and is now restored with its original pillars and vaults.

On the east bank of the Elbe, the extensive Kulturpark Rotehorn has been developed as a recreation centre. There is also a pleasant 3km walk along the embankment from the Lukasturm (Luke Tower) in the north, where a good view of the town can be had, to the Park der Jungen Pioniere (Young Pioneers' Park) in the south, the first public park in Germany, laid out in 1824 by Peter Joseph Lenné and containing many tropical and sub-tropical plants. Excursions on the Elbe by Weiße Flotte pleasure boats are also possible (departures from the Promenade der Völkerfreundschaft near the end of Julius-Bremer-Straße).

Where to stay and eat

Magdeburg has an Interhotel, called the International, at Otto-von-Guericke-Straße 87. Restaurants include Stadt Prag, Karl-Marx-Straße 20; Donezk, Hegelstraße 42; Bördegrill, Leiterstraße 3a; Postkutsche, Leiterstraße 6; several restaurants on the Alter Markt, including the Ratskeller, the Bötelstube, and the Weinkeller Buttergasse; and near the cathedral the Café am Dom at the corner of Danz-Straße and Leibniz-Straße.

Events

The Telemann Festival is held in Magdeburg every three years (1990, 1993 etc); for a week in March a series of concerts is held in various venues across the town.

Information
Tourist information is available at Alter Markt 9.

TANGERMÜNDE

About 50km north of Magdeburg, Tangermünde is a small and pleasant town well-known for its connections with the Emperor Karl IV in the 14th Century. In the middle of the century, Tangermünde became the second centre, along with Prague, of the Holy Roman Empire of the German nation, and between 1373-1378 it temporarily became its capital. The affluence of the town at this time is reflected in a number of buildings, including the Pfarrkirche St Stephan, the town wall and the late Gothic town hall.

The Pfarrkirche (Parish Church of St Stephen) is a late Gothic brick building, begun in 1376 but not completed until the beginning of the 16th Century. It stands near the town hall (around 1430) with its imposingly tall façade and richly decorated gables. A large number of timber-framed houses still stand in the two principal streets, the Kirchstraße and the Leninstraße, although most of them date from after a fire in the 17th Century.

Tangermünde also has one of the most complete town walls in Germany. Much of the wall, including timber-framed houses built in to it and formerly used, if necessary, for defence, dates back to about 1300. Three town gates have also been preserved: the Wassertor (Water Gate — 1470), the Neustädter Tor (1450) and the Hühnerdorfer Torturm (15th Century).

In the area surrounding Tangermünde are two notable buildings: the Klosterkirche (Monastery Church) at Jerichow, 9km southeast of the town, and the Mariendom cathedral at Havelberg 38km north. The Klosterkirche is a 12th Century building famous for its crypt with decorated limestone pillars, while the cathedral dates from the late 13th Century and contains fine Gothic stained glass and a number of attractive statues and reliefs.

STENDAL

Close by too is the town of Stendal, known now mainly for its industry and nuclear power station. In the old town, however, is a notable 14th Century townhall, the Dom St Nikolai (St Nicholas' Cathedral), a late Gothic hall church, and a museum

to Winckelmann (Winckelmannstraße 36), the founder of
modern art criticism, who was born here. It was in admiration
of Winckelmann that the French novelist Henri Beyle took on
the name of Stendhal (the contemporary spelling of the town's
name).

BRANDENBURG

Brandenburg is now a large industrial town on the Havel about
50km southwest of Berlin, but in its town centre preserves some
notable buildings from the time when it was capital of the Mark
Brandenburg region. Although the town was originally a Slav
settlement, it was conquered and then lost several times by
Germanic forces throughout the period from the 10th to the
12th Centuries. In the 1150s it finally fell into the hands of
Albert the Bear, Count of Ascania, who took on the name of
Margrave of Brandenburg and began to develop the town as a
major administrative and trading centre for the whole area.
Under the Hohenzollern Brandenburg declined in importance,
as power passed to the state of Prussia and the city of Berlin.

Despite its rich history, Brandenburg has been widely known
for only one thing: Bach's Brandenburg Concertos. In view of
the story surrounding them, this is ironic. Bach wrote the six
concertos at Köthen in 1717 and dedicated them to Prince
Christian Ludwig, Margrave of the then Prussian province of
Brandenburg, who had asked the little known Bach to compose
some music for his court orchestra. There are no records as to
whether the works were appreciated, or even paid for. On the
death of the prince, his collection of musical scores was sold,
including, in a miscellaneous lot, the Brandenburg Concertos.
The scores were apparently in such good condition that it is
doubtful whether they had ever been played!

A tour of the town could begin on the Dominsel (Cathedral
Island), one of the three islands on which Brandenburg was
originally constructed. Work on the Dom St Peter und Paul
(Cathedral of SS Peter and Paul) began in 1165, shortly after
Albert's victory. Its 13th Century stained glass, a Bohemian altar
and many decorated tombs of local bishops and dignitaries are
all worth seeing. In the crypt a memorial to Christians murdered
in World War II was erected in 1953.

The old town lies to the west of the cathedral on the banks of
the Havel. Here the Altstädtisches Rathaus (Old Town Hall), a
15th Century brick building, is perhaps the highlight. The large
5m high statue of Roland (1474) has stood in front of the town

hall only since 1945; before then it was in Neustadt where it stood in front of the town hall, a building that was destroyed in the final year of World War II.

Other buildings of interest in the old town are the Pfarrkirche St Gotthart (Parish Church of St Gotthart) just north of the town hall, a late Gothic brick church containing wooden Gothic figures and a Renaissance altar; remains of the medieval town wall, including four original towers; and the municipal museum (Hauptstraße 96), a baroque building with an impressive hall and staircase.

The centre of the so-called new town, south of the Dominsel, is dominated by the Pfarrkirche St Katharinen (Parish Church of St Catherine). This three-naved hall church was built between 1395-1401 and has particularly attractive gables and other external decorations.

From Brandenburg it is possible to go for boat excursions on the Havel. A trip to the Kloster Lehnin, 20km southeast of Brandenburg, is also worthwhile. This monastery, founded in 1180, was the first Cistercian settlement in the Mark. The church (1190-1260) is often cited as one of the oldest and best examples of ecclesiastical brick building in Germany. Several parts of the monastery itself are also still intact.

The Bauhaus, Dessau

The East

SPREEWALD

The area known as the Spreewald lies around 100km southeast of Berlin and 100km north of Dresden and is a very popular holiday destination for those who appreciate the charm of lowland landscapes. Between Cottbus and Lübben the river Spree, which has its source in the mountains in Lausitz, divides into hundreds of tributaries. In the Oberspreewald (Upper Spreewald) the tree-lined rivers are surrounded by fields and market gardens growing vegetables and fruit, while in the Unterspreewald (Lower Spreewald) open land, marshes and deciduous trees extend between the many rivers and streams. Although the nature of the land originally made settlement difficult, the Sorbs (see p.11) gradually founded villages such as Naundorf, Leipe and Lehde, some of the land was cultivated, and the unusual flat wooden boats, still used today, were developed. This is the homeland of many Sorbs, and it is still sometimes possible to see women wearing traditional dress, although young women tend to wear it only on special ceremonial occasions.

The most popular way of seeing the Spreewald is by boat from Lübbenau. Trips of various lengths leave from the harbour on Maxim-Gorki-Straße and the boats, mostly propelled, like punts, by a boatman with a pole, glide silently through the countryside. The season extends from May to September, and boats leave the harbour between 9.00am and 1.00pm, although it is possible to arrange special trips outside this period. Local trips last 1 to 1½ hours and longer tours of the area 6 to 8 hours. Local trips and longer trips to the Oberspree (Lehde, Wotschofska and Leipe) and the Unterspree (Schlepzig, Petkamsberg and Groß Wasserburg) also start from near the Strandcafé (Beach Café) on Heinrich-Heine-Straße in Lübben.

The landing stages and the surrounding cafés and restaurants can become very crowded on summer weekends and if possible visits at peak boating times should be avoided. The scene described by the writer Theodor Fontane on a visit to Lübbenau over a hundred years ago can at such times be difficult to imagine: 'It was a Sunday and the tranquillity we found there gave no indication of the busy goings-on that prevail on other days. After a short walk through the town and its park we reached the main course of the river Spree where a gondola, reserved for us, was lying in the shade of a grove of beech trees...'

LÜBBENAU

In Lübbenau (Lubnjow in Wendish) the Spreewaldmuseum (open May to October 9.00am — 5.00pm, closed Tuesdays), formerly a courthouse (built 1745-1748), contains an interesting collection of items relating to the history of the Spreewald as well as local traditional costumes. Another museum has been opened in the nearby village of Lehde, the Spreewald-Freilandmuseum (Outdoor Museum — open May to October 9.00am — 5.00pm, closed Mondays), where visitors can go round a large number of farm buildings, furnished inside as well as in good external condition, showing the daily life of Wendish farmers in the 19th Century.

Lübbenau is a good centre for walking, as well as for boat trips. From the harbour on Maxim-Gorki-Straße it is possible to follow a well-marked footpath to Leipe, some 5km to the southeast, and, like Lehde, a typical Spreewald village. Another walk from Lübbenau starts from the Spreeschlößchen (Spree Castle) inn and leads, an hour or so later, to the Wotschowska inn, and involves crossing 15 bridges on the way. In the parkland round the palace a nature trail 1.5km in length has been set out.

The town itself has been well preserved. The main street, Ehm-Welk-Straße, contains many Renaissance and timber-framed houses. Beyond the Topfmarkt at the end of the main street stands a gatehouse, now used as a court house; under the archway a whale's jawbone can be seen, a gift sent to the town from Hamburg by a merchant, Morzan, who was born in Lübbenau in the 18th Century.

LÜBBEN

Lübben (Lubin in Wendish), like Lübbenau, is a good centre for excursions into the surrounding Spreewald. In the town itself parts of the old town fortifications remain, as well as a castle built in late Renaissance style. An attractive boulevard with a traditional milestone leads from the main street to parkland with walks by the river. Although not as popular as the Oberspreeland, the Unterspreeland which lies north of Lübben contains many picturesque areas and attractive villages such as Schlepzig and Petkamsberg.

COTTBUS

Cottbus (Chosebuz in Wendish) lies on the river Spree south of the Spreewald, and visitors can begin excursions by land and water from here. The town itself grew to prominence thanks to clothmaking, and textiles remain an important industry today, although the coal and energy industries now account for most employment. A few traces of the medieval fortifications remain and the town centre contains some pleasant buildings. The Altmarkt/Stare Wiki (Old Market) still has many baroque and classical houses: nos. 21, 22 and the Löwenapotheke (Lion Dispensary) are particularly attractive. The Oberkirche, east of the Altmarkt, a large brick church, has a spectacular altar by Andreas Schulze (1680) depicting Jonah being swallowed by a large green whale, and an attractive pulpit taken from the Klosterkirche at Frankfurt an der Oder when it was converted into a concert hall. It is possible to go up the tower and obtain a good view of the town and surrounding countryside. The Schloßkirche (Castle Church) to the south, built by the Huguenots between 1707-1714 and the Wendische Kirche, north of the Altmarkt, where services are traditionally held in Wendish, are worth seeing too. Also of note is the Stadttheater (Civic Theatre) on the Schillerplatz, built in Jugendstil by Bernhard Sehring in 1908 and re-opened in 1986 after five years' of reconstuction work.

At the edge of the town the Branitzer Park and the Schloß Branitz, a baroque building now housing a local museum which includes a collection of drawings by the Cottbus artist Carl Blechen (1798-1840), make a pleasant trip. The park in particular is regarded as an exceptional example of German landscape gardening; it includes two pyramids and the tomb of Prince Pückler-Muskau who designed the park during the 1840s.

Where to stay and eat

Accommodation is available at the Lausitz Hotel on Berliner
Platz. Many restaurants, cafés and drinking places can be found
on the Altmarkt, including Lipa restaurant (8), Erich's Bierhaus,
which dates from 1737 (18), Haus des Handwerks (17), a café
and cellar bar (10) and a Weinstube (22). Other restaurants
include Zur Sonne, Taubenstraße 7; Stadt Cottbus, Spremberger
Straße 29/30; Postkutsche on Schloßkirchplatz 1, and Stulle
Skibka on Oberkirchplatz for fast food, snacks and breakfast.

Information

Tourist information office: Altmarkt 29

FRANKFURT AN DER ODER

Like its West German namesake, Frankfurt-am-Main, Frankfurt
an der Oder was largely destroyed during World War II. The
centre has, however, been restored with attention to historical
considerations and has several buildings of note, although within
East Germany itself it is primarily known as an industrial town
(semi-conductors and metal work) and as a border crossing into
Poland.

The brick town hall in the former market place is a striking
example of North German Gothic style. The emblem consisting
of an oblique iron rod supported by a short one which can be
seen on the south gable was used as a symbol by the Hanseatic
League, to which Frankfurt belonged from the mid-14th
Century. The town hall contains the Galerie Junge Kunst
(Gallery of Modern Art) which houses a collection of almost
6,000 contemporary paintings, drawings and sculptures.

Between the town hall and the river Oder in the Faberstraße
is the Kleist Forschungs- und Gedenkstätte (Kleist Memorial
and Research Centre), dedicated to the life and work of
Heinrich von Kleist (1777-1811), the writer of plays such as *Der
zerbrochene Krug* (The Broken Jug), and stories including *Die
Marquise von O*. Kleist committed suicide in a pact with his
mistress on the banks of the Wannsee near Potsdam at the early
age of 34, but was born in Frankfurt. A bronze statue to Kleist
stands in the former cemetry of the Gertraudenkirche (Church
of St Gertraud) near Gertraudenplatz.

Also worth a visit is the former Franciscan Monastery, which
has functioned for the past 20 years or so as a concert hall. The
interior retains its attractive ceiling vaulting and is widely

acclaimed as producing excellent acoustics. Outside, do not miss the Gothic tracery on the west gable.

Where to stay and eat
Accommodation is available at the Stadt Frankfurt Hotel, Karl-Marx-Straße 193. Restaurants include Witebsk, Karl-Marx-Straße 169; Polonia, Wilhelm-Pieck-Straße 296; and Gastmahl des Meeres, Kleine Oderstraße.

Information
Frankfurt Information is located at Karl-Marx-Straße 8a.

MÄRKISCHE SCHWEIZ
Between Frankfurt and Berlin lies a small area known as Märkische Schweiz, a favourite area for weekend trips from Berlin and Frankfurt. The wooded hills and valleys are ideal for walking, and the town of Buckow, close to the Schermützelsee, is a good centre for exploration. Visitors can hire boats on the lake and call at the Brecht-Weigel-Haus (Brecht-Weigel House), a memorial to the writer and his actress wife; Brecht named a cycle of poems, completed in 1953, after the town, *Buckower Elegien* (Buckow Elegies).

EBERSWALDE-FINOW
The towns of Eberswalde and Finow, were brought together for administrative purposes in 1970, and are important primarily as modern industrial and forestry centres, although some older buildings, including remains of the town walls and some timber-framed houses, still stand. It is the monastery at **Chorin**, just north of Eberswalde-Finow, however, that makes the town such an attraction for tourists.

Cistercian monks first founded a monastery nearby in 1258, but moved to the present site next to the Amtssee (lake) in 1273. During the Thirty Years' War the monastery was plundered several times and finally burnt down, but at the beginning of the 19th Century Schinkel began extensive restoration work, and the ruins gradually became a popular place for excursions. Writing in 1863, Theodor Fontane described the strong impression Chorin made on him: 'He who wanders along this path in the twilight and suddenly sees emerging among the poplars, half fairytale-like, half ghostly, this splendid, still and isolated building has been granted the best impression that these ruins, which are scarcely even ruins, have to offer. The poetry of the place envelops him in a romantic dream, before the barren desolation of the interior has had time to destroy the magic created by the fleeting encounter'.

The monastery ranks among the very best examples of Gothic stone building in North Germany. The beautifully restored details of the brickwork and the imposing height for example of the west side, added to the picturesque setting among trees at the lake side, still make a visit to Chorin a truly memorable experience.

Since 1963 various cultural activities have taken place in the monastery, including concerts given by the Berlin Symphony Orchestra and others as part of the Chorin Music Festival held between June and August every year.

About 11km southeast of Chorin at Niederfinkow a completely different experience awaits. For several hundred years, the difference in water levels between the rivers Havel and Oder had been a problem for traders in the area. A series of 17 locks built on the Finow Canal in the 18th Century was not fully satisfactory; nor was a large-scale lock in four stages built on the Oder-Havel Canal between 1906-1914. Finally, therefore, between 1927 and 1934 a large construction to lift boats down the 34m difference in levels was built close by, connected to the Oder-Havel canal by a 157m canal bridge. The lift is still in active use, but has also become a popular attraction as an engineering feat.

To the west of Chorin the Werbellinsee, an 11km long lake, bordered on the west by the Schorfheide (heathland), also attracts visitors interested in outdoor pursuits. The Schorfheide has been a home for deer and various types of game for many centuries, and has consequently been a favourite hunting ground.

The North

THE BALTIC COAST

The Baltic Sea (known in German as the Ostsee — East Sea) runs the full length of East Germany's 340km northern coast, and its varied landscape, which alternates between flat dune land and steep chalky cliffs, has made it a popular tourist area; every year over four million holiday makers, in addition to day-trippers, come to one of the coast's many resorts. Particularly popular are Bad Doberan, an inland resort close to Rostock and famous for its mud baths, the Fischland-Darß-Zingst, a conservation area northwest of Rostock, the towns of Warnemünde, Stralsund, Wismar and Greifswald, and, above all, the islands of Rügen and Usedom.

ROSTOCK

Rostock, the largest town in the north, lies a little way inland from the coast along the river Warnow. Although a major trading centre in the Hanseatic League, Rostock lost importance following the League's demise after the Thirty Years' War and only sprang to prominence again much later when it began to develop as an industrial and international shipping centre. Up to 40% of Rostock was destroyed in bombing raids, but both the old town and the docks were quickly reconstructed, and expansion has continued ever since, with new residential areas now stretching between the old town centre and Warnemünde on the coast.

The unusual Rathaus (town hall) stands in the Ernst-Thälmann-Platz (formerly known as the Marktplatz); the frontage is baroque (1727-1729), but part of the 13th Century Gothic construction is still visible behind it. To the rear of the town hall at Hinter dem Rathaus 5 is the Kerkhofgiebel, a 16th Century house used as a residence for the mayor, with an

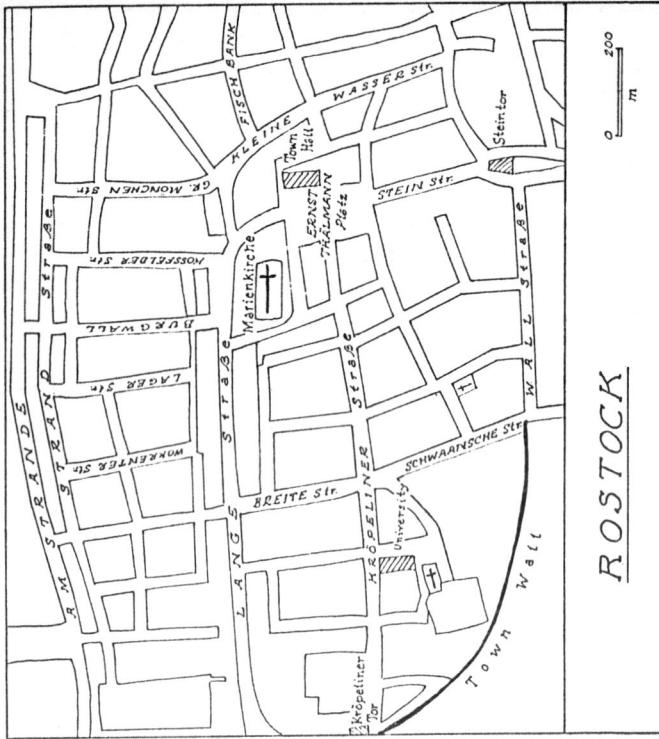

ROSTOCK

SCHWERIN

impressive Gothic gable and Renaissance terracottas. On the square too there is a number of historic gable houses, and to the northwest the Marienkirche (Church of St Mary). The oldest part of this brick hall church dates from 1260 but the interior contains many baroque features. Of particular interest are the bronze font (1290), the 1574 pulpit by Rudolf Stockmann of Antwerp and the high altar (1450). Behind the altar is an unusual astronomical clock, built in 1472 by Hans Dütringer, but re-constructed in 1643 to take account of the latest scientific advances. The clock, with a calendar extending to 2017, shows the day, date, time, phases of the moon and many other details. On the hour it plays a selection of tunes, and at 12 noon the apostles, with the exception of Judas, enter the heavenly gate. The view from the tower over the town and the harbour is one of the best in Rostock.

Heading west out of the Ernst-Thälmann-Platz runs Kröpliner Straße, a pedestrianised street lined with gable houses from various periods. Half way along is the Universitätsplatz (University Square), with its Brunnen der Lebensfreude (Joie de Vivre Fountain). Although Rostock was well-known in the middle ages for its university, the first in northern Europe, founded in 1419, nothing remains of the early buildings. The present university, until recently called the Wilhlem-Pieck-Universität, dates from the 19th Century, and the main buildings lie on the west side of the square. The statue in front of the university is Schadow's 1819 monument to Marshal Blücher, Rostock's most famous son. Next to the university is the Klosterhof, a row of houses leading to the Kloster zum Heiligen Kreuz (Convent of the Holy Cross), originally a Cistercian convent founded in 1270 by Queen Margarete of Denmark, but now a museum.

Three other historic buildings of interest on the Universitätsplatz are the Großherzogliches Palais, the town residence of the grand dukes of Mecklenburg-Schwerin, built in baroque style out of three Gothic houses (1714), the Neue Wache, built for the palace in 1822, and the Barocksaal, a banqueting hall in late baroque style, which has been restored as a concert hall and is open to visitors on Saturday and Sunday afternoons.

On the north side of the square a modern building known as the Five Gable House and based on traditional north German architecture, contains a café and restaurants, and on the corner a glockenspiel, which is played manually at noon.

At the extreme western end of the Kröpliner Straße stands the Kröpliner Tor (Kröpliner Gate), a brick construction which was

once part of the city walls and more recently served as a
municipal museum. Close to the gate it is possible to walk along
a section of the city wall.

Parallel to Kröpliner Straße to the north is the Lange Straße,
the principal shopping street, where the houses which were
destroyed by bombs have been rebuilt in a pleasing combination
of old north German and modern styles of architecture. Between
Lange Straße and the river are several streets with modern
Hanseatic-style buildings, including several restaurants and bars,
and the town information office, located in a converted granary.

The town's associations with the sea are documented in the
Museum of Shipping (Schiffahrtsmuseum) on August-Bebel-
Straße south of the Steintor. It is also possible to visit the
Frieden (Peace), the first ship built for the East German
merchant navy and now berthed alongside the Museum of
Shipbuilding (Schiffbaumuseum) on the river towards
Warnemünde.

Regular motor-boat trips round the harbour include good
views of the Neptun shipyard where cargo, container and other
types of ship are built, and the huge fish-processing factory at
Marienehe.

WARNEMÜNDE

Warnemünde is known for its shipyard, the largest in East
Germany, but also as an attractive seaside resort. It can be
reached in 25 minutes on the S-Bahn from Rostock station. The
Alter Strom (Old River), which flows along the east of the town,
runs through a lively area full of fishing boats, restaurants and
cafés. It leads at its northernmost point to the lighthouse (1897)
and to the West Mole, a long jetty with views usually taking in
ships lying at anchor as well as back over the beaches and town.
Nearby is a restaurant, the Teepott (Teapot), with the same
distinctive shape as the Kongresshalle in Berlin.

A ferry service to Gedser in Denmark leaves from Warnemünde.

Where to stay

Rostock has one Interhotel, the Hotel Warnow on Hermann-
Duncker-Platz. Warnemünde, however, offers several hotels
facing the Baltic, including the Hotel Neptun, which has an
indoor swimming pool and many other sporting facilities, the
Strandhotel Warnemünde and the Promenadenhotel, all on
Seestraße.

Where to eat

Rostock has a number of restaurants serving fish and seafood, including the Gastmahl des Meeres at August-Bebel-Straße 112. Many restaurants and cafés are to be found on Kröpliner Straße. Other restaurants in the centre include the Ostseegaststätte at Lange Straße, the Ratsweinkeller on Ernst-Thälmann-Platz, and a Bulgarian restaurant, Warna, on Lange Straße 7-8.

In Warnemünde, in addition to the Teepott near the lighthouse, there is a fish restaurant, Fischerklause at Am Strom 88, the Atlantik at Am Strom 107 and the Kurhaus, Seestraße 18.

Events

In Rostock an organ festival is held annually between June and September and a musical festival, Music in May, annually in May. In Warnemünde there is an international sailing regatta, and a fishing festival at the beginning of July.

Information

Information can be obtained from the office on Schnickmannstraße, Rostock.

BAD DOBERAN

From Rostock it is easy to make a short trip to Bad Doberan, 15km to the west, to see the 14th Century Gothic minster. The Doberaner Münster (Doberan Minster), sometimes known as the Zisterzienserklosterkirche (Cistercian Monastery Church), was constructed between 1294-1368, although there had been a Cistercian community on the site as early as 1171. The interior of the brick minster houses several precious altars and wooden statues, as well as stone tombs. A few of the old monastery buildings are also still standing, including the pepper-pot-shaped charnel house (Beinhaus), and the brewery (Brauhaus). The minster is open September to June: Tuesdays to Saturdays 11.00am-noon, and for tours at 9.00am, 10.00am, 2.00pm and 3.00pm, and Sundays at 2.00pm and 3.00pm; in July and August Monday — Saturday 11.00am-noon, and for tours between 9.00am-10.30am, and 2.00pm-4.30pm, and on Sundays between 2.00pm-4.30pm.

Close to the minster the municipal museum (called the Möckelhaus) has displays of the history of the town. It is open

Mondays to Wednesdays 10.00am-noon, and 2.00pm-4.00pm;
Thursdays and Fridays 2.00pm-4.00pm and Saturdays 2.00pm-
5.00pm.

Throughout the 19th Century Doberan, as it was simply
called, was known as a rather refined resort, thanks to the
patronage of the Mecklenburg duke Friedrich Franz I. Its race-
track, based on an English model and the first in continental
Europe, was opened in 1807 and was followed by the addition
of another major attraction, mudbaths (1825), using the healing
mud found in the lowlands near Heiligendamm to the north of
the town. In recognition of its popularity as a resort, the name
of the town was changed in 1921 to Bad Doberan.

A narrow-gauge steam railway, built in 1886 and locally
known as 'Molli', runs from Bad Doberan station, along the
main street, and then via Heiligendamm to Kühlungsborn on the
coast.

Where to stay and eat
The Kurhaus hotel, August-Bebel-Straße 2, is located on the
central green, known as the Kamp. A variety of eating places,
including the Zum Ochsen restaurant and the Weißer Pavillon
café, are also in this area. Other restaurants include
Mecklenburger Hof, Am Markt 14; Stadtmitte, Goethestraße;
and the Ratskeller, Rosengarten.

STRALSUND
Stralsund, an important trading station for the Hanseatic
League, enjoyed its heyday at the end of the 14th Century, and
despite recent industrialisation has never again reached the same
degree of prominence in the area. Many of the buildings in the
old town date from this earlier epoch, and their setting on what
is almost an island, surrounded by parks and water, makes this
an extremely pleasant town in its own right, as well as being the
gateway to Rügen island.

The best-known building in Stralsund is the Rathaus (town
hall, begun in the 13th Century) on the Alter Markt (Old
Market). The unusual and imposing brick façade stands out
among secular Gothic buildings in North Germany. Of interest
are the Swedish coats-of-arms on the west side, a reminder that
Stralsund was part of Sweden for almost two centuries (1648-
1814).

Just behind the town hall, the Nikolaikirche (Church of St
Nicholas) is also a Gothic brick building (1270-1350), and from
some angles seems to merge into the Rathaus making a huge and
impressive complex. Unusual features inside the church include
a 14th Century crucifix which is almost 5m in height, the 1611
pulpit and the benches, many of which date from the 16th
Century. At the entrance to the section previously reserved for
the merchants (or Krämer) is the friendly warning in Low
German 'dat ken kramer ist de blief da buten, oder ick schla em
up de schnuten' ('He that's no merchant stay without, or I shall
strike him on the snout!').

The market place, and the town as a whole, contains a number
of burgher houses of interest, in particular no. 5, the
Wulflammhaus, and no. 14, a three-storey baroque building that
originally served as headquarters for the Swedish army.

Other domestic architecture of note is in Mönchstraße and
Mühlenstraße west of the market place.

The Johanniskloster north of the market place was originally
a Franciscan monastery, founded in 1254. After being largely
destroyed in bombing in 1945, however, the buildings have been
made safe but left in ruins as a reminder of the senseless
destruction. In summer concerts and similar events are now held
in the ruins.

Stralsund's museums are housed in the Katharinenkloster,
formerly a Dominican monastery, in the south of the old town.
Both the Meeresmuseum (Maritime Museum), which has one of
Europe's largest collections of tropical fish, and the
Kulturhistorisches Museum (Cultural History Museum), where
early gold jewellery (around 960) found on the island of
Hiddensee is on display, are well worth a visit. They are open
from May to October.

Much of the town wall and other medieval fortifications are
still in place. The sections of the wall south of the museums and
near the Johanniskloster are particularly well preserved, while
the Kütertor (Küter Gate — 1446), which is now a youth hostel,
and the Kniepertor (Knieper Gate — early 14th Century) are
also both in good condition.

From Stralsund it is possible to go by Weiße Flotte to the
island of Hiddensee and to other resorts on the Baltic.

Where to stay and eat

Accommodation is available at the Baltic Hotel, Frankendamm
17. Restaurants include Fiete Dettmann, Kedingshäger Straße

78; Gastmahl des Meeres, Ossenreyerstraße 49; Goldbroiler, Tribseer Straße 21; Grillka, Apollonienmarkt 16.

Information

Information can be obtained from Reisebüro der DDR, Alter Markt 10.

ISLAND OF RÜGEN

Since 1936 the island of Rügen has been connected to the German mainland by a 2.5km causeway from Stralsund. The island, Germany's largest, is regarded as one of the most attractive parts of the Baltic coast because of its variety of scenery ranging from deciduous woods to steep chalk cliffs. The two main resorts, Binz and Sellin, are in the southeast of the island, and between them is the Jagdschloß Granitz, a 19th Century hunting lodge which offers fine views over the whole of Rügen. Further to the north the Stubnitz nature reserve, where yews, holly and rare orchids flourish, borders the coast at the Stubbenkammer, chalk cliffs partly covered with beech trees. From the point on the cliffs known as the Königsstuhl (King's Throne) there is another good view over the Baltic and to Kap Arkona (Cape Arkona), East Germany's northernmost point.

Putbus, also in the southeast but slightly inland, is worth a visit to see its palace and lovely grounds. It was from here that the Prince of Putbus ventured to the nearby coast at the beginning of the 19th Century and founded the first seaside resort on the island. From Putbus it is possible to travel on the narrow-gauge train, known as Rasender Roland (Racing Roland), as far as Göhren 24km away.

Beyond Bergen the road leads on to the Jasmund peninsular and the town of Sassnitz, internationally known for its ferry links to Trelleborg in Sweden, to Rönne in Denmark and to Klaipeda in Lithuania. In addition to the port, other points of interest are a plaque to Johannes Brahms on the hospital wall (it was here that Brahms completed his First Symphony in 1876: at the time the building was a hotel), and two reminders of the time Lenin spent here in April 1917 on his way from Switzerland to Petrograd: a commemorative stone outside the Seemannsheim (Sailors' Home) and an old railway carriage, with original interior decoration, at the station.

Where to stay and eat
Accommodation is available at the Rügenhotel in Sassnitz (Seestraße 1), or, in summer, at the resorts of Binz (Kurhaus) and Göhren (Nordperd).

Sassnitz has a number of fish restaurants including the Gastmahl des Meeres (Strandpromenade).

ISLAND OF HIDDENSEE
The long narrow island of Hiddensee lies off the west coast of Rügen and can be reached by boat from Stralsund or Rügen. Although subject to storms and gales in winter, it is a favourite resort area in summer. Visitors come to enjoy the coast line and also the safe walking — no cars are allowed on the island.

Kloster, in the north, takes its name from a monastery founded here in 1297 during the period when the island belonged to Denmark, although very little now remains of the original buildings. The German naturalist playwright Gerhart Hauptmann (author of *The Weavers*) is buried in the cemetry here; like many writers around the turn of the century, Hauptmann frequently spent his holidays at Hiddensee and died here in 1946. The house where he stayed has also been turned into a memorial to his life and works.

GREIFSWALD
This university town southeast of Rügen escaped any war damage in 1945 thanks to the action of the local commander, Rudolf Petershagen, who surrendered to the approaching Soviet troops without resistance. The old town is therefore largely original, although some reconstruction work has gone on to improve the condition of neglected buildings.

Greifswald played a major role in the Hanseatic League and the old town contains many buildings typical of that period. The Rathaus (town hall) dates back to the 14th Century but was re-built in the mid-18th Century after a fire reduced the brick building to rubble. Nearby on the Platz der Freundschaft (Friendship Square) is a number of burgher houses built in the traditional north German Gothic style.

The centre is dominated by the Dom St Nikolai (Cathedral of St Nicholas), a 13th and 14th Century brick building with a baroque tower, which has preserved some medieval murals in its interior. Two other churches of interest can be found in the old town: the St-Marien-Kirche (Church of Mary — 14th Century) and the Jakobikirche (Church of St James).

Nothing remains of the original university buildings (founded in 1456), but the buildings still used today, and erected in the 18th Century, can be seen in Rubenow-Platz. The square is named after the founder of the university, and a statue of Heinrich Rubenow (by Stüler in 1856) also stands in the square.

For many Germans Greifswald is inextricably linked with the painter Caspar David Friedrich. Friedrich was born here in 1774 and worked here for much of his life; his house has since burnt down but was on the site of Straße der Freundschaft 57.

Just to the east of Greifswald at Greifswald-Eldena are the romantic ruins of the Eldena Monastery (Klosterruine Eldena), which Friedrich depicted many times in his work. The monastery was built for the Cistercians at the end of the 12th Century but was dissolved during the Reformation and subsequently plundered by the Swedish army during the Thirty Years' War. It was as a result of the interest shown in the ruins by Friedrich and other Romantics that they were placed under a preservation order as early as 1828 and maintained in good, if ruined, order. Today the ruins are regularly used for concerts.

In recent years Greifswald has also become known for its Bach Week, held annually in the middle of June. Although Bach had no connection with the town, the cathedral choir has managed to build up the reputation of the festival and it is now an established event, introducing 20th Century music as well as Bach's work.

Where to stay and eat
Accommodation is available in Greifswald at the Boddenhus, Karl-Liebknecht-Ring 1. Restaurants include Am Theater, Platz der Freiheit; Mensa-restaurant, Am Wall; Zur Eiche, Gützowerstraße 1; Goldbroiler, Platz der Freundschaft.

Information
Information is available at Straße der Freundschaft 126.

WOLGAST AND USEDOM
A little to the east of Greifswald lies Wolgast and the island of Usedom, a straggling area of land, the eastern tip of which belongs to Poland. In Wolgast itself, the late Gothic

Gertrudenkapelle (Chapel of St Gertrude) is an unusual twelve-sided brick building, while the Pfarrkirche St Petri (Parish Church of St Peter) is of interest for its interior vaulting and 15th to 17th Century murals and wood carvings. From Wolgast a bridge leads across to Usedom, another popular holiday area on the Baltic Sea. Sandy beaches at resorts such as Zinnowitz, Bansin and Ahlbeck, and wooded countryside and lakes in the east are among the island's attractions. At the western tip around the mouth of the river Peene an area has been set aside as a bird reserve.

Where to stay
Accommodation is available during the summer at the Philipp Müller Hotel in Zinnowitz.

WISMAR
Wismar to the west of Rostock is East Germany's second most important port and is also increasingly popular as a cultural and tourist centre. The town's links with Scandinavia have always been strong: for almost two hundred years (1648-1803) Wismar was under direct Swedish rule and for a further hundred years was leased by Sweden to Mecklenburg, only becoming part of Germany in 1903.

The old town contains many reminders of this connection. Both the Provianthaus (Supplies House — 1690) and the former Zeughaus (Arsenal — 1699) in Ulmenstraße were built as part of Sweden's measures to defend the town, while in front of the Baumhaus (Gatehouse — now belonging to the port authorities and situated in the north of the old town on the quay) stand two cast iron heads known as the Schwedenköpfe (Swedish heads). The name of the oldest remaining burgher house, the Alter Schwede (Old Swede), is a further reminder, although the house, now a restaurant, was built in 1380.

Most of the buildings of interest, including the Alter Schwede, are in and around the unusually large market place. The Rathaus (town hall) is in classical style but dates from the early part of the 19th Century. On the southeastern side stands the highly decorated Wasserkunst (water pump), erected in 1602 in Dutch Renaissance style and surmounted by a bell-shaped copper dome; this pump supplied Wismar with all its water until 1897. Close to the market place the huge red brick tower of the Marienkirche (St Mary's Church — 1339) still stands, although the rest of the church was destroyed by bombing. The nearby 15th Century Archidiakonat (Archdeaconry) has been fully restored, and is one of the most attractive Hanseatic buildings in the whole area.

The Nikolaikirche (Church of St Nicholas) in the north of the old town is built to a design similar to that of the former Marienkirche, and contains the font (1335) that used to be in the Marienkirche. The nave, supported on huge red brick pillars, is the highest in East Germany. Other items of interest inside the church include medieval paintings and a seamen's altar. On the exterior, note the beautifully decorated south gable. The church is open Tuesdays to Sundays 2.30pm — 3.30pm, and half-hour organ recitals are given at 11.20am on Sundays.

On Schweinsbrücke near the Nikolaikirche is the Schabbelthaus, a notable Dutch Renaissance style building in its own right, but also the home of a Museum of Local History (open May to September Tuesday to Sundays 10.00am — 4.30pm; October to April, Tuesdays to Saturdays 10.00am — 4.30pm).

The Weiße Flotte runs trips lasting around one hour to the island of Poel in the Bay of Wismar.

Where to eat

Restaurants include Am Ostsee at Spiegelberg 64 near the harbour entrance; Kulturhaus, Schweinsbrücke; Culinar, Lübsche Straße 29; and on the market place the Alter Schwede and other restaurants, cafés and drinking places.

THE MECKLENBURG LAKE DISTRICT
SCHWERIN (map p.194)

Schwerin is situated on the banks of Lake Schwerin and is surrounded by another six lakes and large areas of forest. In the 16th and 17th Centuries the town developed as the cultural and intellectual centre of the whole Mecklenburg region and from 1815 became the seat of the grand dukes of Mecklenburg. Many of the buildings in the old town were erected in this period from 1815 under the direction of the court architect, Georg Demmler.

The most imposing sight in Schwerin is without doubt the palace (Schloß Schwerin), built between 1843-1857 on a small island in the centre of the town. Visitors who have seen the château of Chambord near Orléans will recognise this as the pattern for Schwerin, although the addition of many towers and turrets and stylistic features ranging from Gothic to baroque and Renaissance, make this pentagonal building a more elaborate affair than its French model. Although the present palace is relatively recent, there have been castles and palaces on this island site for many centuries: the first mention is as early as 973 by the Arab trader Ibrahim Ibn Jacub. The equestrian statue above the main portal bears witness to this rich history: it is of Niclot, the Obotrite chief who died in 1160, an early occupier of a castle on this site.

The present palace is the work of many well-known German architects, including Gottfried Semper, Georg Demmler and Friedrich Stüler. On the second and third floors many of the rooms have been fully restored, including the magnificent throne room, the smoking room and the billiards room. On the second floor there is an attractive café in rooms which previously served as the palace dining room; concerts are given here every afternoon. Both the palace and the café are open Tuesdays to Sundays 10.00am — 5.00pm.

Also well worth visiting are the grounds around the palace, with their rare trees, grotto and orangery, and the extensive Schloßgarten (palace garden), south of the island. This is designed in baroque style with a cross-shaped canal in the centre and a number of statues, mostly copies of works by Permoser.

North of the island lies the so-called Alter Garten (old garden), a square which was once the army parade ground, and which now contains the Staatstheater (State Theatre) and the Staatliches Museum (State Museum). The theatre, built between 1883-1886, is the work of G. Daniel; the nearby bust is of Conrad Ekhof, who in the middle of the 18th Century founded the first German acting academy here in Schwerin. The museum, also dating from the end of the 19th Century, houses one of East Germany's most important collections of paintings. It is particularly strong in Dutch and Flemish old masters (Teniers, Hals, Dou etc), but also exhibits work by contemporary artists. Opening times: Tuesdays to Sundays 9.00am — 4.00pm.

Many of the buildings in the old town have recently been restored, and the streets around the market place now form a pleasant pedestrianised area. The Altstädtisches Rathaus (old town hall) is curiously constructed out of four timber-framed houses (two dating from 1351 and two more recent additions), but has a neo-Gothic façade added by Demmler in 1835. The nearby Neues Gebäude (New Building — 1783) was built for local shopkeepers and has an imposing frontage with 14 Doric columns. It is now a museum of local history (open Tuesdays to Fridays 9.00am — 5.00pm and Saturdays 9.00am — 2.00pm). The nearby cathedral is a fine example of north German Gothic brick building (14th and 15th Centuries). The interior is high and light, painted white with green, brown and grey stripes on the pillars and ceiling. Among the many works of interest inside the cathedral are tombs from the 14th to 16th Centuries, a bronze font (14th Century), a late Gothic altar, an 1871 Ladegast organ, and, in the Marienkapelle, the remains of some medieval wall paintings. It is possible to go up the tower, and organ recitals are given at 8.00pm on Wednesdays in summer.

The Weiße Flotte runs regular trips round the Schweriner See (Lake Schwerin) and also operates routes to more distant destinations, including Neustadt-Glewe, with its 14th Century castle, 17th Century palace and half-timbered houses, and Parchim.

Where to stay and eat
The Hotel Stadt Schwerin, a 3-star hotel, is located at Grunthalplatz 5-7. Restaurants include Haus des Kulturbundes, Wilhelm-Pieck-Straße 8; Altschweriner Schankstuben, Schlachtermarkt; Tallinn, Puschkinstraße; Jagdhaus Schelfwerder, Güstrower Straße 109; Niederländischer Hof, Karl-Marx-Straße 12-13; Weinhaus Uhle, Schusterstraße 13-15.

Information
Information is available at Markt 11.

GÜSTROW
For most of the period between the 13th and the 17th Centuries Güstrow was the residence of princes and dukes. The palace (1559-1598) on Fritz-Parr-Platz, named after the principal architect of the palace, is both internally and externally one of the most impressive Renaissance buildings in North Germany. For the last 20 years it has been the cultural centre of the town, housing collections of 16th Century German, Italian and Dutch works of art, and of classical ceramics, as well as the municipal library and a concert hall.

The Gothic cathedral (of St Mary, St John the Evangelist and St Cecilia), which was begun in 1226, contains many interesting items, including a late Gothic altar with a painting of the *Passion* (1500), the *Güstrower Domapostel* (Güstrow cathedral apostle), the work of the Lübeck artist Berg (1530), and a bronze sculpture by Ernst Barlach, *Der Schwebende Engel* (The Flying Angel).

The sculptor Barlach lived in Güstrow from 1910 until his death in 1938, years during which the Nazi régime tried to eradicate his art. Many of his works can be seen in the Gertrudenkapelle, northwest of the old town, and in the Ernst-Barlach-Gedenkstätte, his workshop at Heidberg 15. The Gertrudenkapelle houses important works such as *Wanderer im Wind* (Wanderer in the Wind), *Mutter Erde* (Mother Earth), *Der Zweifler* (The Sceptic) and *Gefesselte Hexe* (Witch in Chains), while the workshop has a collection of drawings and prints as well as over 100 sculptures.

Where to stay and eat
The Stadt Güstrow Hotel, Markt 2/3, offers basic accommodation. Restaurants include the Ratskeller, Markt 10; Fischerklause, Lange Straße 9; Marktkrug, Markt 14.

LUDWIGSLUST
Although the area around Ludwigslust is known as the 'Grey Area', because of its lack of scenic interest, the town itself is frequently called the Potsdam of Schwerin, because of its palace and palace gardens. The late baroque palace (1772-1776) was designed by Johann Joachim Busch, court architect to the dukes of Mecklenburg. Although the basic construction is of brick, the façade has been faced with sandstone, and the front of the palace, decorated with larger than life statues and classical vases, is an impressive sight. Close to the palace is a church (1765-1770) containing several unusual features, including a massive *Adoration of the Shepherds*, an organ painted on the wall and candelabras which appear to be made of silver but are actually papier-maché. Two bell towers built in the ancient Egyptian style stand apart from the church around 200m to the east.

To the north and west of the palace is an extensive area of park land, originally baroque but extensively transformed by Lenné in the 19th Century. Features of interest include the canal and its stone bridge, a Swiss House (Schweizerhaus), many unusual foreign trees, and a catholic church, the first neo-Gothic brick building in the Mecklenburg area (1803-1809).

Where to stay and eat

Basic accommodation is available at the Parkhotel, Straße der Deutsch-Sowjetischen Freundschaft 19. Restaurants include the Schweizerhaus in the Schloßpark and the Rostocker Hof, Schweriner Straße 39.

MECKLENBURGER SEEN

The area known in English as the Mecklenburg Lake District stretches southeast from Schwerin and Güstrow across a large area of northern Germany to Neustrelitz and Templin. In total it contains over 1,000 lakes, surrounded in parts by wooded hills and in parts by farmland and meadows. Many of the lakes are connected by rivers, such as the Elde, Havel, Peene and Warnow, or by canals, and there are many possibilities for boating and camping holidays,

Although the whole area attracts visitors, among the most popular lakes are Lake Schwerin (Schweriner See) and, East Germany's largest lake, Lake Müritz. Both lakes, like many others in the district, are ideal for swimming and for sailing, or for trips by motor-boat; there are also many opportunities for fishing. Paths around the lakes mean too that it is good walking country. Lake Müritz has been a conservation area for many years, and the east bank often attracts rare birds such as cranes, sea-eagles (there are currently around 130 pairs nesting in East Germany) and ospreys. In the same area are bisons, Voronezh beavers from the Soviet Union, mud turtles and adders. The flora is characterised by the dense heath of dark green juniper shrubs, while the meadowland supports ten varieties of orchids, as well as gentians, butterwort and many other rare plants.

Camping sites in the area include Krakow am See, on the northwest bank of the Gruber See; Dahmen, on the Malchiner See; Röbel, on Lake Müritz; and Plau am See, on the west bank of the Plauer See.

MECKLENBURGISCHE SCHWEIZ

The area between Güstrow and Neubrandenburg, just north of Lake Müritz, is known as Mecklenburgische Schweiz (Mecklenburg Switzerland). As its name implies, it is a scenic district, characterised by sudden and steep hills, interspersed with lakes and flat land. Because of this, there are particularly good views from some of the higher points, including the Röthelberg near Burg-Schlitz and the memorial at Heidberg near Teterow.

NEUSTRELITZ

Neustrelitz is best known for its Stadtpark (town park). The park land was originally attached to Neustrelitz Palace, but since the destruction of the building in World War II only the park remains. Although traces of the original late 18th Century layout can still be seen, the park was substantially modified in the course of the last century. Of particular interest are the Path of the Gods (Götterallee), with its statues of classical gods and the four seasons, a bust of Marshal Blücher by Rauch (1816), and a classical temple built in honour of Queen Luise.

It is also convenient to use Neustrelitz as a starting point for visits to the nearby lakes: to the northwest lies Müritz and to the south the smaller lakes around Fürstenberg and Rheinsberg. Also nearby are a number of monuments worth visiting. Near Fürstenberg at Ravensbrück stands a national memorial to the 130,000 or more women and children from 20 countries in Europe who were brought to camps in this area during World War II. 92,000 prisoners lost their lives; many were murdered and others died as a result of the terrible living and working conditions. To the southwest at Rheinsberg, an 18th Century palace is picturesquely situated in extensive park land on the banks of the Grienerick Lake. The original baroque Wasserschloß (Water Palace) designed by Knobelsdorff was later modified by Langhans in rococo style, and since the last war has been converted to serve as a sanatorium. Finally, at Ankershagen, 20km northwest of Neustrelitz, is a memorial to Heinrich Schliemann, the archeologist who discovered Troy and who was responsible for bringing to Germany many of the exhibits now on display in museums in Berlin.

NEUBRANDENBURG

Although over 80% of the centre of Neubrandenburg was destroyed in one night in April 1945, many of the major historical buildings have been restored and the town has regained its reputation as one of the most complete fortified towns in Germany. Most of the 13th Century walls surrounding the old town can still be seen. In many places half-timbered houses, known as Wiekhäuser, are built into the wall. The houses were originally lived in by those responsible for the defence of the town, and in case of emergency became part of the town's fortifications. The town gates, beautifully decorated brickwork constructions dating from the 14th and 15th Centuries, are also intact, and one, the Treptower Tor (Treptow Gate), is now a museum of early history. At another gate, the Stargarder Tor, the original tannery has been turned into an attractive restaurant known as the Forsthaus (Forest House).

Three churches are also of particular note. The Stadtkirche St Marien (town church of St Mary) in Ernst-Thälmann-Straße is a 13th Century Gothic brick building, rebuilt since 1945 and now used as a concert and exhibition hall. In the same street a monastery church dating from the same period, St Johannes (St John's), has a particularly attractive pulpit (1588). Finally, in the north of the old town, are the remains of the Franziskanerkloster (Franciscan Monastery), founded in 1260: the north wing (now the local registry office) and the cloisters.

The modern tower which dominates the skyline is the so-called Culture Finger, or more properly the House of Culture and Education. The building is a centre for arts of all types, and at the top has a panoramic café.

Where to stay and eat

Neubrandenburg has one international class hotel, Hotel Vier Tore at Ernst-Thälmann-Straße 16. Restaurants include Gastmahl des Meeres, Straße der Befreiung; Zur Klause, Turmstraße 28; Kosmos, Karl-Marx-Platz; Sandkrug, Malzstraße.

Information

Tourist information can be obtained from Ernst-Thälmann-Straße 35.

NEURUPPIN

Both the writer Theodor Fontane (1819-1898) and the architect
Karl Friedrich Schinkel (1781-1841) were born in Neuruppin,
and both are commemorated by statues in the town and by
rooms dedicated to their life and work in the Heimatmuseum in
August-Bebel-Straße. The house where Fontane was born (the
Löwenapotheke — Lion Dispensary) can also still be seen at
Karl-Marx-Straße 84.

Schinkel has also left his mark on Neuruppin's most famous
building, the Klosterkirche (Monastery Church), the only
remains of the Dominican Monastery founded here in 1246.
Between 1836 and 1841 the church was substantially restored
according to Schinkel's plans, although both towers were added
more recently.

To the north, the area known as Ruppiner Schweiz (Ruppin
Switzerland) offers pleasant lake and woodland scenery. The
forest museum at Stendenitz on the Zermützel Lake, 11km north
of Neuruppin, is particularly prettily situated.

One of the "Swedish Heads" on the quay at Wismar

View of Schwerin

Patrician houses and church of St Mary, Rostock

Biographical Appendix

Listed below are a few of the people connected with East Germany, whom you are likely to encounter in street and place names.

Bebel, August (1840-1913) Founder member of the Social Democratic Workers' Party.

Becher, Johannes R. (1891-1958) Founder member of the communist party, writer, minister of culture from 1954.

Brecht, Bertolt (1898-1956) Writer and dramatist who worked in the USA during World War II but returned to East Berlin in 1948 and remained there until his death.

Dimitroff, Georgi (1882-1949) Communist activist accused of playing a part in the Reichstag fire; he successfully defended himself against the charges; later became Bulgarian leader.

Ebert, Friedrich (1894-1979) Mayor of East Berlin from 1948-1967.

Fontane, Theodor (1819-1898) Realist novelist, also known for his descriptive *Walks through Mark Brandenburg* around Berlin.

Goethe, Johann Wolfgang von (1749-1832) Poet, dramatist and writer who also had a distinguished political career; spent a large part of his life in Weimar.

Grotewohl, Otto (1894-1964) Imprisoned by the Nazis; instrumental in the formation of the SED of which he remained leader until 1964.

Hauptmann, Gerhart (1862-1946) Realist dramatist and novelist.

Honecker, Erich (1912-) Imprisoned by the Nazis in 1935; held various positions of authority from 1946 onwards until he became first secretary of the SED in 1971 (and general secretary in 1976) and thus East Germany's effective head of state; removed from office in 1989 amidst allegations of political corruption.

Honecker, Margot (1927-) Married Erich Honecker in 1953; minister of education from 1963. Lost office at same time as her husband in 1989.

Kollwitz, Käthe (1867-1945) Artist and early German socialist-realist.

Lessing, Gotthold Ephraim (1729-1781) Critic and dramatist.

Liebknecht, Karl (1871-1919) Communist politician murdered (along with Rosa Luxemburg) by anti-revolutionaries.

Liebknecht, Wilhelm (1826-1900) Friend of Marx and Engels and founder member of the Social Democratic Workers' Party.

Luxemburg, Rosa (1871-1919) Communist thinker and activist murdered (along with Karl Liebknecht) by anti-revolutionaries.

Nagel, Otto (1894-1967) Painter whose work was suppressed by the Nazis but who became president of the GDR Academy of Arts in 1956.

Pieck, Wilhelm (1876-1960) President of the GDR 1949-1960

Schiller, Johann Friedrich (1759-1805) Poet and dramatist, friend and contemporary of Goethe; associated with Jena and Weimar.

Thälmann, Ernst (1886-1944) Communist leader imprisoned by the Nazis and murdered in Buchenwald.

Ulbricht, Walter (1893-1973) Fled to France during the Nazi period; after holding various offices became general secretary of the SED in 1950 and first secretary in 1953 and remained so until 1973 and was thus effectively head of state.

Weigel, Helene (1900-1971) Collaborator of Bertolt Brecht; they married in 1928.

Zetkin, Clara (1857-1933) Early communist and leader of the feminist movement in the 1920s.

INDEX

Accommodation 16, 21
Ahlbeck 203
Allstedt 133
Altenburg 151
Ankershagen 209
Annaberg 154
Architecture 11-12
Arkona, cape 200
Arnstadt 13, 138-139
Aschersleben 174
Augustusburg 154

Bach, Johann Sebastian 13, 24, 25,
    47, 99, 102, 118, 137-139, 145, 180,
    185, 202
Bad Blankenburg 145
Bad Brambach 25,157
Bad Doberan 197-198
Bad Elster 25, 157
Bad Frankenhausen 133
Bad Gottleuba 152, 158
Bad Schandau 158
Baltic coast 8, 193-204
Bansin 203
Bastei 158
Bauhaus 12, 100, 178-179
Bautzen 162
Bebel, August 5, 46, 138, 158, 213
Becher, Johannes 14, 61, 213
Berggiesshübel 152
Berlin 28-71
East Berlin 41-71
West Berlin 31-41
- Akademie der Künste 32
- Alexanderplatz 50
- Alte Bibliothek 46
- Altes Museum 59
- Aquarium 34
- Archenbold Observatory 67
- Bellevue Palace 32
- Berlin Cathedral 48
- Berlin Museum 38
- Berliner Ensemble 65, 68
- Bode Museum 58
- Botanical Gardens 39
- Brandenburg Gate 31, 44
- Brecht House 61, 66
- Bröhan Museum 39
- Charlottenburg Palace 35
- Checkpoint Charlie 15, 31
- Comic Opera 57
- Court 62
- Dahlem (museum and gallery) 38
- Deutsche Oper 34, 40
- Deutsche Staatsoper 46,68
- Deutscher Dom 55
- Dorotheenstädtischen Cemetry 65
- Eating, East 69
- Eating, West 40

- Egyptian Museum 35
- Entertainment, East 68-69
- Entertainment, West 40-41
- Ermelerhaus 63
- Ernst-Thälmann Park 64
- Europa Centre 34
- Französischer Dom 55
- Friedrichsfelde Palace 67
- Friedrichshain 64
- Friedrichstadtpalast 65, 69
- Friedrichstraße 18, 44
- Friedrichswerdersche Kirche 45, 54
- Grunewald 36
- Hansaviertel 32
- Huguenot Museum 55
- Humboldt University 45-46
- Information, East 70
- Information, West 41
- Kaiser-Wilhelm-Gedächtniskirche
    33
- Kleinglienicke 37
- Klosterkirche 62
- Köllnischer Park 63
- Kongreßhalle 32
- Kurfürstendamm 33
- Le Corbusier House 36
- Lenin Memorial 64
- Marienkirche 49-50
- Markets 39-40
- Märkisches Museum 63
- Martin-Gropius-Bau 33
- Marx-Engels-Forum 49
- Marx-Engels Platz 48
- Maxim Gorky Theatre 47, 68
- Ministerrat 62
- Müggelsee 71
- Museum of Antiquities 36
- Museum of German History 47
- Museum of Working Life in Berlin
    60
- Musical Instruments Museum 39
- National Gallery 59
- Natural History Museum 60
- Neptunbrunnen 52
- Neue Nationalgalerie 33
- Neue Wache 47
- Neues Museum 59
- Nikolaiviertel 52-53
- Olympic Stadium 29, 36
- Otto-Nagel-Haus 60
- Palace of the Republic 48
- Pergamon Museum 57
- Pfaueninsel 37
- Philharmonie 32, 40
- Planetarium 64
- Platz der Akademie 55
- Plötzensee 39
- Postal Museum 60
- Radio Tower 36

- Reichstag 31, 121
- Rotes Rathaus 52
- St Hedwig's Cathedral 54
- Schauspielhaus 56, 68
- Siegessäule 31
- Socialists' Memorial 67
- Spandau 37-38
- Spittelkolonnaden 62
- Staatsrat building 54
- State Library 45
- Sugar Museum 39
- Synagogue 66
- Television Tower 51
- Transport, East 70
- Transport, West 40
- Treptower Park 57, 66
- Unter den Linden 44-47
- Wall 7, 30, 31, 56
- Wannsee 37
- Weißensee 64
- Weltkugelbrunnen 34
- Zeughaus 47
- Zoo, East 67
- Zoo, West 34
- Zur letzten Instanz 62
Bernau 71
Bernburg 180
Binz 200
Blankenburg 174
Bode river 172
Bode valley 172
Border crossings 18-19
Brandenburg 8, 185-186
Brecht 13, 45, 61, 65, 191, 213
Brocken 171
Buchenwald 112
Buckow 191
Burgk 145

Chemnitz (Karl-Marx-Stadt) 149-150
Chorin 191-192
Colditz 124-125
Cottbus 8, 11, 189
Cranach, Lucas (The Elder) 38, 58, 59, 90, 99, 102, 104, 106, 121, 137, 139, 169
Culture and the Arts 11-14

Dessau 10, 11, 178-179
Dimitroff, Georgi 31, 92, 121, 213
Dornburg 146
Dresden 11, 12, 79-97
- Albertinum 85
- Altmarkt 82
- Altstädter Wache 89
- Blockhaus 92
- Botanical Garden 92
- Brühlsche Terrasse 85
- Dreikönigskirche 93
- Frauenkirche 84

- Gallery of Modern Masters 85
- Gallery of Old Masters 89
- Gewandhaus 83
- Golden Horseman 93
- Green Vault 85
- Historical Museum 90
- Hofkirche 87
- Hygiene Museum 92
- Japanese Palace 94
- Johanneum 86
- Kreuzkirche 83
- Kulturpalast 83
- Landhaus 84
- Langer Gang 86
- Luther Monument 84
- Museum of Early Romanticism 93
- New Town Hall 82-83
- Opera 88
- Palais Marcolini 90
- Pillnitz 94-95
- Royal Palace 87
- Zoo 91
- Zwinger 89
Drink 22-24

Eberswalde-Finow 191
Economy 9
Eisenach 2, 5, 13, 135-138
Eisleben 170
Elbe river 9, 79, 159
Eldena 202
Erfurt 11, 127-131
- Anger Museum 130
- Augustinerkloster 129
- Cathedral 128
- International Horticultural Exhibition (IGA) 130
- Krämerbrücke 129
- St Severus 128
Erkner 71
Erzgebirge 8, 151-152
Ettersberg 112

Fichtelberg 152
Fontane, Theodor 55, 60, 117, 188, 191, 211
Food 22-24
Frankenhausen, battle of 2
Frankfurt an der Oder 190
Freiberg 12, 152-153
Friedrich, Caspar David 12, 35, 85, 93, 103, 202
Friedrichroda 134, 139, 140
Fürstenberg 209

Geography 8-9
Gera 12, 143
Goethe, Johann Wolfgang von 13, 93, 99, 100, 106, 109-112, 117, 140-141, 145, 172, 213
Göhren 200

Görlitz 12, 163
Gotha 139-140
Greifswald 12, 201-202
Greiz 157
Grienerick lake 209
Gropius, Walter 12, 100, 178-179
Güstrow 206-207

Halberstadt 171
Halle 8, 12, 175-178
Handel, George Frederick 13, 24, 25, 176
Harz 8, 13, 171-174
Heiligendamm 198
Heiligenstadt 133-134
Heine 13, 134, 172
Heldrungen 133
Herder, Johann Gottfried 4, 104-105
Hiddensee 199, 201
History 1-8

Ilm river 99, 109
Ilmenau 140-141
Information sources 26-27
Insurance 18

Jena 13, 144

Karl-Marx-Stadt See Chemnitz
Klingenthal 157
Kloster 201
Kochberg 112
Königstein 158
Köpenick 70-71
Köthen 13, 180
Kühlungsborn 198
Kyffhäuser 174-175

Language 22
Lauscha 135
Lausitz 11
Lausitzer Bergland 8, 162
Lehde 187
Leipe 187
Leipzig 114-125
- Alte Waage 117
- Alte Börse 117
- Auerbachs Keller 117
- Bach Archives 118
- Battle of the Nations Monument 122
- Georgi Dimitroff Museum 120-121
- Gewandhaus 119
- Gholis Chateau 121
- Messe 115, 122
- Museum of Fine Arts 121
- Museum of Local History 116
- Naschmarkt 117
- Nikolaikirche 119
- Opera 120
- Sachsenplatz 118
- St Thomas's Church 118
- Schiller's House 121
- Town hall (new) 120
- Town hall (old) 116
- University 119
- Zoo 121
Lenin 46, 64, 122
Liebknecht, Karl 49, 67, 74, 214
Liebknecht, Wilhelm 5, 138
Life and people 9-10
Lilienstein 158
Liszt 13, 47, 110, 145
Literature 13-14
Lübben 189
Lübbenau 188
Ludwigslust 207
Luther, Martin 2, 13, 50, 120, 127, 129, 136-137, 165, 167-170, 176

Magdeburg 181-184
Mansfeld 170
Märkische Schweiz 191
Markneukirchen 157
Marx 46, 49, 139, 144, 149
Mecklenburg lakes 9, 208
Mecklenburgische Schweiz 209
Meiningen 141
Meissen 135, 159-162
Melanchthon, Philipp 168
Merseburg 175
Money 17-18
Moritzburg 96
Mühlhausen 131-133
Müntzer, Thomas 2, 25, 131-133
Müritz lake 9, 208
Music 12-13
Music holidays 24-25

Naumburg 11, 146-147
Neisse river 163
Neubrandenburg 210
Neuruppin 211
Neustadt-Glewe 206
Neustrelitz 209
Niederfinkow 192
Nordhausen 172, 174
Nossen 162

Oberhof 135
Oberwiesenthal 156
Oder river 9, 190
Opening times 24

Parchim 206
Peasants' Revolt 2, 131-133, 167
Pillnitz 94-95
Pirna 158
Plauen 157
Poel 204
Politics 10-11
Population 1

Porcelain 135, 161
Post 21
Potsdam 12, 72-78
- Alexandrovka Settlement 77
- Cecilienhof 76
- Dutch Quarter 77
- Einstein Tower 77
- National Film Museum 77
- St Nikolai 77
- Sanssouci 74-76
Pretzsch 170
Putbus 200

Quedlinburg 11, 173
Querfurt 174

Radebeul 96
Radeburg 97
Railways, narrow-gauge 26, 97, 156, 159, 172, 198
Rathen 158
Ravensbrück 209
Reformation 2, 25, 165-169
Registration 17
Religion 10
Rheinsberg 209
Rostock 8, 193-196
Rübeland 172
Rudolstadt 145
Rügen 200

Saale river 9, 145
Saaletal 145
Saalfeld 142
Sassnitz 200
Saxon Switzerland 8, 157-158
Schiller, Friedrich 4, 13, 108-111, 141-142, 144-145, 214
Schumann, Robert 117, 155
Schwerin 204-206
Schwerin lake 9, 206
Seiffen 155
Sellin 200
Shopping 22
Sorbs 11, 79, 82, 162-163, 187, 189
Spas 25, 135, 152, 157
Sports 25, 135, 152, 156
Spreewald 8, 11, 187-189
Stendal 184-185
Stendenitz 211
Stolberg 133, 170, 174
Stralsund 198-200
Suhl 142

Tabarz 139
Tangermünde 184
Telephones 21
Thale 172
Thälmann, Ernst 61, 64, 67, 84, 112, 214
Thüringer Wald 134-135

Torgau 180
Transport 19-21

Usedom 202

Visas 15-16
Vogtland 8, 157

Wagner, Richard 13, 115, 136, 138, 145
Waltershausen 139
Warnemünde 196
Wartburg 2, 13, 135-137
Weimar 6, 13, 98-113
- Belvedere 110
- Bertuchhaus 106
- Central Library of Classical German Literature 102
- Free School of Drawing 100, 102, 106
- German National Theatre 107
- Goethe's Garden House 109
- Goethe's House 100
- Goethe Museum 100
- Goethe-Schiller Archives 111
- Goethe-Schiller Memorial 108
- Goethe-Schiller Tomb 110
- Gelbes Schloß 102
- Grünes Schloß 101
- Herder Kirche 104
- Hotel Elephant 103
- Jakobskirche 105
- Kirms-Krackow House 105
- Liszt's House 110
- Lucas Cranach's House 102
- Natural History Museum 111
- Park on the Ilm 109
- Residenzschloß 103
- Rotes Schloß 102
- Schiller's House 108
- Shakespeare Memorial 109
- Stadtmuseum 107
- Thuringian Museum of Early and Pre-History 111
- Tiefurt palace 111
- Von Stein's House 101
- Wieland's House 101
- Wittumspalais 108
Wernigerode 172, 173
Wieland 101, 105
Wismar 8, 11, 203-204
Wittenberg 2, 165-170
Wolgast 202
Wörlitz 179

Zermützel lake 211
Zille, Heinrich 51, 53, 63
Zinnowitz 203
Zittau 159
Zittau mountains 2, 159
Zwickau 155-156